ROBBO
NOW YOU'RE GONNA
BELIEVE US

ROBBO

NOW YOU'RE GONNA
BELIEVE US

Reach Sport

www.reachsport.com

Reach Sport

www.reachsport.com

Published in Great Britain and Ireland in 2020 by Reach Sport, 5 St Paul's Square, Liverpool, L3 9SJ.

www.reachsport.com
@Reach_Sport

Reach Sport is a part of Reach PLC.
One Canada Square, Canary Wharf, London, E15 5AP.

Hardback ISBN: 978-1-911613-80-0
eBook ISBN: 978-1-911613-87-9

Photographic acknowledgements:
Andrew Robertson personal collection,
Liverpool Football Club, PA Pics, Getty Images.
Every effort has been made to trace copyright.
Any oversight will be rectified in future editions.

Printed and bound by CPI Group (UK) Ltd,
Croydon, CR0 4YY.

CONTENTS

TOGETHER, WE CAN MAKE A DIFFERENCE

T HE first step towards becoming Premier League champions was also the most painful. On the final day of the 2018/19 season, Liverpool faced Wolverhampton Wanderers in the knowledge that victory would bring the title back to Anfield in the unlikely event of Manchester City losing or drawing at Brighton.

For twenty-one minutes that dream scenario became our reality with the 'as it stands' table reflecting our 1-0 lead and City's 1-0 deficit. The atmosphere at Anfield was electric. At one point I had to tell supporters in the Sir Kenny Dalglish Stand to calm down. We still had a job to do and we couldn't afford to get carried away.

It also felt too good to be true and that was how it turned out as City went through the gears to ensure that Liverpool's twenty-nine year wait to become champions would enter a thirtieth. Coming so close only to be denied could have demoralised us but it ended up doing the opposite. It galvanised us, motivating us to be even better, and the emotion that we saw, heard and felt at Anfield that day was one of the catalysts. I drove away from the ground that night thinking: 'If we win the Premier League, this place is going to go nuts.' No further inspiration was needed.

A little over a year later, at the culmination of what Jürgen Klopp described as "one of the greatest stories in football history," our mission was finally accomplished. As someone who either records, memorises or details pretty much every moment, I wanted to document our journey from believers to achievers in a book that would capture it all. I've needed a bit of help to make it happen and I have to thank those who have contributed in various ways.

As ever, my family have been massively supportive and everything I do is for them. Between them, the ownership, management, coaches, staff and my team-mates at Liverpool created a wonderful story that deserves to be told. Our magnificent supporters provided non-stop inspiration, whether they were in the ground or not. Reach Sport, my publisher, supplied guidance, encouragement and assistance throughout, none more so than Steve Hanrahan, Paul Dove, Chris Brereton and Chris McLoughlin.

Matty McCann did what he always does while Tony Barrett helped with the writing – both are much more intelligent than they look.

In the background, Liam O'Donnell, Ricky Gillies, John Paul Mowberry and Tyler Alexander-Arnold looked out for my best interests as ever. I am grateful to all those mentioned and many more besides.

I hope that anyone who reads this book enjoys it as much as I enjoyed writing it.

For those who have been generous enough to buy it, you should also be aware that by doing so you are supporting my new charity – AR26 – which aims to offer young people the opportunity for an equal start in life whether that's through access to training, support or jobs. In addition, it will provide life-changing experiences for children who are battling critical health conditions.

I was brought up to believe that if we stand together, we can make a positive difference and the goal of AR26 is to prove that this is true.

On and off the pitch, unity is strength.

Andrew Robertson, 2020

**This story is dedicated to the unsung heroes
at Anfield, Melwood and Chapel Street**

ONE NIGHT IN MADRID

I T was six o'clock in the morning when the lights finally went on. First I blinked as my eyes came to terms with the brightness. Next, I did a double take as my focus returned. For a Liverpool player, lifelong Celtic fan and Scotland international, there could be no greater sight. But a combination of lager-induced brain fog, lack of sleep and outright surrealism made it difficult to take in. Stood in front of me was Sir Kenny Dalglish, the hero of all heroes. Not only that but he was being told by his lovely wife, Marina, that no, he couldn't carry the party on because they had a flight to catch and if they didn't leave right now they would miss it.

For a boy from Clarkston who had grown up on tales of King Kenny, told to me over and over again by my dad who worshipped him, this was as good – and as bizarre – as it gets. Except it wasn't. Seven hours earlier I had been stood on the pitch at the Wanda Metropolitano, blinded by the floodlights as I thrust Liverpool's sixth European Cup into the Madrid night sky. 'Go on Andrew,' I thought to myself. 'How do you even begin to make sense of all this?'

If I'd never experienced anything like this before then I'd wager the Madrid Eurostars Hotel hadn't either. This was our base for 48 unforgettable hours around a fixture that would change all of our lives forever. We arrived back there in the early hours, dancing down an escalator chanting 'Allez Allez Allez' with Alisson Becker carrying the European Cup into a crowded room. This had been the party to end all parties. Not in the sense of what was drunk – although I have to be honest, this was one of those rare nights when the lads could let our hair down – but in the sense of sheer jubilation.

For everyone who was lucky enough to be there – players, staff, families, supporters – the feeling of euphoria that all of us were sharing was much more intoxicating than whatever we were consuming. I'm not a big drinker but that night I indulged without ever getting to that stage where you start feeling a bit unsteady on your feet. I just didn't want the night to end. I wanted it to carry on forever. Management at the hotel had other ideas, which was why they turned the lights on, sending Sir Kenny and his family for their plane and leaving the rest of us looking for somewhere else to get a drink.

For me, that meant heading up to my room with Adam Lallana. The pair of us went up in the same lift that had brought us down the previous evening, but now we were different people. Our personalities hadn't changed but our status had. Just like King Kenny gets to be called 'Sir' after being knighted, we would now be known as European Cup winners. It's something you could never get sick of hearing. 'European

Cup winner Andy Robertson.' Wow. I have to stress that I don't go around describing myself like that and I'd fully expect a slap from one of my mates if I did, but I'm not ashamed to say that it gives me a buzz when a TV commentator says it or I'm announced as a guest at an event with those five wonderful words. It's not just personal pride either, especially as I know I'm only part of a team and I know better than anyone that there are many others who helped me along the way. More than anything, I understand what it means to my family and everyone else who has been part of my journey. But how could a footballer not take something out of being in the company of the Lisbon Lions, the legendary Liverpool teams and the greats of Real Madrid, AC Milan, Bayern Munich and Barcelona? No wonder Lallana and myself needed another drink!

The problem was, we literally couldn't get one. The rules on European away trips are quite simple – players cannot order alcohol to be brought to their rooms and our mini-bars are always emptied before we've even arrived. As far as these strictly enforced regulations go, our new status counted for nothing. There were no deals to be done, no Michael Edwards-style negotiating to get what we wanted, rules are rules and no amount of pleading, begging or bargaining was going to change that. I love Lallana, he's one of my best mates, but at this point he was, like me, absolutely useless. So we did what all footballers do when they can't get what they want, we turned to members of staff for help. In this case we were lucky.

In our company were Mark Leyland and Harrison Kingston, members of the club's analysis team who had helped plot our victory over Tottenham Hotspur. Not only are these lads outstanding at their day jobs, they are also hugely resourceful, so we tasked them with obtaining the beer that, up to that point, was eluding us. They had room service sent up to their rooms and as soon as it arrived they brought it along to us. Simple but effective. Obviously it wasn't anywhere near as important as their work in the build-up to the final, or in the weeks and months previously, but at that point in time there was nothing they could have done that would have mattered so much and it gave us yet another reason to be grateful for the efforts of the team behind the team.

We'd decided to pull an all-nighter for two reasons. The obvious one was that we were all determined to savour every minute. But there was also a realisation that if we went to bed for an hour or two before flying home, we'd only wake up feeling terrible. It wasn't just the tiredness of being up all hours that would have been a problem, it was the fatigue from the game that was going to kick in at some point. I just wanted to delay that feeling for as long as possible. I'm not sure the conversation that morning would be widely considered as being of the highest standard. There was a lot of small talk about what had happened the night before and what awaited us back in Liverpool but, in the main, we just had a laugh.

At one point I was sitting on the bed with Ads and we both started staring at our medals at exactly the same time. We just looked at each other and burst out laughing because the ribbons round the medals aren't the best and you could see both our necks cutting up. I couldn't tell you what Ads was thinking but for me it was a moment of reflection, compared to where we'd been the year before with the silver one. Now we had gold ones and the only problem was they were irritating us like mad. We were trying to scratch our necks and wrap our hoodies around the ribbons but we were never taking them off. Not a chance.

Just thinking of that silver medal brought back some bad memories from almost exactly a year earlier. The difference between the aftermaths of our two Champions League finals couldn't have been greater, which was why I had so much sympathy for the Spurs players we had just beaten. I knew exactly how they were feeling. Strangely, it was still possible to almost have a sense of déjà vu about our own experiences from 2018, even in the midst of the rush of ecstasy that 2019 was giving us. I say strangely but I suppose in some ways it's totally natural, simply because it was the pain that had been inflicted when we lost to Real Madrid twelve months previously that drove us on to this success. We kept it with us, using it as a motivation whenever we needed it because, to a man, we knew that we didn't want to feel like that again.

How bad was it? It wasn't the kind of defeat you get over quickly that's for certain.

Probably the worst thing about losing a Champions League final is that you are left with a whole summer to stew on it. It's not like a big league game when you have the chance to put things right within days. Lose the big one at the end of May or early June and you know it will take a year, at the very least, to put the record straight. On top of that, you have the best teams in Europe standing in the way as you go in search of redemption.

That was one of the reasons why I took it so badly when Real got the better of us. I respected them as European giants and on the night they had been deserving winners but I also knew that, for various reasons, we hadn't done ourselves justice and we weren't interested in being the kind of team that gets plaudits for reaching the final. If we were going that far in the competition, only one thing mattered and that was winning.

There was no shame in falling short and, of course, you take the positives from all that we achieved on the road to Kiev but the dull ache that only defeat can cause was etched onto all of our souls that night, which was why I recalled that terrible feeling as I sat in Ads' room even though the feeling itself had now been taken away.

I remembered the flight home more than anything. Kiev is a long way from Liverpool so we were sat on a plane for four hours with all of us having thoughts of what might have been. As with Madrid, I didn't sleep a wink. As usual, I was sat next to James Milner – probably because nobody else would! Basically, Ads and Hendo had to sit together because they were inseparable and then Milly and myself had the next two seats with Ox and Trent just behind. In fairness to Milly, he's actually an ideal travelling companion. Whatever the situation and whatever the mood, he knows exactly how to play it.

Some of the lads like to snooze, Lallana was one of them. He would put his headphones on, go to sleep and wake up in a different country. Me, Milly and Hendo don't really sleep on flights so Milly brings out his wee speakers and puts on his music. He tries to stay down with the kids with Chris Brown stuff but I'm not sure he really likes it. We all love a bit of Westlife and then, more often than not, we will have a game of cards with Trent, Jimbo and Matt McCann, the club's Head of Press. Six of us play cards, we always do that. Milly is very good at judging the situation and the environment.

This time, though, there was no music and no-one was interested in playing cards. I sat with Milly and we debriefed the final and what had gone wrong. Hendo joined in too. I have a vivid memory of lying on the floor of the plane talking to those two about the game for most of the time we were in the air. None of this was making us feel any better but we knew we had to do it. I suppose in some ways that's the start of the healing process, not that it felt like any healing was going on at that stage. Our wounds were too raw for that.

When we landed in Liverpool at around 6am we had some breakfast and then I waited for my mum, my dad and Rachel to land on their plane which had taken off not long after ours. Obviously the hope had been that we would be returning to a heroes' welcome on Merseyside but as I drove back home with my family I knew that all we had to look forward to was a day of introspection having had zero sleep. Real and ourselves had both reached the same stage and played in the same game but from the moment the final whistle had gone, we instantly occupied totally different places. They had the glory and the joy, we had the pain and the regret.

I got back into the house at around seven o'clock and my kids were just up. Everybody else went off to bed because they'd been flying in at different times throughout the night. I wasn't in the mood for lying down so I did what anyone else would do in that kind of situation: I headed to Homebase as soon as it opened and bought a barbecue so that I could take my frustrations out on some unsuspecting sausages and burgers.

The other shoppers must have been wondering what I was doing because it's probably not too common an occurrence that a footballer will turn up in his local DIY store less than twelve hours after losing a major final but I knew I had to do something with myself, otherwise I would've just ended up stewing on things all day long. I also knew that 2017/18 had been a big season for me.

The last six months of the campaign had kind of proved that I was a Liverpool player and could be a Liverpool player so in that respect, it made sense to have a bit of a get-together regardless. There wasn't too much of a party but it ended up being a decent night because the weather was good and it was a chance for myself and the rest of my family to enjoy being in each other's company. The Real Madrid players might have been painting the Spanish capital red – and I would have given anything to have been doing likewise in Liverpool at their expense – but I had the people who matter most around me and that's never a bad consolation.

It's because of what our families go through with us – whether it's putting up with our bad moods when we have a bad result or looking after things at home when we're away for long periods – that it's so important to share the special moments with them. I don't think anyone who was at the Wanda Metropolitano around a year later on June 1, 2019 could have been left in any doubt about what our loved ones mean to all of the Liverpool players.

In my case, I was lucky enough to have my family at the stadium and my mum and dad were able to get onto the pitch afterwards, while my fiancée and son were also in the ground. I feel extremely fortunate that I was able to share that time with those closest to me, especially as this was the very least they deserved. My youngest was back at the hotel with Rachel's gran because she was only four months old at the time but I got to see her afterwards and that was special in itself.

I tried to phone home to speak to my grandad but he didn't pick up. I later found out he was in his bed because he wasn't well. He watched the final and went straight to bed. He was meant to be going to a family party but they were unable to go, so I tried to ring my gran back home but that didn't work either. I thought about them a lot, even though we were unable to speak because they are the kind of people who helped make me what I am so it's only natural that I feel like I owe them a great deal.

I also thought about one of my aunties who I had been really close to but who died before her time. I doubt very much that I'm alone in this. You really do start thinking about everyone who has played a part, big or small, in getting you to a position in which you are standing on the pitch at the end of a Champions League final coming to terms with the fact that you are a European Cup winner. It is an incredibly emotional time and I was fortunate to have so many special people with me, either in the stadium or in my thoughts.

I never cried but I came close to shedding a few tears when my dad came on the pitch because he was crying like a baby and that was the first time I had ever seen him like that. I've seen him upset but more at funerals and at sad times, both of which are totally normal to see. My mum is an emotional character but my dad is more like me, so seeing him crying summed up how much it meant to him and all of my family.

When Rachel ran on with Rocco I was excited to see them rather than emotional. My little boy was just buzzing to be on the pitch and I became a dad at that point. My priority, as usual, was to make sure he was okay as he charged around on the same playing surface on which goals from Mo Salah and Divock Origi had made all of our dreams come true just a matter of minutes earlier. People often get asked when and where they were happiest and for me those precious moments would have to be right up there.

Another moment that really hit me came when we were all stood on the podium waiting for Jordan to collect that wonderful trophy which was about to become ours for a year at least. I was stood there with the medal around my neck and I turned around and saw Jürgen. The first thing I said to him was: "This one's a lot better than last year." I couldn't help thinking about the contrast and I've no doubt it was the same for the gaffer and all of the lads. This was our moment of personal and collective redemption and just by being a different colour, those medals instantly came to represent the journey we had all been on together.

From that moment on, Kiev became the back story to our success; a reason for what we were achieving rather than the game that would define us. That was important for all of us and I know it was exactly the same for all of our supporters who had supported us in unbelievable numbers once again. Only the lads on the pitch are lucky enough to get a medal but those in the stands were equally deserving because without them we would not even have been in Madrid. It really is that simple.

Back in the dressing room, those who were not fortunate enough to be out in Madrid were bombarding me with messages and my phone ended up buzzing almost as much as Rocco. I received loads from friends back home in Glasgow, lads who I had gone to school with and known since I was two years old. Usually they would be slagging me off or trying to make fun of a picture of the trophy above my head, but their texts were all quite emotional. If my mum or dad or my fiancée had sent me an emotional text, which they did, it still gets you but you kind of half expect it. But when it is from one of your mates who you're just used to joking around with then it probably affects you a little bit more. It showed how much it meant to us and what we mean to each other as friends. I just wouldn't ever tell them that!

The scenes in the dressing room will live with me forever. We were all dancing around singing 'Campeones', champagne was spraying all over the place, some of the lads were dying their hair red and it was basically just a scene of total and utter delirium. Every now and again you would see one of us just sat there, staring at our medal or taking pictures of it, just trying to take it all in. Then the European Cup got brought in and it all kicked off again.

The good thing is that a lot of the footage taken inside the dressing room made it out into the wider world so people were able to see just how much it meant to us. No doubt there were Scouse parties breaking out all over Madrid and back in Liverpool. I just hope that everyone else enjoyed it as much as we did. Judging by some of the videos that were doing the rounds in the weeks afterwards I'm pretty confident that they did. It seemed like every day there was a new one emerging. All the lads shared them on WhatsApp because the scenes were so unbelievable that we wanted to see them for ourselves.

I'm just glad nobody was filming on the team bus back to the hotel afterwards because if they were, a DJ malfunction involving yours truly would probably have gone viral. I'd wanted to put a bit of a mix on just so everyone could get into the swing of things with songs that we all knew and could sing along to, but it didn't quite work out. Neil Diamond's 'Sweet Caroline' was first up and that was a great start because everyone got into it straight away, belting out the 'woah-oh-ohs' and agreeing that, yes indeed, good times had never seemed so good.

The problem was that the good times never stopped. Instead of putting the playlist on shuffle, I'd put it on repeat so 'Sweet Caroline' kept on coming on over and over again. Everyone was banging on the bus, though, so they must have been happy enough with it. I thought about going down to the front to sort it out and I would have done, only the gaffer was there and I didn't really want to put myself under that kind of pressure. So, by accident rather than design, 'Sweet Caroline' was the only song we heard all the way back to the hotel and that didn't change until we went down an escalator to the reception and all the lads broke out into 'Allez Allez Allez', dancing down the stairs with Alisson carrying the European Cup at the front. The big fella took the trophy off the bus and he looked like he never wanted to let it go, which was fair enough seeing as he hadn't let much go all season.

Jamie Webster performed on stage which was brilliant in itself because he had played a big part in terms of creating the kind of atmosphere that had inspired us to reach successive finals and the lads had all got into his songs. We were all up on the chairs and tables when he played 'Allez Allez Allez'. I had managed to get the European Cup off Alisson by that point and I was slamming it about as everyone sung about us conquering all of Europe for a sixth time. I'm not sure my dancing was up to much but no-one could question my passion. As anyone who saw the footage would know, the drinking had begun in the dressing room but I wouldn't say anyone ended up being drunk. I think everyone was just happy with life and why wouldn't we be? We had our friends and families with us and there were plenty of supporters about who had found their way in one way or another, so life felt great.

I think the enormity of what we had just done hit me quicker than a couple of players. I remember sitting with Hendo at that party and you couldn't really tell if he was on the winning team or the losing team because he was still processing it all.

Hendo has such a strong sense of responsibility and is so selfless but, all of a sudden, he had joined an elite group of European Cup-winning captains. That's a lot for anyone to come to terms with. I was just a left-back, a backing singer in the band, so I was able to just enjoy the party in the knowledge that I'd been part of something truly special. There was no point where I was in shock but I think some of the lads were in the same boat as Hendo, which is totally understandable. Making an arse of yourself by dancing on a couch with the European Cup when you've just experienced the greatest moment of your career isn't for everyone after all. That couch became my base for most of the night. I was able to sit there with my dad, my brother, my mum and my fiancée. We were toasting me becoming a champion of Europe.

To be honest, my initial plan had been to take the trophy to bed with me but one of the security lads, big Dave, took it away. He protected it like it was his kid but that was no bad thing as it meant someone who knew what they were doing was looking after one of the most precious pieces of silverware in world football. Big Dave or me? I know who I'd trust.

Had I been able to keep my hands on the cup I probably would have sneaked it up to my room and got a few hours' sleep but things worked out for the best because I ended up in the company of Sir Kenny. That was one conversation I never wanted to end – which was why we were still talking when the lights came on. At one stage he said to me: "In a couple of weeks, you'll realise what you've done," and that really hit me because of who was saying it. If there's one person who knows about success and how it affects you, it's him.

We were joking about the fact it was no surprise that it was the Scottish still going until the very end. Looking back on that moment, it is a bit surreal. At this club, he has a stand named after him, he is now a 'Sir' and in Scotland he is one of the biggest, if not *the* biggest, icon in the game. So for us to be sitting talking at six o'clock in the morning about me becoming a champion of Europe is something that will live with me for a long time. It must have been even more special for my dad.

On the day I signed for Liverpool, my dad spoke about Kenny Dalglish. That period in the 1970s and '80s when Sir Kenny was in his prime was the perfect era for my dad. My dad and my grandad were going to Celtic games every week and Kenny was my dad's hero. Actually, my dad ending up hating Liverpool for a time when they stole Kenny from Celtic but that dislike turned into a love for them because he couldn't resist watching him play. Thirty-odd years later, he is stood with his hero and his son while the pair of us discussed what it means to win the European Cup. As a dad myself, I'm not sure it could get much better than that.

In the hours that followed, the hardest thing I had to do was a radio interview. Usually I'm fine with media duties because in the modern game they're almost as much a part of the job as training ground rondos and shuttle runs. I've lost count of how many I have done in my career so far but this was the first time I was doing one without any sleep and on the back of a few beers, so it wasn't ideal.

I was committed to it, though, and I doubt the BBC would have been impressed if the club had contacted them to say that I couldn't do it because I wasn't in the best condition. So I jumped in the shower to freshen up, packed my bags and headed down to the breakfast room from the 29th floor so that I could do my bit. The gaffer was sat at the next table to me making his own plans for leaving the hotel as I prepared to do a pre-record with Jonathan Overend for Radio 5 Live.

I know the interview definitely happened because I can vividly remember looking out over Madrid as it took place but God knows what I said! I've never heard it back and I don't think I want to either. I remember being on the phone for fifteen or twenty minutes. I wasn't drunk but you can still tell when someone has been up all night.

I was doing everything I could to concentrate so that I at least sounded professional. Before it started I said to myself: 'Whatever you do, don't sound like you've been up all night.' The first question? 'Have you been to bed?' My answer: 'No!' At least the question had been put to bed even if I hadn't. Like I say, I don't remember another word of that interview but Jonathan is a top operator so no doubt he kept the conversation flowing. I hope so anyway!

There was only one major topic of conversation from then on – the parade. The final itself was secondary by that stage, simply because of the excitement about what might lie ahead.

As usual, I sat by Milly on the flight home and we did speak about the game for a bit, mainly about how we felt we had it won in our own minds during the build-up because we had been in such a positive place mentally and our preparation had been so good, but we didn't speak about a certain chance Tottenham had or a certain moment they had.

We maybe spoke about Milly's shot and my shot – for the record, mine was better and closer than his – and we took the mickey out of each other but other than that, we didn't sit and say 'we were lucky' in this or that situation or 'we should've scored here'. It wasn't long before we landed and the talk had already started about what the parade would be like. It changed from what had happened the night before to thinking 'we're probably about to see something really special here.'

I know people won't believe this in hindsight because everyone now knows what unbelievable scenes greeted us on our return, but I don't think we would be human if there wasn't a part of all of us that was thinking: 'What if it isn't that big?' I was ninety-nine per cent sure it would be massive because I'd seen the footage after the Liverpool players brought the European Cup back from Istanbul in 2005 and I also know full well how passionate and committed our supporters are but, still, it's totally natural to wonder because none of us had been in a situation like this before. What if the weather is bad? What if everyone is hungover? What if people did the modern thing and chose to participate via social media? What if.

Before the parade could start, we had to go back to Melwood so that we could have some food and put our 'Champions Number 6' t-shirts on. Then we got onto a bus which took us out to a military barracks in the south of the city.

Nobody was thinking straight by then, we were all knackered. We drove through some pretty deserted streets that made the feeling that it could turn out to be a damp squib take hold a little bit more. The fact we had avoided the parade route itself hadn't occurred to us and there was definitely an anxiety that it might not be that good.

Sensing the mood, Milly did what he had done countless times before only usually in the dressing room rather than on the top of an open top bus and gave us all a rallying cry. "Right lads, come on, we need to give this our everything." The chants kicked off, even though the route ahead looked dead. We were going to make the most of it, no matter what lay in store.

There were three buses, the front bus, the secondary bus for staff and other people and the third bus was for media to cover the event. Everybody just piled onto our bus. I was at the front with Hendo, Milly, Ads, Trent, Studge and then Alberto came up. We're a team but you gravitate to certain players on nationality and stuff and though we were in our wee groups we were all together really.

I remember we had a lorry in front of us with confetti. That took off and we followed. The next thing, people on the media bus were shouting because that had been left behind and, of course, that needed to be at the front. We were in this non-descript car park and there were three buses and two trucks reversing and jockeying for position. It was a shambles but that was exactly what was needed because it was so surreal and all we could do was laugh.

Apart from Trent, none of us knew whereabouts in Liverpool we were. So we didn't know where the bus was going. We were nowhere near the city centre, we were nowhere near Anfield because we'd never seen this part and we were nowhere near Melwood. It wasn't as if our preparations for the final had involved parade planning.

We were told that we were heading down Queens Drive, one of the major ring roads dividing the city, but again, other than Trent who had grown up there, we didn't really have an idea just how long that road is so we set off on a bit of a journey into the unknown. We were driving for a bit before we reached the start of the route and I ended up saying to one of the staff: "What's this going to be like? Everybody is knackered." I was probably one of the most upbeat but then Milly started banging the side of the bus and everything started to make sense to all of us.

I took a picture on my phone as we set off and sent it to Tony Barrett from the club. 'You promised us something big' I said because that was exactly what he had done the night before and he replied: 'Wait till you get to where I am'. I remember turning to the lads and saying: "Don't worry, Tony Barrett is somewhere in this parade and he says it's even busier where he is, just wait till we get to that point."

It was when the bus took us around Allerton Maze that it became clear it was going to be massive. The crowds on the pavement were ten to fifteen deep, there were people in gardens, up trees, up lampposts, in the middle of the roundabout itself, hanging out of windows. The difficulty was we didn't know how long we would be on the bus so at that point we were all thinking 'ok, we'll do a lap around here, head to the barracks and then go back'. That would have been amazing itself because of the amount of fans that had come out to see us even in that short section but we carried on, everyone on the bus got going, the beers were being flung around and the party started again.

Maybe because I have the loudest voice but somehow I became the instigator of all the songs. We must have sung 'Allez Allez Allez' about five hundred and fifty times on that bus but if I wanted to change it up to Sí Señor or Virgil Van Dijk then I'd do it and everybody would join in.

When I wasn't singing I was just sitting back and thinking: 'This is big'. We all knew it. I think we got on the bus thinking we were going to make the most of it so we never really chatted and even if we'd wanted to we probably wouldn't have been able to hear each other. It was more a case of thinking 'wow, look at this'.

There was a moment when Gini was videoing the crowd but he dropped his phone and one of the fans threw it back up to him. It probably made for a good video to be fair. Somehow I had a massive flag on a pole which I put out of the side of the bus. I was trying to wave it about but the wind was so strong. Scarves and balls were getting flung at us with pens so that we could sign them but we ended up having to punt most of them away because we didn't have time to sign stuff. Usually the lads are great when it comes to autographs and things like that but we all wanted to drink this experience in because it was so incredible.

There was one toilet on the bus – that was fun! I'd heard a story about one of the Everton players once having to get off their open-top bus to answer a call of nature at one of the houses that they had been passing but, thankfully, things never got to that stage with us, although it probably wasn't far off on a few occasions.

As we headed down Leeds Street towards the Pier Head, I saw all of my mates outside a big BMW garage. They'd all just flown back from Madrid, seven lads from Glasgow who I'd gone to school with and played football with, and they were stood by the traffic lights where it was easy for me to pick them out. They had driven three hours out of Madrid to catch their flight and then come across to Liverpool from Manchester once they had landed so they were worried they wouldn't get here in time. The fact there were so many people on the streets did them a favour because it slowed the parade down.

They were looking at me and laughing as we went past. At this point my hand was red raw from skelping and I was absolutely shattered because of how much energy we were putting into the parade but I also sensed that it was coming to an end as there were fewer people on Leeds Street than there had been in other parts of town. It had been quite emotional seeing my mates waving up at us. We hadn't seen our families yet as they were in a rooftop bar waiting for us.

We were two hours late so we must've been on the bus for four or five hours by that stage. But as we came through the traffic lights and turned onto the Strand we heard this roar. It was so loud that none of us had ever heard anything like it. We had already seen probably 500,000 people in that first four or five hours, so to go around that corner and see another 300,000 in that one street was totally incredible. There were flares going off, everyone was waving their flags, everyone was maybe having a wee drop and the noise was ear splitting. That moment touched everyone and I think the lads probably shed some tears because it was so emotional.

I'd imagine a lot of people who had come out for the parade carried the party on that night and it was the same for us as the club put on a bit of a celebration for us back at Anfield. First we had to head to Melwood. Everything felt right with the world, except for the fact that I could no longer speak. I tried to talk but I couldn't. All that came out was a Glaswegian croak. That's what happens when you're the idiot who starts all the songs on the bus, I suppose. Not having any sleep since my pre-final nap ended at four o'clock the previous afternoon hadn't helped either. That combination of tiredness and drink all rolled in to one to leave me literally speechless.

All of the lads were going to meet their families at the party but not one member of my family were in sight and nor were any of my friends, so I was wondering what was happening. We had created a WhatsApp group for everybody in Madrid and I messaged them: 'What's going on, where is everyone?' The replies came in and it turned out that my family had gone home to get refreshed and ready for the do. I was like: 'Yous better hurry up because I am done here!' I wasn't exaggerating either. I had nothing left in the tank.

Just as in Madrid, I got myself onto a couch as soon as I got to the party, only this time there was no chance of me bouncing around like a kid who's been eating Skittles. I sat myself down and I can't have been the only one who was shattered because some of the lads started to leave before my family had even arrived. I got a bit annoyed about that, to be honest, because everyone else was with their loved ones who had come in all dolled up while I was sat on my own stinking of B.O. and beer after swinging a scarf above my head on a bus for six hours.

When they finally turned up I'd slid halfway down the couch and could easily have fallen asleep if I'd been allowed to. I perked up straight away, because this was the first time I'd been with my mates since before the final. It was also the first time I'd seen my uncle and aunties. It was all quite emotional.

I was knackered though. There was a band on and I felt sorry for them because they must have been expecting a room full of energy and they got the opposite. The gaffer is always the life and soul of any team party but even he came over to me and said: "Robbo, I can't. I'm done. I need to go home." He left and it soon got to the point where I was the last man standing for the second night running – if only because I hadn't seen my family and I wanted to spend some time with them. But then I hit the wall. I turned to Rach and told her: "You can all stay if you want but I need to go home." She came home with me and my mum, dad and brother and I just went straight to bed. They'd put balloons in the house and decorated it but by that point I couldn't even stand through exhaustion.

There was no hangover the following morning. My body had pretty much shut down so I slept like a baby and the only pain I had when I woke up was caused by metal rather than alcohol. I had obviously managed to take my trousers and my shoes and socks off before getting my head down but I'd gone to sleep with my Champions of Europe top on and with the medal around my neck. The ribbon had been rubbing against my neck while I was out for the count and I could feel the soreness as soon as I woke up. At least my voice had come back so that was a big relief to me, if no-one else.

Rocco took the medal off me and put it on with my boots so he could walk around the house like he'd just won the European Cup. Those moments at home with Rachel, Rocco and Aria were as good as it gets. I know it's usually me who's wearing the boots but without their love and support I don't think things would be going as well as they have since I joined Liverpool.

That Monday was my most emotional day. I wasn't crying but I just felt emotional. It felt like we had been on a mad rollercoaster for months and all of a sudden it had come to a halt. Now there was time to think and reflect. I thought about getting beaten 3-0 by Barcelona and then turning it around at Anfield on a night that will live with me forever. I remembered staying up all night after that second leg because I had an injury and I was worried I'd miss the final, so sleep was out of the question.

It was during those sleepless hours that I texted Trent because obviously that was his famous game and I said to him: 'You're the best right-back in the world.' Between those two games against Barcelona, we had gone to Newcastle and scored a late winner to keep our title dreams alive. Bobby missed that game through injury and then Mo got injured. Then, after Barcelona, we had won our last league game of the season but missed out on the title and had gone on to win the Champions League. A run like that, with so many twists and turns and highs and lows, is going to leave your emotions all over the place and I spent the day kind of letting it all out.

A lot of that process involved getting in touch with the other lads, mainly to check in with them and see how they were feeling but also to look back at what we had achieved together and what we still hoped to achieve in the future. Lee Nobes had joined us as Head Physio in the previous November but in that short space of time he had made a big difference because he had slotted in so seamlessly, so I wanted to let him know how much we all appreciated him. I was just on a mad one, texting everyone. I sent Milly a message saying how special this must be for him because he had already won some big trophies but the Champions League is probably the biggest of all so that was perfect for him.

My most important message went to Hendo. It was a long one, which is never a good sign, but looking back it's probably one of the best texts I've ever sent. I think it was partly because I'd been with him in the hours after we won the Champions League and it felt like he hadn't been able to take it all in, but it was also because I wanted him to know what a magnificent captain he is.

One of the great things about Hendo is he's the type of person who puts others first, he's never selfish or driven by his own ego, he wants what's best for the team and that's it. At times, this has meant that he hasn't been appreciated anywhere near as much as he should be outside of Melwood, simply because he's not into self-promotion and doesn't have people around him who'll ensure he is always in the limelight. I don't think this is a problem in itself because he has the absolute respect of his team-mates and everyone else who is able to see what he does at close quarters but I've always thought some of the assessments of him have been unfair and, in some cases, downright disrespectful.

Obviously, he inherited the captaincy from Steven Gerrard who was the toughest act of all to follow given what he had achieved for Liverpool and sometimes the comparisons with Gerrard had been unfair seeing as they're different players and different people.

So I sat there with my phone in my hand and thought: 'You know what, send him a text and let him know what you think of him'. The wording was pretty straightforward and to the point …

You know I'm not a very serious guy Hendo but I hope you realise you are now a Liverpool legend! In the history of this club only five captains have lifted that trophy and you are one of them! Could not happen to a better person, you are a leader on and off the park and drive these lads forward in ways you won't give yourself credit for! I know you've dealt with a lot since being captain and I hope now you are appreciated as much as you are by the lads that have the pleasure of playing alongside you! It was emotional watching you lift that trophy so can't imagine what it felt like for your friends and family! You are the man skip ♥

Hendo being Hendo replied humbly and with a few kind words for myself but I wasn't finished. 'Thank you skip,' I typed. 'Now let's go and win that Premier League trophy next season.'

ROBBO

SUMMER BITES BACK

"**T**HIS could lead to sepsis."

Of all the things to associate with the summer after winning the Champions League, I wasn't expecting it to be this.

Like most players, July is my month of normality, a time when it's all about family, friends and chilling out and I did my fair share of that but I also had an encounter with a spider that left me fearing for my health and the place that I had worked so hard to earn at Liverpool.

The mad thing is, all I have to show for it is a small scar on my right hand. When anyone sees it, it doesn't look like much, just a tiny mark that could have been caused by something pretty minor but, to me, it is a constant reminder of a couple of weeks that I will always associate with physical pain and a fair bit of largely self-inflicted mental anguish.

It had all started so well, too. My memories of how the season had ended were still so fresh and so vivid that when I closed my eyes I could experience them all over again. It wasn't just Liverpool either, Scotland had given me the perfect ending to an unforgettable campaign when we beat Cyprus 2-1 in Steve Clarke's first game in charge. It had been a difficult season for us and that remains a disappointment for me but that was a good day for Scotland as a team and as a nation.

It was also a particularly memorable one for me given I was captain and I managed to score the first goal of Steve's reign. Looking back, that was a game that perhaps I shouldn't have played in. It had been a long, hard season and when I joined up with the squad I had a few aches and strains. It's fair to say that if this had been autumn or spring I probably would have had to pull out but as I had a break coming up, I was determined to play. I also didn't want to let my country down. I might not have been in peak physical condition as there was a fair bit of wear and tear going on but my motivation to play and perform for Scotland was as great as ever.

I arrived a few days after the other boys because of my involvement in the Champions League final. When I arrived I got clapped in at the dinner table, all the lads recognising my achievements with Liverpool. That was a lovely touch. Although I'm not usually comfortable with being the focus of that kind of attention it did make me feel good about myself mainly because these were all lads who I had either grown up with or got to know well from playing football at international level. To have them show me that kind of respect was really nice and it would be great if I could return the favour for a few of them in the years to come.

But it wasn't long before things got back to normal and I

was getting my fair share of stick, as is right and proper. I didn't help myself on that front when everyone found out I had forgotten my regular boots. All of a sudden, I was the bootless European champion and I ended up having to wear my personalised Champions League final boots. Still, they turned out to be lucky for me so maybe there was a bit of fate involved – not only did I win the European Cup in them, I scored for Scotland in them. I might need to bring them back out again!

Even though it was a must-win game for us I was very relaxed within myself because of what had happened in Madrid and when I came out onto the pitch at Hampden the fans gave us a bigger cheer than usual, which was lovely. I scored the first goal and pretty much everything went for us that day.

I should have had one more game to play but by then my body couldn't take any more. I had gone into the Champions League final with an ankle knock that had forced me to come off in the second leg of the semi-final against Barcelona. I came out of it with a tight hamstring that I carried on feeling in training, all the way up to the Cyprus game. I was on such a high and such a buzz after Madrid that I was able to forget any pain I was feeling. I also had a fair bit of adrenaline coursing through me because I was representing Scotland.

So I was desperate to carry on but after playing against Cyprus my hamstring was a wee bit worse so I had to be honest with myself and the gaffer because there was a strong chance I would have let people down if I had declared myself fit to face Belgium. To be fair to Steve, he said: "I don't want you making it worse and then you missing six weeks, having a disrupted pre-season then an injury-prone season for Scotland and Liverpool." I still went over to Belgium and trained the night before, just to see if there had been a miraculous improvement. I couldn't even sprint. I told the gaffer, even though I still wasn't ready to give up. I said: "Gaffer, I can play at fifty per cent if you want me to and I will do it," but between us we made the call to take me out and it was absolutely the right one.

It's bad enough playing against any team when you're not fully fit but if I'd gone up against the likes of Romelu Lukaku, Kevin De Bruyne and Eden Hazard on one leg it would have been carnage. I would almost certainly have spent the following month undergoing rehabilitation. I hate missing training, never mind games, but I had no choice.

A break from football was needed but I still needed to wean myself off the buzz of winning that I had been fortunate enough to get used to in April and May.

Luckily enough, I still had one of the sporting events of the year to look forward to – my annual race day with my brother, Stephen, and our mates. We regard it as one of the highlights of the sporting calendar.

Ayr Racecourse was the setting and we booked a box so we could enjoy each other's company. I made sure I didn't make the same mistake as the previous year when I allowed my name to be put on a sign hung outside the box. Stephen, being Stephen, decided this was an unmissable opportunity to have a joke at my expense. He put the sign around his neck and ran around with it while everyone fell about laughing. This time, *his* name was going on the sign.

Paul Hanagan, the jockey, called in to see us and that helped turn a good day into a great one. I was a bit star struck when he came in, to be honest. We were at a sporting event and the jockey wanted to come up to our box and meet us?! He came up and spoke to all of us and I got a picture with him before my dad shouted over to Paul, asking if he had any tips for the day. He told us one of his had a chance and he wasn't wrong. It absolutely romped home.

With everyone having won a few bob, the trip back to Newton Mearns was even more lively than usual. There are twenty-five of us who go to the races and we always hire a bus, sorted out by one of my mates. One year we even got the Celtic team bus. My mate came to us and said: "I've got this amazing deal for £300, it's a big bus." We climbed on this team bus that had a big kitchen and all the mod cons. When you leave your friends in charge of booking stuff, this kind of thing happens.

This time around, my dad and all my uncles were buzzing. Everyone had picked winners and we all ended singing Celtic songs as the bus carried us back to a curry house called Zyka. I know the owners and staff pretty well. We always go there because it's part restaurant/part pub so we can have a couple of drinks too. Usually, it's pretty low key in the sense that it's just a gang of mates getting together and nobody pays us too much attention but on this occasion the owner came over and told me how proud he was of me for what we had achieved at Liverpool.

I'm definitely not complaining about that because it was a lovely thing to happen but it did serve as a reminder of how much things had changed for me. Only a few years earlier, I could sit in there and no-one would bat an eyelid. Now I was deemed worthy of recognition. It all goes with the territory, of course, and mostly it's positive because people are generally well-meaning but for someone whose life is built around friends and family, it can take a bit of getting used to.

That's one of the reasons that getting away from it all has become so important. Switching off mentally is absolutely vital, especially after a rollercoaster season of extreme emotions, and so is spending quality time with your loved ones. Most of the time you are either on the road with club or country or else so focused on games that it's hard to relax. Add the fact we're constantly in the public eye and it can all be challenging to be a family man in the same way as other dads. I'm not complaining because I'm well aware that the rewards far outweigh the drawbacks but I have come to cherish the basics of fatherhood and any time I am able to spend with Rachel and our close circle of friends.

A gang of us found ourselves on a boating holiday off the coast of Spain and Portugal at the height of summer. That was a trip that sort of happened by accident, even though there's no question I bought it myself.

I'd like to blame James Milner if I could but it wasn't really his fault. Every year, Milly puts on a charity ball and it's a brilliant event which raises a lot of money for his foundation. Most of the lads go because it's always an occasion to look forward to and it's nice to be part of something that results in so much good work being done for people who need it.

The auction is one of the highlights of a great night. That is partly because we're all naturally competitive, partly because we like a bit of fun and partly because we want to help Milly raise as much money as possible, but we all get heavily involved – which is how I ended up buying a holiday on a yacht.

I'd already bid for a piece of memorabilia and missed out because a rival bidder offered more. Getting involved gets the juices flowing which is obviously the whole idea. But most of the guests are clever enough to go for stuff that they really want. Me? I'm the perfect attendee at an auction because I just want to win, so when the opportunity to bid for a holiday on a yacht came up I was all over it. This wasn't entirely logical. Being out on deck in the Mediterranean would be ideal for most people but for a lad with freckles from Scotland it doesn't make too much sense. That didn't matter. The bidding had started and my right hand was shooting up like it had a mind of its own.

Winning the yacht holiday meant that Rachel and a group of our closest friends could enjoy a little break away. It cost around £6,000, except I didn't read the small print – that was before food and fuel – the £6,000 was just for getting on the boat! It ended up costing me closer to £15-16,000 because I also had to pay for flights and boat tax in the harbour where we were getting on.

The boys and myself stayed below deck for most of the time. Not many of us take a good tan and there were at least three gingers, so we were taking no chances. We sat inside playing cards and helped each other out with Factor 50 while all the girls sunbathed. We would venture out for ten or fifteen minutes and occasionally jump in the water before going back inside. You can't take any chances with the sun when you come from Glasgow!

I'm not exaggerating when I say that my mates and myself moaned about the boat for three days solid but really we loved it. We were out at sea, away from everything and we could just let our hair down, though that's not always easy for me. After the first day, with the boat docked, I still got up early and ended up going for a run. I just thought I should because I had been eating and drinking. It is probably the athlete's instinct in me. I didn't need to do it, but I *had* to do it.

Like anyone else who works hard through the year, I had earned the right to a holiday and to let my guard down a little but I think the urge to get out and do a bit is always in me. It may not be the same for players who have made their way to the very top by virtue of their God-given talent, but when you have had to scrap to join them you can't afford to allow standards to slip or else it might not be long before you go back to square one. That may not be entirely logical and it might actually make more sense to have a complete break when you rely so much on intensity but it works for me and, for better or worse, it makes me the player I am. There may also be a bit of Catholic guilt involved, too, in the sense that I feel the need to atone for the 'sin' of enjoying myself a bit too much.

Whatever it is, I'm not changing any time soon so it's better to embrace it and make the most of it rather than wasting time wondering what life would be like if I was different.

As a blow-out, the boat trip couldn't have been better. It was only brief but it was exactly what was needed after a long, hard season. No sooner were we home than we picked up the kids and got on another plane to Portugal for our family holiday. Like everyone else with kids, this was something Rachel and myself had really been looking forward to. We had a villa booked for two weeks and both sets of parents were coming with us, so it was a rare chance to have some uninterrupted family time, or so I thought.

While we were flying out, my hand started itching. I started scratching it to make it go away because my first instinct was that it was just something trivial. But the itching didn't stop and there was a wee red spot developing. I still thought nothing of it because you don't, do you?

We got to our villa, settled in and I went to bed that night with a little bit of irritation but nothing more than that. I was fully expecting the itching to stop overnight and then for everything to get back to normal the following day. That was the plan anyway. But the next morning I woke up and the first thing I felt was this prickly, throbbing sensation. I looked down at my hand and it had almost doubled in size. It looked like a joke shop hand.

I felt pins and needles and then looked at it, brought it out from under the pillow and thought, 'Jesus Christ'. It was bright red and massive. At first, I thought I'd just slept on my hand and it was dead and had no blood in it – but there was no sign of the swelling going down so I ran downstairs. I put it in an ice jug straight away, picked my phone up with my other hand and Googled 'bites' because by then I'd realised there was more to it than a bit of discomforted sleeping. After I'd had my hand in ice for 15 minutes, I read that: 'Ice is the worst thing you can do for an insect bite'! There's me thinking I was getting the swelling out but it turns out heat is the best thing to draw out the infection, so my wee hand was already 15 minutes behind.

Even then, my instinct was to get on with things. This was our family holiday and the one period in the summer when we get to be together so I focused my energies on being a father and husband when maybe I should have gone to hospital. I even played golf with it that morning and I wasn't too bad, although the quality of opposition wasn't the best given it was my dad, Rachel's dad and my brother. The big thing for me was I didn't want to ruin the holiday for everyone else. I played in the pool with the kids, played tennis with my dad, basically did all the things that I would normally do. My hand was bugging me but no more than that, so I was happy just to carry on.

Four or five days passed and I was still feeling it, so I got in touch with the doctor at Liverpool and he emailed me a letter to take to a nearby pharmacy so that I could get some antibiotics. The Portuguese pharmacist gave me the tablets and told me that if I completed the full course that should be enough to kill the infection effectively. By then my hand was numb and sore.

I like to think that I have a high pain threshold. I'm used to getting hit or having ankle pain or whatever but the difference with this was it felt a wee bit out of my control. I couldn't trace it back to a knock and all I could think was that it must have happened while I was asleep on the boat because nothing else made sense. It was all a bit mysterious and, in my mind, that made it more troubling.

All I could do was try to put it to the back of my mind and get on with the holiday as best I could. I doubt the kids even noticed something was wrong. They were quite rightly too busy enjoying themselves in the pool and eating ice cream and they were still a bit young to realise that their old man was struggling a bit. That helped me because it meant I didn't have to worry I might be letting them down. At that stage, it wasn't pre-season that worried me, I was just concerned about my hand. Touch wood, up until this point I have been very lucky. I've not had any serious injuries or illnesses, so this was all a bit new.

I finished the course of antibiotics as instructed but my hand was no different, it was still swollen and, if anything, it probably felt a wee bit worse. Then it started turning purple and it looked a bit of a mess so my dad took me to see a doctor in Portugal. I think when the doctor first saw my hand he didn't want to touch it and I couldn't really blame him.

He put me in a sling – which made me laugh because I looked like someone out of a comedy show – but obviously he wanted me to keep my arm raised. It all felt a bit surreal. When I walked back into the villa everybody started laughing at me and I couldn't help laughing at myself. I had been playing tennis half an hour before going to see the doctor and now I was in a sling like an eight-year-old kid who's fallen off his skateboard.

With the infection showing no real signs of clearing, I sent a text message to Johnny Gordon, the Scotland team doctor, because I was becoming increasingly concerned. Johnny also works in the NHS.

I told him that I would be flying back into Glasgow ahead of the start of pre-season training in three days' time. He asked me to send him a picture, which I did, and he also wanted to know whether I'd taken any medication so I told him I'd been on antibiotics but they hadn't really worked.

One of Johnny's friends is a hand specialist so he got him to look at it and the next question was: 'When do you land?' That started panicking me a wee bit. Suddenly, it all seemed a bit urgent.

The fear that was running through my mind centred on having to have an operation because I had never had that kind of surgery before. I had had dental surgery a few months earlier but an operation to clean out an infection in one of your limbs is obviously on another level to that so it really started playing on my mind. I don't think any of my fears were out of the ordinary and I'd expect most people would have experienced them at one time or another, but it was definitely the first time in my life that I'd ever felt in any way vulnerable where my health is concerned.

On top of that, I'm not good with needles – I hate getting my blood taken so I wasn't in a good place. I called Johnny, probably looking for a bit of reassurance as much as anything else because he knows what he's talking about.

But even though I got top class guidance and information from one of the best operators I've come across in football, I never got the comfort I was looking for. I told him that the antibiotics still weren't having any effect and Johnny went into full-on doctor mode. "Whatever you do," he told me, "don't stop taking them." I was about to reply with something daft like: "Why, will my hand drop off?" but before I could even turn to gallows humour he shut me down.

"Don't stop taking them, you might not think they're doing anything but they're keeping it in that area. Without them, it could spread up your arm and you could get sepsis."

I couldn't kid anyone and pretend that this didn't hit me hard because it was so obvious that it had. Again, I turned to Google, searching for 'spider bite sepsis'. The first result that came back was a newspaper headline: *Mum bitten by spider in garden nearly dies after contracting sepsis.* So I kept taking the tablets.

I flew back into Glasgow later that day, landed, went to see Johnny straight away at about six o'clock, had a consultation with him and his hand specialist friend and no sooner had I got into the room with them that they booked me in for an operation the next morning.

I came back from the hospital with a big arrow up my hand. I was massively embarrassed. I said to Rachel: "I'm getting an operation tomorrow, I need to go to sleep," and to everyone it was just a laugh. Even I was laughing. It was a spider bite, for God's sake!

Looking at it now, though, every time you need an operation, it's serious. Even if it's just a clean-up, you're getting put to sleep for a reason and getting cut open where you shouldn't be getting cut open, so I look at it like that.

That night wasn't the best sleep I'd ever had if I'm honest. I wasn't panicking but the medical experts clearly felt this was urgent enough for surgery to be necessary straight away and there was also a risk of the infection spreading. When my head hit the pillow, I knew it would be the only thing on my mind. Rachel's obviously given birth to two kids so she must have been wondering why the prospect of a hand operation was bothering me so much but this was all new territory for me. I just wanted it over and done with.

The following morning I went to the hospital, put my glamorous hat and gown on and waited for the fun and games to begin. In my mind, the first bit was going to be the biggest challenge – getting the general anaesthetic and confronting my fear of needles. "You'll just feel a little scratch," said the anaesthetist. 'Oh aye,' I thought as she came at me with this Olympic-sized javelin that she was about to plunge into my arm like I was a character in Trainspotting.

I took it like a man, though. No tears, no shouting, no wailing. I'm actually not sure many have ever taken it better. Next thing, I'm asked to count to ten but I only got to about four or five and I'm flat out while the surgeon got ready to go about his business.

From what I was told afterwards, the operation only took about 45 minutes. He had to slice my hand open, clean all the tendons and take all the infection out. The infection was everywhere; it was really quite deep. It wasn't going to drain, they had to cut it out and make sure all the tissue was healthy.

Rachel stayed with me and it was only a small surgery but it was something that was well out of my control and my comfort zone. All of this was new to me. Some footballers might be used to having minor operations but I'd never had anything. It was just a stupid infection in my hand but it needed an operation and I was more than happy to get it over and done with and, more importantly, the doctor was happy enough with the outcome.

Not that my anxiety was over. If anything, it was only beginning. On the morning of the operation, I had been panicking about getting it sorted and, being totally honest, I also had a nagging concern about waking up, as stupid as that may sound. When I did wake up, my concern shifted from the personal to the professional. I knew my hand was fixed, which was great, but the next thing on my mind was 'when can I be back training and back involved?' That question dominated my thoughts as I lay in a hospital bed.

I know a lot of my fears might not have been entirely rational but if you speak to any footballer they will tell you that one of the things they worry about most is falling behind in pre-season and then struggling to catch up. It's not as if I was playing for the Dog & Duck either, I was playing for the reigning European champions, so I knew I couldn't take my place for granted. I also knew that I would have to prove my fitness just to get myself involved in training. I've never had a fear of spiders but right at that moment I definitely didn't like them.

A lot of the lads were not even due to report back until a fortnight after me because they had played international football well into the summer, so logically I probably did not need to worry as much as I did. This isn't about logic, though.

If it was about logic I probably would have taken the hint when Celtic released me as a teenager because they didn't think I was good enough to make the grade. If it was about logic, I would have looked for another career when it looked like football wasn't going to work for me. If it was about logic, the other lads and myself might have accepted our fate when we had to beat Messi's Barcelona by four goals to nil.

Being illogical and irrational isn't just part of being a professional footballer, it's sometimes absolutely essential, but it can work against you as well as for you and when you add in the kind of insecurities that I have, it can become a recipe for fearing the worst. I need that, though. It drives me on and means I can never settle for what I've got or accept my fate. It made me restart my career at Queens Park after my Celtic dream died. It makes me carry on fighting when it seems like everything is against me. It makes me put on a pair of trainers and go on a run when I could be putting my feet up. It's not an easy mindset to have because you are never allowed to settle or think that you might have done enough but it has made me the person and the player that I am and for that reason I wouldn't change it for the world, even if it does mean I have some days that are tougher than they need to be.

What added to the anxiety during that period was the fact the transfer window was open. I'm definitely not alone in this as a player either. We all know that we could be one signing away from being replaced. I suppose a part of me was thinking that if I am out for three weeks then what happens? Does the club look for back-up? Does the manager start thinking that maybe he can't rely on me as much as he had? Does the fact that the problem was caused while I was on holiday rather than on the pitch count against me?

For those reasons and many more I didn't want to miss a single day, never mind a couple of weeks. Maybe my outlook would have been slightly different if I was a more laid-back character. Someone like Virgil would see all the possibilities and all the risks but he is so cool, calm and collected that he would probably just take it all in his stride. I've never been that confident. I've always known I've been decent at football but at the core of what I do is an ethic built around hard work and positive attitude. I am never going to be the type who could get any kind of injury, accept it for what it is and then expect to get my place back whenever I returned to fitness.

My way of seeing things is that an injury could be the beginning of the end. There are countless examples of players who have been flying, only for some sort of physical setback to change the direction of their career. That's why I take nothing for granted. A Champions League winner's medal wouldn't keep me in the team. Only hard work on the training ground and good performances on the pitch would prove that I still deserve to be involved and, if not, there would be no shortage of left-backs who would be willing to give up their current club to join a team that was now widely viewed as Europe's best.

I knew that I was the only recognised left-back in the first team squad and, up to then, the club had shown no real signs of doing much in the market but it seemed like everyone was saying we needed a back-up because I'd had to go off against Barcelona with an ankle injury. So the timing with my hand problem couldn't have been worse. I didn't want to give the club reason to go and do something. Like most players, I welcome competition but it is always better for it to arrive when you're fit enough to react positively. It was Alberto Moreno's misfortune with injury that brought me into the team so I knew that it wasn't beyond the realms of possibility that my own injury could allow someone else to do the same to me.

All of these thoughts – and many more besides – were going through my mind in the hours after surgery. I knew that this was in my head and that it probably wouldn't be in anybody else's. The club couldn't have been planning for anything just in case I got bitten by a spider and the gaffer did his best to put my mind at rest. He had told me to let him know how I was as soon as the operation was done. I texted him straight away just to tell him that, physically at least, it had all gone well. Even though I knew he was on holiday himself at the time, he replied almost immediately saying he was really happy that it had been a success. But he couldn't resist a little joke. 'No throw-ins for a while,' he said because, as everyone knows, we had been working with a throw-in coach. Ever since that started, everyone decided I was bad at them. Still, it made me smile and that was something I definitely needed.

The next message I received didn't have the same effect. It came from the surgeon who told me that I was facing 14 days with no activity. I just looked at him and said: "That's not going to happen." I knew straight away that I had to get a second opinion so I spoke to Andy Massey, the Liverpool club doctor, because although what I was told by the surgeon was clearly standard advice for all patients it was important to me to have someone to give me a prognosis through the lens of someone who works in football. It wasn't that I thought the NHS doctor was wrong, but I did wonder if there might be a fast-track for professional footballers.

The problem was that the wound was open as the surgeon couldn't stitch it, in case the infection came back. There was a piece of cloth stuffed into the wound to protect it and Andy warned me that I would have to take it easy due to the risk of re-infection and also because of any lingering after-effects from the anaesthetic. I ended up going back to pre-season as planned but I didn't actually get involved until the following week. I was also told I wouldn't be involved in our second friendly away to Bradford City. That was probably for the best because I definitely wasn't ready. I still needed to have the cloth removed, too, and I was a bit uptight about that, so much so that the doc had to give me a couple of diazepam to settle me down before it got done. They did the trick because I was almost falling asleep but the peace didn't last long as I was in agony when the cloth got pulled out.

All of which meant that on the back of the longest holiday I'd had since becoming a professional footballer, I was going to have my shortest pre-season. Lads like Milly and Lallana were back and they always hit the ground running – I don't actually believe Milly has any kind of holiday because he always turns up at Melwood on the first day like he's about to take part in an Iron Man competition – so I knew I was behind. This wasn't good. Every minute, every second counts at the highest level and we had just finished a season in which we had missed out on the league title by the smallest of margins, so anything that added to the risk of us falling short again wasn't welcome. We were going to America on tour and I didn't want to miss out on that because then I really would have been in trouble. We were having three games out there, one in Scotland, one in France and that was it before the Community Shield against Man City. I ended up flying out to America with the rest of the squad but I only trained for the first time when we got out there.

The memory of how I felt during that first session is something that will live with me for a long time. We were out in South Bend, Indiana, and the weather was scorching. The lads were two weeks into pre-season so they weren't about to hang around for me. This is a competitive environment with elite athletes, so you either step up or you get left behind. I ended up blowing out of my arse. My touch was alright but my energy levels were well down. Maybe it was down to a combination of jet-lag and the anaesthetic not quite having worn off. I was also still on antibiotics. I just felt zapped.

Afterwards, I pretty much fell on the doc when I went to see him. I told him I felt run down and he said that was normal and to be expected. I had only been out for a couple of weeks on the back of a hand operation but I was nowhere near the levels I needed to be at, which made me appreciate even more how the likes of Ox have returned from major injuries after a year or so on the sidelines. I haven't got a clue how he did it and, to be honest, I don't ever want to find out.

I spent most of my time in the USA wearing a massive bandage on my hand. If it was any of the other lads they would have looked even dafter because most of them catch the sun and a tan would only have made the strapping stand out even more. For once, my pale skin worked in my favour as it was hard to see where my white arm stopped and the equally white bandage started. Not that it was inconspicuous to the lads. To them, 'the bandage' became an object of fascination, something for them to give me stick about on a regular basis because, in their minds at least, there was nothing going on underneath.

When the day arrived when it had to be removed towards the end of the tour, it turned into a big event. It was like a gender reveal with a crowd of mates gathering around to see what it was going to be. I could have played pass the parcel so they could all take a bit of the bandage off but they were already having enough fun at my expense anyway. To Virgil, Ads, Hendo, Milly, Trent and Ox this was a box office event and they were milking it for all it was worth. To a man, they were buzzing. This was their chance to cane me and every single one of them had a look on their face which told me they were enjoying this almost as much as anything they had ever done. Then the bandage came off.

I knew it was bad because I had seen the doc's face change as he unravelled it but they'd been too busy making fun of me to notice, so I had a pretty good idea what was coming. Milly said: "Come on, let's see what all the fuss is about." I lifted my grotesque, discoloured, swollen hand with a hole in and all of a sudden they weren't so keen to see it. Trent and Ox were nearly sick, backing away as if I had the plague. It was bloody and fleshy. The big reveal hadn't gone as they'd planned. All they could say was: "What the hell is that?"

I was thinking exactly the same thing. The wound closed over three or four weeks later. The scar it left behind is not exactly the biggest and then it was: 'Is THAT it?'

That was all part and parcel of the healing process. It was strange for a footballer to have and the lads were all like, 'only you could get this'. Most importantly, I was able to get back playing while I continued my recovery because the doc had a lightweight protective strapping that I was able to wear.

I did okay in my first game back against Borussia Dortmund, nutmegging a guy twice and almost scoring with a half volley, so in my mind I was alright. We lost 3-2, though, and we followed that up with another defeat to Sevilla and a draw against Sporting Lisbon.

I found those games a lot tougher physically and as a squad we were also struggling to find our rhythm, which wasn't really surprising because a lot of us had come back at different times, some of the other lads weren't even back and we were still in the process of getting our fitness levels to where they need to be. Add in a bit of jet lag, some inevitable rustiness and some seriously hot weather and peak performance is out of reach. In a competitive environment like that, you might recognise the context and understand that peak fitness doesn't come straight away. That doesn't stop it from being frustrating when your levels seem a fair way off. It's totally natural to want to perform at what you see as your normal standard and we were nowhere near that.

There was also a bit of a hangover from the Champions League final which, in hindsight, probably didn't help. The crowds in the USA were absolutely brilliant, as they always are, and the welcome we got at each venue was a bit special. This was an opportunity for our American fans to celebrate our success and, quite rightly, they made the most of it.

We even had the trophy with us, which was a great idea because the more supporters who could see it the better. There had been queues of fans getting their picture with it in Liverpool for days on end and it was right that we took the European Cup to the USA so that people over there could see it too, especially as we were visiting Boston, where our owners, Fenway Sports Group, are based.

We would go out to check the pitch before games and as soon we came out of the tunnel, the Champions League winners parade video would be on a big screen. We were selling a lot of tickets in big stadiums and it's understandable the fans wanted to see the parade but by the third time it felt like a bit of a distraction. The new season was only a couple of weeks away. We would carry those memories for the rest of our lives, that video is going to be there in twenty or thirty years when we're old and sitting back and looking back on memories, but now it was time to create new ones. The time had come for us to draw a line between the past and the present, otherwise the future might end up being compromised.

Luckily, one of the gaffer's biggest strengths is sensing the mood amongst the lads and knowing when to intervene. He certainly didn't want everything to revolve around what we had done in the Champions League and the mantra of all of the coaching staff that summer was: 'It's not about what you've won, it's about what we are trying to win next'. It wasn't quite the legendary Ronnie Moran going around the Liverpool players in the 1980s pointedly telling them that he'd see them next season after they had won the league but the sentiment was exactly the same. Don't rest on your laurels, don't think you've done enough and never, ever allow contentment to set in. Winning once is great but it's nowhere near as good as winning over and over again and the only way to have a chance of doing that involved fighting against complacency.

As usual, the gaffer led from the front. We were at an event at the Four Seasons Hotel in Boston that was for the FSG partners and it was great. I had been selected to go with Trent, Virgil, Gini, Milly, Hendo and Ox and we were really well looked after. It was nice for us, too, as it gave us an opportunity to express our gratitude to the owners for their efforts and to hear what the club's progress meant to them.

One of the partners asked a question which had become fairly standard for us by then about what winning the Champions League meant. It was a totally reasonable thing to ask but as a manager, the gaffer has to come at it from a totally different angle to most other people and, like us, he was becoming concerned that a celebratory tour of the USA could soften us up, so he answered the question on our behalf. His response was diplomatic and respectful and it was also intended for our consumption rather than anyone else because he basically said that our focus now was on attempting to be champions of Europe again and champions of England for the first time in far too long. Message received, loud and clear.

From then on, we just switched off from it and as soon as we got back to Liverpool the gaffer drilled the point home again. "Okay, we will remember that for years to come but now isn't the time to sit back and reflect, now is the time to kick on. Try to forget about the Champions League, carry the memories with you, carry the feelings and memories with your families and friends but we need to kick on and forget about it."

It had to be said but by then our focus was shifting from past results to the fact that we hadn't won during pre-season. It is all about getting fitness and rhythm back, but you still don't want to get into the habit of not winning games and it did start to annoy me. We still had Alisson, Firmino, Sadio, Fabinho and Mo to come back so nobody was panicking but it was an irritation and there was worse to come.

We landed back from the USA at around 10.30am on the Friday and had the rest of the day off. We hadn't seen our families for a couple of weeks so it obviously all gets a bit hectic with the kids when you get home and, although we'd been on tour time, you can't avoid jet-lag.

The next day we had a tough afternoon session at Melwood, went home for a night's sleep and then flew to Edinburgh on Sunday morning. For me, it was a big deal because I was playing in Scotland. It was only a friendly against Napoli but this was my home country and I knew quite a lot of my friends and family would be in the crowd. We never stood a chance, though, because as early as five minutes in we all knew that we were knackered. We ended up losing 3-0 and it could have been more. Judging by what they'd seen, the fans who had packed out Murrayfield were entitled to be worried. We had context, though – we knew we were tired.

While the supporters would look at it as us being battered by a team that we should be competing with at the very least, our perspective was that we had not prepared for the game against Napoli, we had prepared for the ones coming up in the league. Most of all, we knew our legs would never feel that bad again. I think sometimes the manager tests us in at least one game pre-season where he basically says: 'If you can play through this, you can play through anything.' You play with an empty tank, you play with the tired legs, you play with a tired mind and then, during the season over the Christmas period where we have maybe six games in fourteen days or whatever, that's not a massive problem because it's not as bad as what we did during the summer.

I know Pep Lijnders has a theory that having such a testing July was the perfect way for us to move on after winning the Champions League and I think there's definitely something in that. It may have annoyed us at the time but failing to win those friendlies helped ensure that our hunger and desire returned stronger than ever and it also gave us a reminder that previous success would count for nothing.

There was no doubt in my mind about our attitude but because if there's one thing I can guarantee about this team, it's that we never turn up thinking a game will be a walk in the park. That's just not us. Everything about us is built on hard work and giving everything in every game. If you take that away, we know better than anyone else that we won't be winning games. It's that simple.

We all know how fundamental training is to what we do in games. Every training session is different with Pep and credit to Pep, Peter Krawietz and Vitor Matos – and the gaffer, of course – because we do something different every day and that's what keeps training so interesting. The 'Young v Old' games we play are always massively competitive. I'm right on the cusp in terms of age. If a couple of lads are injured, I'll be on the 'old' team but usually I'm on the 'young' side.

Pep is the referee and he loves the 'play on' shout. That winds me up because I think 'just referee the game, play to the whistle!' That always makes us lose our heads a wee bit and I've probably apologised to him at least fifty times during the season over his refereeing – just his refereeing, not his coaching, I have nothing to complain about there! I know there is method to his madness, though. It's all about creating situations in which we suffer adversity and how we deal with that.

So while we struggled against Napoli, Borussia Dortmund, Sporting Lisbon and Sevilla, our competitive edge was sharpening at the same time as we were regaining our fitness. There was a sense of adversity and a feeling of needing to put things right. It might only have been pre-season but when we stepped off the pitch after losing heavily to Napoli we had all gone well past the point where we might be prepared to accept that results in friendlies don't matter.

To put it bluntly, I don't think I've ever been in a dressing room where there was such an emphasis on winning a pre-season game. The next one didn't just matter, it was crucial because not only did we need to reassert standards, we also had to put down a marker for the season to come.

From Edinburgh, we flew straight to Geneva before heading to our training camp in Évian, south-eastern France. The good news was this would be the first time that everyone would be back together since the homecoming parade in Liverpool because Mo, Sadio, Bobby, Fabinho and Alisson would all be joining up with us.

This was always going to be the real start of pre-season.

ROBBO

BEYOND THE BRINK

I AM totally under water. Outright distress has not set in yet but I know it's not far off and the feeling of discomfort is growing with every passing second. Fears are escalating and no matter how hard I try to shut them out they find a way in. When I summon up the courage to open my eyes, the chlorine stings them and all I can see through my blurred vision is a group of my team-mates who are all in the same predicament.

This isn't nice. It's actually horrendous. It is all I can do to focus on my breathing but I know that when I do, it just makes me even more aware of how much I need oxygen so my strategy changes again. Blank everything out, that's the one. No thinking of how much longer I can take this, no wondering how the other lads are coping and no wondering what the hell I'm doing down here; just shut the world out and embrace the darkness. Then the voice kicks in again: *You can't take much more of this you know. Your lungs can't cope any longer. You need fresh air. You need to get out of this water and you need to get out now.* Before I can even make a conscious decision, I'm heading back to the surface, gasping as I arrive and feeling a strange mixture of failure and achievement that I've never experienced before. At the water's edge, there's the man who put us down there – the gaffer – and he's looking incredibly pleased with himself.

Hotel pools are supposed to be fun. At worst, they are places where you work on your stamina and fitness if splashing around and acting daft is out of the question. But for one morning/afternoon during pre-season, our hotel pool in Évian turned into a test of everything from our endurance to our willingness to put our faith in the gaffer's methods. For those outside the club who couldn't get their heads around the entirely logical idea of us using a throw-in coach to improve our technique in that area, God knows what they would have made of the thought that a league title bid could be given added impetus by an entire squad being forced underwater.

Never mind marginal gains, this was significant pain and the mastermind behind it was a German surfer who none of us had heard of before Jürgen introduced him to us. Having spent a couple of hours in a pool with him, I can guarantee that we won't ever forget him. Like Thomas Grønnemark, who was brought in to give us something extra at throw-ins, Sebastian Steudtner was viewed by the gaffer as someone who could help both our breathing technique and our mental durability. He made us suffer. He made us crave oxygen like we'd never craved it before. But, by taking us to the brink, he also underlined how much we had to give and how far we could go. There was method to this madness and we would only come to realise just how much in the weeks and months that followed. There is no doubt in my mind that the suffering was all worthwhile.

The whole point of the exercise had been to improve our ability to cope with extreme situations and extreme pressure. The gaffer was thinking outside the box and after sharing his experiences of surfing incredible waves with us, Sebastian moved onto the breathing exercises that both he and Jürgen believed would be beneficial. As soon as Sebastian explained his thinking and how he believed that putting us into an extreme situation would enable us to trigger new coping mechanisms, it made total sense. The only problem, as far as I was concerned, was that ever since I was a kid I haven't liked being underwater. Swimming is fine. I'll splash along with the kids all day long when we're on holiday and get my lengths in when I'm training but I'm really uncomfortable about having my head under the water and not being able to breathe. In my book, that makes me pretty normal.

The challenge was to shut off your brain and not allow negative thoughts to creep in. As soon as I went under, I wanted to get myself back up again. Staying under water to my maximum did scare me at first but by the end I was fine with it, even though it was much more of a challenge for me than it was for most of the other lads. Ultimately, I was able to control my breathing and send different signals to my body from my brain.

We all improved the amount of time we were able to stay underwater, whether it was by ten or twenty seconds. By the end, some of the lads were clocking up almost three minutes. It was incredible to see the difference that your mind can make and it turned into a great session because we all took it so seriously and committed to what we were doing, even if it felt so unnatural to some of us. Sebastian kept telling us that when we think we are at our limit, we can still find something more and all we have to do is tell our bodies that. He told us there would be times during the season when we would need to burst through a pain barrier, when we would literally have to suck it up and find a way to deal with whatever challenge we were facing. Having any kind of coping mechanism was only going to help us.

We had just come off the back of a season in which we only lost once and finished with ninety-seven points so the gaffer wanted us to be able to find a happy place under stress. Given what followed, I don't think that was a bad idea. As a player, there are times when you sit in meetings and it seems like the coaching staff are coming at you from left field so you can wonder what it's all about but this wasn't one of those occasions. We all got it and bought into it. Everything the guy said made sense from a sporting perspective.

While there's no way we could measure the impact of what we were doing, there's no doubt that subconsciously it definitely helped us in the weeks and months that followed. If I had to pinpoint one fixture when it really made a difference I wouldn't hesitate in going for Leicester away. This was a game when we were coming back off the Club World Cup in Qatar having flown thousands of miles around the world with Christmas in between. The expectation outside of the squad itself was that we would probably struggle.

As it was, we produced arguably our best performance of the season and blew them away, even though they are clearly a very good side. When you've been under water, wondering

Magic of Madrid: I'll never get tired of being called a European Cup winner. Beating Spurs 2-0 laid to rest the disappointment of the year before

You're the man: I sent a special message to Hendo after he lifted the European Cup telling him that he was up there with the greatest Liverpool captains in history

Bus ride to heaven: Hard for some people to believe but we worried that no-one would turn up for the victory parade –I guess we got that wrong! Spotting my mates in the crowd was a special moment

Bringing it home: *(Left)* Adam and me in our Madrid hotel – getting our heads around the fact we are European champions. *(Right)* on the plane back to Liverpool with Milly and the trophy

THAT spider bite ...

No easy ride: In Évian in 2018 – pre-season is always about pushing us to the limit

Lucky boots: *(Left)* I ended up having to wear my personalised Champions League final boots for Steve Clarke's first game in charge of Scotland – but they proved a good omen. I scored and we beat Cyprus 2-1. *(Right)* star struck meeting jockey Paul Hanagan at Ayr racecourse

Stepping up: Despite the result, our Community Shield performance against Manchester City in August proved that we were ready to compete with Pep Guardiola's side for the big prizes

Hitting the ground running: Back at Anfield and celebrating with Mo after he had scored in a 4-1 win over Norwich in our first league game. It wasn't all good news – Alisson had to leave the pitch injured

The battle of Istanbul: Competing for possession with Chelsea's César Azpilicueta during the Super Cup final in Istanbul which turned into a scrappy affair – but we showed our resilience to come through and lift another trophy (*below*)

Saints and winners: There were no big celebrations after the Super Cup final. We had a quick turnaround with a tough trip to Southampton and a reunion with an old friend – Danny Ings

You're Gunner do it: Mo scored twice and Joel got on the scoresheet as we blew away Arsenal at Anfield. Joel played a vital role for us over the course of the season

Team spirit: The press made a lot of the Mo and Sadio incident at Burnley which was amusing. I was with them afterwards and they were laughing about it. Our dressing room is first class

Tough to take:
With Belgium's Romelu Lukaku after Scotland had lost to Belgium in a Euro 2020 qualifying game. We were bitterly disappointed to get nothing from our two home games – we also lost 2-1 to Russia in September

Friends and rivals:
(*Above*) Virgil looks on as I compete for the ball with Gini during a friendly against Holland from a couple of years ago. Scotland can follow the same path as Liverpool and build a bright future

Back on track:
(*Left*) Martin Dubravka denies me a goal against Newcastle as I put my Scotland disappointment behind me. Bobby was on fire that day as we won 3-1

Grinding it out: Celebrating after Bobby had just put us two up at Stamford Bridge. But we had to dig in during the second half to get the result at Chelsea

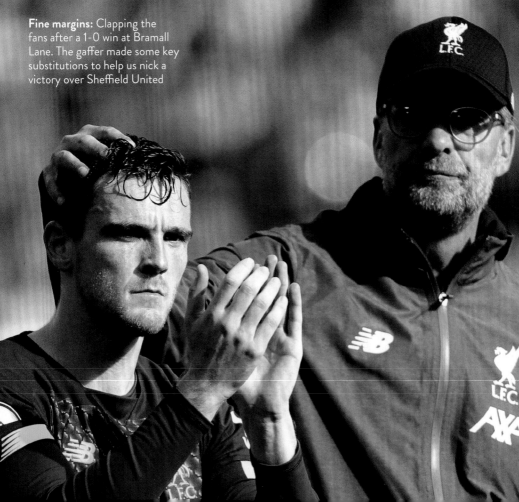

Fine margins: Clapping the fans after a 1-0 win at Bramall Lane. The gaffer made some key substitutions to help us nick a victory over Sheffield United

how long it will be until you can breathe fresh air in again but knowing you have to stay down for as long as you can, it makes dealing with stuff like fixture congestion and fatigue a little bit easier than it would otherwise.

I know a lot of people believe that, as a squad, we resolved to win the league the season after we lifted the European Cup. Apart from the individual messages that we shared with one another, it wasn't really like that as a group. I think we might have all had that feeling but nobody was vocal about it.

When you get that feeling of being a champion, you want it a lot more, whether that be the league or the FA Cup or whatever. But I don't think straight after Madrid we were all saying to each other "next season, Premier League." We were the champions of Europe and stayed in that bubble rather than thinking about losing the league or how close we had come. Our focus shifted during pre-season, though, and it wasn't just a case of saying so either, there was a definite change of demeanour. From the manager downwards, there was an extra determination to scratch the itch that was bugging all of us and to do whatever it would take, even if that meant being pushed to the very brink.

That message was reinforced in word and deed while we were in Évian, most powerfully of all during a team meeting which took place later on the same day that we had given our all in the pool.

Up to that point, the gaffer had been comparatively relaxed; the players had been coming back at different times and there had definitely been a sense that the second phase of pre-season would be a different level to the first. So when he stood in front of us all in a small meeting room on the ground floor of the hotel, it quickly became clear to all of us that the gaffer saw this as his opportunity to really set out his stall for the season. For me, this is where he really comes into his own because I don't think I've come across many people in any walk of life who are better able not just to sense the mood, but to take advantage of it.

"In twenty, thirty, forty years from now, everyone will know that we were Champions League winners in 2019," he said. "That is in the record books and nobody can take that away from us. In Madrid we made it six times for this wonderful club and that is a fantastic achievement but now we want more. We want to be Premier League winners for the first time, we want to be European Cup winners for the seventh time. As a group, we want to keep on winning." It's no exaggeration to say the hairs on the back of my neck were standing up as he spoke.

For the gaffer this wasn't about taking the memories away from us, it was about keeping them with us and using them for inspiration going forward. He wanted us to keep the images of Madrid in our heads as a constant reminder of what we had achieved and what we want to achieve again, but there was also a dividing line – that was then and this is now. Basically, he was creating a hunger in us to become serial winners.

The other message was that we were going to need to stick together more than ever and that we had to have the kind of unity which means that, if you cut one of us, we all bleed. He said: "One of the problems that we are going to face is that we only lost one game last season and we still fell short. If we lose one or two in the first ten games or so there will be pressure from outside, but we have to recognise that we won't be in a bad position. Every season is different. We need to forget what happened last season and not use it as a constant comparison."

I would say without hesitation that this was one of the best team meetings I've been in. I literally could have started the season that night. We walked out and I guarantee everyone, to a man, was thinking that this could be another special season – maybe even more special than the one before. Over the course of a day in a French hotel, our minds had not only accepted the challenge ahead, they had embraced it.

Psychologically, we could not have been in a better place. Physically, the hard work was only just beginning. In terms of setting, scenery and so on, Évian is one of the nicest places we go to. It really couldn't be much more picturesque but appearances are deceptive because it is where things get really tough. Before we even arrive, we know that it's going to be five or six days of really intense, unforgiving work. I wouldn't describe it as a boot camp but it's not far off in terms of required attitude because we all have to be right at it.

Even the manager's demeanour changes. He puts on his game face and it's as close as any of us see him to when he's on the touchline during the biggest matches. For him – and the rest of us as well – Évian is the moment that we flip from one stage of pre-season to another. The phase in which we do a lot of media, public appearances and basically get ourselves going again is done, and now we have to step up physically and mentally without any distractions. It is a tough time, but in the best possible way because we know what the aim is. It involves double sessions and, on the odd occasion, a triple session, so you have to be ready for it. Otherwise you could easily fall by the wayside.

Worst of all is the 400-metre running track that circles the pitch. I only have to see that and I get a shiver down my spine. Like most other footballers, I hate running. Not as much as

Virgil hates it, but not far off. Put me on a pitch with a ball and I'll run after it like a dog chasing a stick all day long but running for the sake of running is a different thing entirely. It's only the oddballs, the Milners of this world, who embrace that element of pre-season, the rest of us view it as the necessary evil that it is.

We switch between 500-metre and 1000-metre runs and as anyone who has done any kind of track work would know, they're punishing distances because they're a horrible mix of running flat out for speed and building up stamina. We all have to work to our maximum and there is no hiding place because we have to wear heart monitors.

Every pre-season I have the same conversation with the sports scientists. "Please don't put me in a group with Milly," I ask but they must like inflicting a bit of pain on me because as sure as night follows day that's the group I end up in. It's like doing karaoke with Frank Sinatra. There's only one performer out there who is going to blow everyone away and it isn't going to be me.

While the rest of us are puffing and panting away, straining just to stay in his slipstream, the Yorkshire Express is biding his time, giving us the false impression that we are keeping up with him. Then he produces this ridiculous burst to pull away and leave us all trailing in his wake. It can be quite annoying to see a thirty-four-year-old man half a track ahead of you but it also sets a standard for the rest of us as well and that's never a bad thing.

The point of it all is that this is where it all starts. The manager never tires of telling us that we can't just switch it on in games and the same goes for pre-season. If you want to achieve anything, you have to build up to it and prepare for it and that is what Évian is all about. When you have those moments in games at the height of winter when you feel like you've got nothing left to give, the physical and mental toughness that you've built up in Évian allows you to go again.

It's also during these trips that team spirit really builds up again and I think it's now widely recognised that this has played a big role in our success. I roomed with Milly while we were there. Usually, the rooms are drawn but this time we got to choose between ourselves.

There were six of us who were in the mix for three rooms – Milly, Hendo, Adam, Trent, Ox and myself – and we were going to pull names out of a hat but Milly didn't want to share with Trent or Ox because they tend to be awake a bit later than the rest of us, so I went in with him. I knew exactly what I was doing, though, because the captain and vice-captain get a wee upgrade on their rooms which means I benefit from Milly's seniority.

Unfortunately, my partnership with Milly wasn't extended to the table tennis pairs tournament which featured every member of our travelling party. When the draw took place, I came out of the hat with Matty, our Head of Press, which meant my dreams of glory were dashed before the competition had even started.

Against all odds, we got to the quarter-finals before an unnecessary change of tactics cost us and all we could do was watch on as Hendo and Mo were declared Évian 2019 winners following victory against Ox and Harrison in the final. The sense of disappointment was strong, I can't lie, but in any game of pairs you are only as strong as your weakest link and I could at least comfort myself in the knowledge that I couldn't have done any more.

I also knew that I wouldn't have to take part in the annual karaoke challenge because it was only for the new boys and I'd made my singing debut a couple of years earlier with a stunning rendition of 'Sweet Caroline' that brought the house down. This time it was the turn of Harvey Elliott, our new signing from Fulham, and Lee Richardson, our sports psychologist. It was Lee who stole the show for the wrong reasons with a song that he had written himself. I'm all for creativity and it definitely takes bottle to stand up and sing in front of a load of footballers who you've only just met but as performances go his was definitely more Watford away than Barcelona at home.

That wasn't the only noise going on during that period as there was a fair bit of talk about our lack of form during pre-season. Even though we were away from England and we're used to shutting voices out, we knew questions were being asked about our results and performances because we hadn't won a game. There were also those who were accusing the club of resting on its laurels because we hadn't been too active in the transfer market. I'm not criticising anyone who held those views and even though they were not shared by us, we knew that we needed to put a bit of a marker down just to settle things a bit.

That's why our friendly against Lyon while we were in France took on greater importance than it would have done normally. Yes, it was just a friendly and yes, we knew enough about ourselves and what we are capable of not to get drawn into any unnecessary negativity but we didn't want our run of poor results to extend any further. That was why we put pressure on one another going into the game. We wanted to carry on improving our fitness but there was also a heightened emphasis on winning and we achieved that objective with a fairly comfortable victory. Even more importantly, there were quite a few signs of a things starting to click again. It doesn't matter what time of year it is, that is always a good feeling to have as a team. To put it simply, that was the moment when we knew we were ready for the new season.

It was just as well that we found our form when we did as Man City were next up in the Community Shield. It was a bit of a weird scenario for us because we hadn't won anything to qualify for that game. The only reason we were playing in it was that City had cleaned up domestically and we were given a place as runners-up in the Premier League so, mentally at least, it was definitely a bit odd. But the fact that it was City and we had enjoyed such a great battle with them in the league ensured that everyone viewed it as a competitive game regardless of its status.

Another thing that helped focus our minds was the fact that we were staying at a hotel just across from Wembley so when we went out for our pre-match walk on the morning of the game, we saw supporters of both clubs swarming around. It created this huge sense of occasion. I know the Community Shield is a curtain raiser but as it got closer to kick-off it had the feel of a cup final and the quality of the opposition certainly helped in that respect too.

Externally, the perception is that there is a strong rivalry between us and City but, for the players, any rivalry is built on mutual respect. We know how good they are and I would hope they can see our qualities too. It's probably fair to say that on this occasion there were alternate spells when we saw the best of each other. In the first half, we struggled for rhythm and they were on top but in the second we took control, creating chances and cancelling out their goal. If anything, we were stronger on the day and the fact that we eventually lost on penalties did not change that. This was important to us, especially after being pipped by City just a few months earlier. We had beaten them previously, including a 3-0 win in the Champions League, but this felt like more of a complete performance and it gave us confidence that we could go on and mount an even stronger challenge.

The kind of flow we had in the second half inspired that feeling more than anything else. Of course we had wanted to win, particularly with 45,000 Liverpool fans in the crowd who you want to send home happy, but we took something even more important out of that game – belief. City were the benchmark and they deserved that status because of everything they had achieved but we had been stronger than them and I think it was the first time, certainly since I had been at Liverpool, that we had been entitled to believe that we were on a par with them. That isn't to take anything away from City, who remain an incredibly talented team, but football is about moments and the ebb and flow that goes with competitive sport and at that point in time we felt that we were going from strength to strength, just as they were experiencing a wee bit of transition.

There had been games previously when we had deservedly beaten them but in our heart of hearts we still knew they were a more complete team than us, so the fact that it felt differently at Wembley was a big thing for us. We had been comfortable out there, we had felt like we were their equals at the very least and it was up to us to show that throughout the course of the season, albeit in the knowledge that a team like City wasn't about to roll over for us or anyone else.

It was after the game that Simon Mignolet let all of us know he would be returning to Belgium to join Bruges. I know people outside of the squad may not attach any great importance to a second choice goalkeeper leaving but to us it was a big thing because Simon had been a big part of what we were doing. Obviously he had lost his place to Alisson and there's no shame in that because Ali is arguably the best in the world, but Simon's professionalism and commitment to the cause never wavered. Also, we are such a tight-knit group that my natural inclination was that I didn't want to see any of the lads depart but, understandably, Simon wanted to play having been number one for so long and none of us could blame him for taking up the offer from Bruges.

His departure led to Adrian coming in and the widespread expectation was that, like Simon, he wouldn't get too much playing time but that he would also need to be ready to step up because you never know what can happen in football. I knew that myself because I had needed an injury to Alberto Moreno for me to get my chance and it is the same for so many players but, even so, Alisson was looking like an immovable object. Adrian took his place on the bench for our first game of the season at home to Norwich City and the expectation was that he would remain there but that was not how things turned out.

In the dressing room beforehand, there was a real sense of anticipation. This was the first time that we would be running out at Anfield as champions of Europe so the buzz was definitely different. The first game of the season is always exciting anyway and I could feel the electricity as soon as the team bus approached the stadium.

I wouldn't say there was an edge to the atmosphere, it was more of a happiness, a collective feeling of pleasure about what we had achieved together and excitement about what the new season might bring. I know it was a big thing for the supporters and it was also a big thing for the players. It was something that had been talked about pretty much since the European Cup had been won and the cheer that we got when we ran out before kick-off is something that will live with me for a long time.

As usual, I charged to the Kop which looked even better than ever because the supporters had created this brilliant mosaic reminding the world that Liverpool had won it six times. The sights, the sounds, the feeling – you take it all in as much as you possibly can because these are truly special times and there is nothing better than being able to share them with your own people at your home ground. It made me feel ten feet tall. I'm not one who needs extra motivation but I do have the kind of personality that gets lifted and inspired by a passionate crowd. I think the Liverpool fans saw that in my first season when I chased all over the pitch trying to get the ball from Man City and it's something that I would never want to lose because being able to feed on the energy of the crowd is definitely a quality that helps my game.

Judging by the way the entire team reacts to a big game atmosphere, it's fair to say that the same goes for the rest of the lads as well. I know this isn't unique to Liverpool – I saw it through a fan's eyes at Celtic Park – but it does seem to be accentuated here and there is ample evidence to suggest that when our supporters are right at it and we're on our game, it makes for a really powerful collective. There's a banner that gets flown on the Kop that says 'Unity Is Strength' and there's definitely a lot to be said for that.

As well as feeling the passion of our supporters, we were

also aware of the pressure of the situation. Our fixture was the first of the season in the Premier League and we were playing the day before most of the rest, so all eyes were on us. We knew that anything other than a win would be viewed as an early setback but we were also aware that, having just been promoted, Norwich would come right out of the traps and have a proper go. Our status as European champions would mean nothing to them and rightly so. They would just view us as a big scalp to try and take in front of a big TV audience on a Friday night and they also knew that, in terms of expectations at least, they had nothing to lose.

The good thing was that, as a team, we had become used to being in this kind of situation. In a short space of time, Liverpool had gone from being a side which could be unpredictable from one game to the next – and sometimes even from one moment to the next – to one that was expected to win, especially at Anfield, because more often than not that's what we did. It almost feels like a muscle memory in the sense that we keep repeating the same situation over and over again and regularly achieving the same outcome.

Norwich came and had a real go, something that I don't think they were given enough credit for, but the comfort that we had in our own surroundings and the confidence we had developed there meant we had too much for them on the night. In almost any other circumstances a 4-1 win in our first game of the season would be viewed as a perfect start but the loss of Ali to injury meant this was far from perfect. It goes without saying that you don't want to lose any player at any time but seeing the world's best goalkeeper being helped off after 39 minutes of a new campaign is a massive blow, there is no getting away from that.

I was probably closest to Ali when it happened because it was a goal kick on my side and, like everyone else, I thought it was bad straight away as he's not the type to go down and he's definitely not the type to stay down. When he went off, I was fearing the worst but I had no idea what he had done. I just knew we had a problem on our hands.

It's at times like that that you have to place your trust in the club, though. The reason why Adrian had been brought in was exactly for this kind of situation so Michael Edwards and the gaffer clearly thought he was good enough to play in goal for Liverpool or else he wouldn't be here. When he ran on to replace Ali, we were all pretty confident that he would be fine and I've got no doubt that his own belief was boosted massively by the enormous roar that he received from the Kop. He couldn't have asked for a better vote of confidence than that. I'm sure he'll remember that reception for much longer than he'll recall the fist pump welcome that I gave him, put it that way!

The real positive was that he acquitted himself so well and he deserves a lot of credit for that because he had only been training for us for a few days and most of us had been on recovery after playing against City, so it wasn't as if he'd had plenty of time to work with his new team-mates. That's testament to Adrian's own professionalism and his attitude because if he'd wanted an excuse for having a game in which he had a few teething problems there were plenty available to him. Thankfully, for him and us, he made a good first impression.

It was only afterwards that I found out that Ali had felt something go in his calf and, without being a physio or anything, I knew he was facing at least a few weeks on the sidelines. That fear was then confirmed and it was clear to everyone that we would need Adrian's positive first impression to last for the foreseeable future because we had some big games coming up during the period when we would be without Ali. None more so than the Super Cup in Istanbul, which was massive for us.

The European Super Cup final was another one of those games that you don't realise how big it is until you get there. Whereas a competition like the FA Cup has a century of history and every club has its own story to tell, only a select group have contested the Super Cup because the qualification criteria is so elite. Not only do you have to be one of the best teams in Europe, you need to be one of two clubs to have won a big European trophy the previous season so it doesn't lend itself to mass interest – ninety-eight per cent of teams haven't had the opportunity to participate in it.

It did seem a bit strange because it was a Premier League clash against Chelsea but we were also going for another trophy in a foreign country and the chance of winning another cup so soon after our last one was a big incentive for us, no matter what some were saying. Sometimes the value of this kind of fixture can be over-analysed anyway. If you boil it down, we are competitive sportsmen and ever since we were kids we have played in games and tournaments with trophies on offer and that kind of scenario never stops being a big deal as long as you're able to pull a pair of boots on.

It turned out to be a long slog of a game and we were never quite at our best but the fact that it wasn't straightforward only added to our sense that winning really mattered. If it had been a walk in the park there might have been a few shoulder shrugs but it was the exact opposite of that; it was highly competitive and the game could have gone either way. I would defy anyone who had decided beforehand that the Super Cup wasn't that important to watch our game and still stick with that belief. Both teams ran themselves into the ground. There wasn't a moment when either of us felt comfortable out there. That only happens when a competition is meaningful and both teams are determined to win.

Ultimately it was Adrian who turned out to be the difference for us after we scrapped our way to a 2-2 draw. The penalty shoot-out that followed was typically tense and our new boy became an instant hero when he saved Tammy Abraham's effort to win us the trophy. It had been different playing without Ali because we had become so accustomed to the way he plays and he's obviously a special goalkeeper, but Adrian performed incredibly well on the night and we couldn't have been happier for him. It was a great feeling in general.

It is these kind of victories, tough and hard earned, where your winning mentality can only grow and with a trophy being involved it also added to our sense of momentum that had been building from the previous season. I'm not going to lie and say that my Super Cup winner's medal is the most cherished I have because the Champions League was out on its own in that respect at that stage, but it was still a big deal to me. There were no great celebrations afterwards, though. The fixture schedule put paid to any thoughts of letting our hair down as we were playing away to Southampton less than seventy-two hours later, so our focus was on nothing other than recovery.

We went back to our hotel, had dinner and went to bed. There was no drinking and the only indications that we had just won another trophy were the smiles on our faces and the medals around our necks. We knew we had a big Premier

League game coming up and, even if we hadn't, it was the start of the season rather than the end so this was no time to be enjoying ourselves.

Given how limited our preparations were, Southampton became a massive test. This was us putting our heads under water, holding our breath and trusting ourselves to get through on sheer determination and focus all over again. The only method we had to fall back on came from previous experience of having matches in quick succession but this was on another level again because of the travelling involved and the quick turnaround. So it became an endurance test and also an examination of our ability to switch from one challenge to another with very little time for adjustment.

We flew back on the Thursday, had a night in our own beds at home, then flew down to Southampton on the Friday. Thankfully it was still early in the season so mentally we were still refreshed from having time off but physically it was tough and I would imagine the sports science lads wouldn't want a repeat of this situation at any time in the future. Ideally, you don't want to rely on whatever resistance you have built up at such an early stage, but we had no choice. We knew the standards that had been set in the previous campaign and we either met them in every circumstance or else we would fall by the wayside. The gaffer made a few changes just to freshen things up a bit and we acquitted ourselves well, taking a 2-0 lead before Southampton came back into it and we ended up hanging on a bit towards the end after Danny Ings grabbed a goal back.

This was a funny situation because we didn't know who to have a go at – Ingsy for doing damage to his old mates or Adrian for getting a bit slack at a time when focus was all important. Ingsy was only doing his job for his new club, though, and Adrian had been brilliant since coming in so we took it in our stride and moved on. It was a reminder for all of us about the standards that were required and it probably helped Adrian too because he hadn't been with us in the previous season when we had learned the hard way that every goal and every point can determine who becomes champions. As a team, it is always better if you're able to learn from your mistakes when it doesn't cost you any points and, luckily for us, this is what happened on that day.

To be honest, I was more concerned with my own form than anyone else's at the start of the season. It's normal for me to be harsh on myself. Like most players, I'm my own biggest critic and I know better than anyone that I tend to struggle through pre-season simply because I thrive on the rhythm of games. If I'm getting forty-five minutes here and there, stopping and starting, I know I won't be at my sharpest but I also know that the approach we have is in the best interests of myself and the team. I have to accept that if I want to be flying when the season really gets going it doesn't make sense for me to start the campaign like I'm on fire, as that just isn't sustainable.

So it is a grind early on and all I can do is hang on in there by battling through matches until I get my rhythm. At some stage in my career, I hope that I will have enough experience to deal better with this side of things because I am aware of why I have these issues, I'm just not so good at putting them in the kind of context that they deserve when it happens. Maybe that ongoing internal battle is something I need to bring out the best in myself, though, so I don't want to get rid of it altogether. It would just be a bit easier, especially for those closest to me, if it didn't affect me quite so much.

When I get something wrong on the pitch I don't need anyone to tell me but it happens anyway. Whether it's a glare from Virg or a bollocking from Hendo, it's all part of what we do and who we are. Stuff like that happens so often in games that everyone is used to it – it hardly ever provokes any interest and when it does, it tends to be nothing more than a few funny gifs on social media. As we discovered at Burnley, though, there are exceptions to that when a brief spat between team-mates is made out to seem so big that it overshadows everything else. Ask anyone what they remember about that game and it will almost certainly be Sadio having a bit of a rant when he was taken off because Mo hadn't set him up for a shot on goal a minute or two earlier.

The mad thing is, this was our most complete performance of the season to that point. The control we had, the chances we created, the goals we scored, how tight we kept things at the back against a difficult opponent – it pretty much had all of the qualities that we strive for. The only problem is it isn't recalled for those reasons, not outside of the club anyway. All anyone talks about in relation to that game is Sadio falling out with Mo.

I can't think of too many other workplaces where everyone can perform at their best but it's forgotten about because a couple of blokes had words with one another. That kind of disagreement is part and parcel of every walk of life but in football it makes headlines and I don't think that is going to change any time soon, so as players we just have to accept it.

The lads themselves found the reaction funny which puts it in its proper perspective. In an ideal world we would avoid sounding off in front of the cameras because we know the fuss it can bring and the scrutiny that can follow. The incident itself was pretty standard and the kind of thing you would expect. As someone who doesn't get into scoring positions too often, I'm probably not best placed to judge it. It's safe to say that it was the kind of thing that you see on the football pitch all the time, with one player opting to shoot when another is expecting a pass.

Mo was accused of selfishness in some quarters but his single-mindedness in front of goal is one of his greatest assets and it's certainly helped us to win countless games. Similarly, Sadio was entitled to want the ball because he was in such a good position. If Mo had scored, Sadio would have been the first to congratulate him but it didn't work out that way and Sadio let his frustration show. It was brilliant for the lads at the back. We have dozens of arguments every game so we got to enjoy this one, especially with it becoming a national talking point within seconds. It was something and nothing but the main thing was we had got another win to maintain our perfect start to the season.

I was in the shower with Mo and Sadio afterwards. I was right in between them and they were both laughing and joking. People don't see that – they only see what happens on the pitch, but behind the scenes the spirit in our dressing room is top class. Yes, we will have disagreements on the pitch. Like any other industry, football has a creative tension and that inevitably leads to moments when we will disagree but as long as that's all it is it's not a problem.

That was the way the gaffer saw it and we moved on from it straight away which was important because it didn't give anyone the opportunity to stir things up. In hindsight, it may well have been a good distraction too because while everyone was focusing on Mo and Sadio, no-one was really talking about how well we had played which was helpful as it allowed us to keep going about our business without our form getting as much attention as it would have done otherwise.

The Burnley game had come the week after our 3-1 dismantling of Arsenal at Anfield. That had brought a different kind of scrutiny as more and more observers began to start to speak openly about the possibility of us taking City's title. If that's what they believed, good luck to them, but there was not a chance of us getting carried away and becoming involved in that kind of talk. Not only was it far too early for that, we have far too much respect for City and also for ourselves to get drawn into any premature excitement. Which is not to say we didn't feel confident, because we did.

Arsenal were seen as dark horses and the expectation was that they would have a good season under Unai Emery because they had spent a fair bit of money in the summer on some good players. We could also feel that there were those who thought this was the game when we could stumble but we were in no mood to give them the satisfaction of allowing their predictions to come true.

As it happened, Arsenal gave us a lot of space in the wide areas and we took full advantage of that. They had obviously decided to defend the middle but that meant Trent and myself were able to get forward almost at will. The front three came into their own as we were able to dominate as a team and the outcome was never really in any doubt. There was a spell in the second half when we had them pinned back for so long that it felt like there was nothing they could do to get out. I've been on the receiving end of that myself and it's not a good place to be because it's like you're being suffocated and goals almost come as a merciful relief because it means you can at least get up the pitch and start again from a kick-off on the halfway line. So I knew how Arsenal felt but I wasn't about to start feeling sorry for them. This was an opportunity for us to show our ruthless side and we did that to put down another marker.

We managed to limit them to just a couple of chances so it was even more frustrating that we conceded from one of them but any feeling or irritation was totally secondary to the sense that we had been right at it as a team. With that result, a good start to the season became a great one.

I was never overly worried about conceding goals during that period because we were winning games. It was annoying but the fact that we were winning was more important than anything else. We all knew that we wanted to get back to keeping clean sheets and there is no question that we were having a few teething problems early on. I suppose we were victims of our own success in some respects as we had gained a reputation for being tight defensively and not giving too much away but the reality is that everything doesn't just click straight away. Passes go astray, maybe our pressing as a team isn't as co-ordinated and effective as it has been, a lack of match practice undermines teamwork – football is a game played by human beings and it is totally normal for there to be times when a little bit of ring rust sets in and it becomes harder to achieve peak performance.

Being Liverpool means you're not allowed to show these kind of frailties, though. We are held to a higher standard than most but that is one of the great things about playing for this club. Maybe at other clubs a slight drop in standards won't be as noticeable but here it immediately becomes a matter of national interest. Whether we agree with all the criticism or not is irrelevant, we know that playing for Liverpool comes with a responsibility to be at our best on all fronts and at all times. This is something that we all thrive on and it was for that reason, rather than any need to disprove our critics, that we were all so determined to cut out the minor mistakes which were costing us clean sheets.

In a season that we were expecting to be decided by small margins, we knew that if we continued giving cheap goals away it would eventually cost us but we never lost faith that we would get back to keeping things tight. The same players were still here, the approach was still the same and the manager definitely isn't the type to allow our performance levels to drop so it was just a case of remaining patient, working as hard as ever at Melwood and trusting one another.

The club had been clear throughout the summer that we would not be doing too much business in the transfer market and besides Adrian, who arrived as a free agent, and two youngsters, Harvey Elliott and Sepp van den Berg, no more reinforcements would be arriving. Andy Lonergan was the exception – brought in a few days after Alisson got injured.

This prompted another external debate with many questioning whether we were missing a trick by not building from a position of strength. My own view was that a new face or two is always good because it brings a different personality into the dressing room and, if things work out, different qualities to the team. So I can see why there was a bit of a clamour for us to make more signings. But when we were out in America and France, I was also looking around the dressing room thinking 'this squad is good enough to win the Premier League'.

In pre-season we take away about thirty players and obviously throughout this season people will come to see how good they are but maybe some didn't know that at the start of the season. The gaffer always looks inside for solutions first and places a lot of emphasis on developing young players, so this was a case of both him and the club as a whole placing a lot of faith in the players that we already had. That kind of vote of confidence can be a shot in the arm in itself because it tells all of us that those who matter most believe we are good enough for the challenges that lie ahead. The club remained very strong despite the pressure that they were coming under to make a big signing. When you actually look at the squad and take time to look at how many positions we have covered and what the squad depth is, they were absolutely right.

There had been a bit of a clamour for us to bring in a left-back to provide cover for me and I had been pretty relaxed about that. If we had brought another one in, it would have been a chance for me to go and prove myself again because then there is added pressure on my position. I would know, like every other player, that if my standards dropped or the new guy turned out to be a quality addition, my place in the team would be in jeopardy. You can't shy away from these type of challenges in football.

Every step of the way I have had coaches who did not rate me as highly as they rate others, I have had clubs who either did not want me or did not want to keep me and I have had critics who have questioned whether or not I was good enough for club or country. I would like to think that I have proven I'm the type of player who thrives on adversity and has the kind of belief that allows you to kick on even when others expect you to fall by the wayside. If I didn't have those qualities, I wouldn't be at Liverpool, it is as simple as that.

Thankfully, the club agreed with my assessment because they obviously thought they had cover for every position. For me, that would almost certainly mean Milly playing a couple of games filling in for me at left-back and a couple at right back as cover for Trent as well – although Neco Williams has also come in and shown what a talent he is.

When you look at our starting eleven and bench for the final against Spurs there wasn't much room for improvement. Among the substitutes, we had Ox who had come back from injury a few weeks earlier, Milly whose importance speaks for itself, Divock who came on to score another huge goal in another huge game; Lallana, Joe Gomez, Dejan Lovren, Xherdan Shaqiri, I could go on and on. Ours wasn't a squad that needed an overhaul, it wasn't even one that had obvious weaknesses and, most importantly, the club obviously felt there was more to come from us as a group.

When the transfer window closed and no more incomings had arrived, the onus was on us to prove them right and the only way we could do that was by carrying on in the same way we had started.

ROBBO

MIND GAMES

THE only problem with a perfect start to the season is it means you're not conditioned and not prepared for a downturn in results. Never mind the new campaign, we'd been pretty flawless all year. From January 3rd – when Liverpool were narrowly beaten by Man City – I went almost nine months without experiencing defeat in this country.

Injury forced me out of a couple of Scotland defeats I would rather have played in but the only time I was on the losing side for club or country was when Barcelona beat us 3-0 at the Nou Camp and even that turned out to be the start of a miraculous comeback rather than the end of a dream. It was an incredible run and the kind I'm not expecting to be repeated.

Even though I never took it for granted, it inevitably left me struggling to recall how it felt to be on a losing side. I never felt invincible, if anything it was the opposite because fear of losing is something I need, but it did make it harder for me to recall how low I can get when results go wrong. I was riding the crest of a wave and that meant at some point I would inevitably come crashing down. I tried to steel myself, I did everything I could to stay even and put potential setbacks into perspective, but when they did arrive it hit me hard and I needed all of my powers of recovery and a pep talk from Jürgen Klopp to get me back on track.

I know there are those who believe that players who enjoy success with top clubs might not suffer as much when international football doesn't go well but if anyone of that view saw the state I was in after Scotland lost back-to-back games at the start of September, they would struggle to justify that opinion.

Like any proud Scot, I want my country to win at everything and that feeling is multiplied by God knows how much when I pull on a blue shirt. The fact I am captain of my country amplifies that still further. When it comes down to it, I'm a lad from Glasgow who is part of a team that carries the hopes of our nation. We are representing family, friends, people we know and people we don't know. I don't think anyone would argue that the Scotland team has been of vintage standard in recent years and we don't have the same reserves of quality that other countries have, but our desire to do well is definitely not in question. That's why I always look forward to the international break and, again, the other lads are the same.

Just on a human level, it's always good for me to go back up the road to join up with the squad, simply because I'll be seeing so many close friends who I've got to know really well coming through the Scottish system. So the club versus country issue doesn't really apply to me. I want to play for my country and the only things that will stop me from doing so are fitness problems or suspension. What can be difficult, admittedly, is when the break comes really early in the season because that is a time when you are just finding your rhythm with your club and it would be an ideal scenario if we were all given a bit longer to keep on doing that. Equally, given how packed the football calendar is, I understand it can't be easy to find dates that suit everyone. So, it is what it is, and all we can do as players is get on with it as best as we possibly can, giving our best for whichever team we are playing for and taking care of ourselves so that we are available for club and country.

It is mainly a question of adaptation. It doesn't matter who you are, the main challenge is to switch from one team that has its own style, players, strengths and weaknesses to another with qualities of its own. At least, as I say, quite a few of my Scotland team-mates are lads I've played with since we were under-11s and under-12s. Also, a lot of our players either play in the Premier League or have played in the Premier League so even if we're not in the same club side, we do know each other's games pretty well.

It is the contrast in styles that can sometimes be the biggest test. At Liverpool, I am used to being part of an attacking team. Individually, I have a lot more license to get forward and collectively, we tend to have more possession than the opposition. So I will see Ali roll the ball out to Trent and I will automatically know that I can start pushing up the line because the chances are that if Trent doesn't pick me out himself with one of his trademark switches from right to left, the ball could get to my side quickly and I have to be ready for that. With Scotland, we have to be a wee bit more conservative and sometimes we have to sit back and defend, so my own game becomes more about positional discipline than adventure. It's not straightforward, I absolutely accept that, but I feel I adapt much better than some tend to suggest.

There are times when I get the feeling there are those who look at the Liverpool team I am part of and think that I should be going and winning games for Scotland from left-back but, realistically, I am needed to defend and to help keep clean sheets. If I do that then we hopefully have players at the other end to score because the likelihood is that, as a team, there will be occasions when we have less possession than most and that means it's about me doing the right things in defence. In basic terms, for Liverpool I might bomb forward fifteen times in a game, for Scotland there will be games when it might only be four or five. The individual challenge, for me, is to make sure that I do my utmost to make those times count.

The big similarity between Scotland and Liverpool is expectation. The period when our country was regularly qualifying for major tournaments and sometimes even having dreams of winning them may have passed, but that doesn't mean the hopes of our nation have diminished altogether. It can be easy to view this as a negative and I know as well as anyone there have been times when our quality has not been able to match our aspirations but we can't ever want expectations to be lowered just to reduce the pressure on us as players.

We are all human beings and there will be times when we have been beaten by one of the best teams in the world and the criticism that confronts us feels incredibly harsh, given what we have been up against, but the time to really worry will be when we aren't held to such high standards. If the criticism is fair, constructive and not personal, none of us can complain. It's only when that line gets crossed that I have a problem with it but in the main we have to take it on the chin.

My own performances are probably questioned a bit more than most because I am captain and also due to the way I play for Liverpool. Again, I don't mind that because it means if I'm in the firing line, the other lads aren't. But I do sometimes wish that our harshest critics would realise that no-one is more disappointed than we are when things don't go well for Scotland.

When I look back at the 2018/19 season, one which ended with me winning the European Cup with Liverpool, I might have a huge feeling of satisfaction from what I achieved with my club, but this doesn't remove the personal sense of regret caused by falling short with Scotland. That was my first season as captain and, to be frank, we just didn't kick on and I would be the first to say that we did not do well enough as a team. To go further, I didn't do well enough for Scotland as an individual and that is something that bugs me. For club, it might have been the season of my dreams but for country it was very different and I wouldn't want anyone to be under the misapprehension that doing well with Liverpool makes it easier to deal with Scotland falling short. If anything, the exact opposite is true. The defeats hit you harder because you have become so accustomed to winning, the feeling of letting people down is even stronger because that is not something that I am used to and, yes, the criticism does hurt more because I am fortunate enough to be part of a club side that gets a lot of praise.

I know what is at stake and I also recognise that my personality makes it impossible to take lurches from high to low in my stride but this is something I have to fix. I can do that one of two ways – by doing my bit to help Scotland improve, so that any tough times are fewer and further between or else change my personality so that I am better able to compartmentalise success and failure. I desperately hope it turns out to be the former, not least because I think it is much more achievable than the latter.

There have been times when I have struggled coming back to Liverpool. It has probably taken me a couple of days to get back into the swing of things because I'm still carrying a sense of disappointment with me into an environment where pretty much everything is hunky dory. I have sometimes arrived back at Melwood and the lads must recognise the face but not much else because I am so down that I can't even contemplate the usual banter. I'm like a teenager who's just been finished by his girlfriend while the lads who've been away with England, Holland and Brazil tend to be buzzing.

As a footballer you are almost pre-conditioned to respond to a positive dressing room. That's not because you forget your troubles as soon as you walk through the door or see a familiar smiling face and everything suddenly feels okay. It's down to the basic fact that training grounds are incredibly competitive places and you know that if you let your guard or your standards drop for just a day or two because your morale is low, you could easily find yourself sitting out the next game. It really is a case of sucking it up and getting on with things. There is no alternative.

I am striving to ensure that when I come back from internationals, I am as content as the English and Dutch lads. The best way to do that is by achieving positive results, something that I'm increasingly confident that the current Scotland squad is capable of.

Being inside the camp, I see the quality, I see the emergence of young players who have the potential to have a big impact at international level and I feel the growth of a team spirit that should stand us in good stead for years to come. Don't forget, it was only five years ago that people in football were questioning whether or not Liverpool would ever restore former glories so I've seen close up what is possible when the right ingredients start falling into place. As a nation, now is definitely a time for Scotland to dare to dream.

Liverpool had only played four league games when the first international break of the 2019/20 season came around which, from a club point of view, probably wasn't ideal. We were just hitting our stride as a team and we could all feel the momentum building, both individually and collectively. The next thing, we are all heading off to the four corners of the world. All you can do is hope we will be able to pick up where we left off when we return to Melwood. We know that won't be straightforward because travelling always take its toll and the chances are that at least one or two will return with knocks. In my case, I would return fine physically but my mental state would turn out to be another matter entirely. If I headed north of the border with high hopes, I returned south with my head all over the place.

Our aim had been to take a minimum of three points from our two qualifiers against Russia and Belgium in order to maintain our chances of automatic qualification for Euro 2020. We ended up taking none. It was massively disappointing for us. We hadn't made the best of starts to the group and the talk all week leading up to the Russia game was that this was a must-win.

On paper that was an easier fixture than the one against Belgium, although we still knew that Russia would be tough opposition, and we simply couldn't afford to slip up. Maybe that pressure played a part in the way we performed. Maybe this was an occasion when the expectation that comes with being the Scottish national team also had a negative impact. Maybe, maybe, maybe…

The truth is, I could search for loads of reasons and if I looked hard enough I could probably find them, but when it comes down to it we didn't produce when it mattered. We didn't come up with the kind of performance that the situation demanded and we didn't take our chances when they came. I was disappointed about that and I was also disappointed with the way I played because this definitely wasn't an occasion where I could look myself in the eye afterwards and think I'd done myself justice. It may have been our first competitive defeat at home for four years but it could not have come at a worse time, especially with Belgium, the world's number one ranked team next up. Ideally, we had hoped to be going into that game level on points with Russia and with everything still to play for. As it was, we left ourselves needing a miracle against the toughest opponents we could wish for.

The miracle we needed didn't happen. It felt possible at the start because we were the better side early on and things looked promising until we left ourselves wide open on the counter and Romelu Lukaku gave Belgium the lead. From being in their faces, winning our tackles and generally making things difficult for them, we found ourselves on the back foot.

Being 1-0 down not only gave us a mountain to climb, it also played into Belgium's hands because they knew we would have to carry on coming at them, meaning they could use their quality to pick us off. It all unravelled quite quickly from then on and we ended up on the wrong end of a 4-0 defeat, which hurt a lot. The logical thing to do is to find context, to acknowledge what a great side Belgium are and to accept that we are not at their level, but the whole point of playing football is to find ways of holding your own against better teams and finding a way to beat them. Given what was at stake and how much playing for my country means to me, this one hit me hard. The only thing I had to hold on to was that there was still a possibility we could qualify through the play-offs, but even that couldn't prevent me from reaching a bit of a low ebb.

The other saving grace was that I had four days to get my head straight before Liverpool's next game against Newcastle United. I can only imagine what it's like for the gaffer after international breaks. Usually a team shares the same highs and lows but players come back in different moods, depending on their country's results.

Luckily, we have the kind of manager who likes to meet these kind of problems head on. One of the first things Jürgen did after I got back was to invite me into his office to talk about where I was at. Everything he said made perfect sense. He told me I couldn't carry the burden on my own, that the only way to respond to these kind of setbacks is to get your boots on and get playing again and that even though the pain I was experiencing was totally normal and understandable, I couldn't allow it to affect my form with Liverpool. It is the kind of common sense stuff that I had been trying to tell myself but it is always better to hear it from someone else.

I was still a bit quiet afterwards but there was no point in hiding how I felt or pretending that I was over it when the reality was that I still had a bit of suffering to do. I just had to get through it in my own way and in my own time. It probably wasn't until the Thursday before we played Newcastle that I started to feel like I was getting my head straight. The key to that change in my mental state was the gaffer's message that I could not afford to let what happened in my last game to affect my next one. I had to deal with my own disappointment or else I would be letting my team-mates down.

Some managers have a knack of saying the right thing at the right time to get you to respond in the right way. The gaffer at Liverpool is obviously like that and another is Steve Bruce, who was a big influence on me at Hull City. This time, as manager of Newcastle, he wouldn't be giving me any motivational speeches to spur me on. But he did manage to give me a fit of laughter in the heat of the game.

I was taking a throw-in just in front of the dugouts when I heard his familiar Geordie tone. "Hey Robbo, any chance you could stop running?!" I turned around and there he was, grinning from ear to ear. I couldn't stop myself from bursting out laughing. "Sorry gaffer," I said, before launching the ball up the line and racing forward to join the attack. Some apologies are more genuine than others.

Knowing Steve, he wouldn't have expected anything else from me. He played such an important role in my career, bringing me into English football with Hull City and helping me improve my game to such a level that a club like Liverpool ended up signing me. Hull came in for me when I was at Dundee United and, to be honest, English football scared me a bit at that time but Steve convinced me, telling me I was definitely good enough and that he would look after me. I genuinely think that if he had not been so positive and encouraging, I would have stayed in Scotland. Some managers have that ability to get you on board just through their own integrity and Steve definitely falls into that category. I'm definitely indebted to him, just not enough to stop running because he tells me to!

The thing is, me bombing about wasn't even Newcastle's

biggest problem. Bobby was on fire that day and the highlights of his performance are like a YouTube showreel that captures some of the best moments of a great player's career. No-look passes, through balls, back heels, flicks, spins, you name it, he did it and pretty much all of it came off. Bobby hadn't even started the game either. The Brazil lads had come back from international duty last and they'd also had the longest journey, so the gaffer decided to start him on the bench. Then he had to come on after 37 minutes because Divock picked up a knock. At that stage, the score was 1-1 but we were nowhere near our best and Bobby's arrival transformed us. It was like someone had flicked a switch, it was that instantaneous.

On the pitch, we could feel the excitement in the crowd whenever he had the ball because it seemed like anything was possible and when a team-mate is on fire like that, it raises everyone's level, especially when it's one whose role is as instrumental as Bobby's. I would go as far to say he is irreplaceable. I get people look at strikers and the first way they assess them is by how many goals they score but the way Bobby brings others into play, the intelligence of his movement and the ability he has to act as foil for both Mo and Sadio makes him priceless to us. The fact that he chips in with goals as well, starts our defending from the front and works harder than any other striker I've seen, means he is pretty much the perfect package. Maybe outside Liverpool he is not appreciated as much as he should be but no-one would need to tell us how important Bobby is, we recognise it every time we play. I've no doubt the Newcastle lads would agree with that, too, because his arrival took the game away from them that day and we ended up winning 3-1. They couldn't live with him and there is definitely no shame in that.

That victory lifted a weight off my shoulders. It also helped that I got my first assist of the season, which came as a relief. I'd gone four games without creating and although I'm a defender first and foremost, I also have a responsibility to make things happen going forward. The type of assist also mattered. It wasn't a case of whipping a ball into the box and hoping someone would get on the end of it. After breaking through a challenge from Fabian Schär, which actually left me nursing an injury, I lifted my head up and picked a pass in to Sadio and he did the rest. This is an area of my game where I think I have really improved since joining Liverpool. I had to improve, too, because although I had a reputation for being an attacking full-back when I arrived, I needed to refine my approach. It often appeared better than it actually was.

I've always played the same way in terms of getting forward, right back to my Queen's Park days. If you asked coaches who worked with me when I was younger they would probably say I had a decent cross and that I was capable of picking areas.

What I would say, though, is that right up to my first season at Liverpool, a lot of my balls into the box looked like good crosses but actually weren't because while they were going into good areas, they were not necessarily finding a team-mate. They were flashing across goal and the crowd would get excited but no-one was getting on the end of them. Again, I may be being overly critical but I look upon those deliveries as being about style rather than substance.

In that respect, my second season at Liverpool was really important because I started to find more accuracy and that allowed me to actually pick people out when they were in good positions. I went from hoping that someone would get on the end of a cross to believing that I was capable of finding someone with a cross. That might not sound like a big difference but it changed things enormously for me.

My debut against Crystal Palace was a really good example of this. I put in seven or eight crosses that I think most people in the ground, including myself at the time, would have thought were good balls but only one of them led to a team-mate having a chance. The other six or seven came to nothing and that was a learning experience for me. Instead of thinking of my delivery in isolation, I had to start thinking more of how I linked up with the players in front of me, particularly Bobby, who will always look to give you an option to feet if he possibly can. It was about becoming more effective rather than looking good, which is not to say I didn't play well because I think I did okay. But I also recognised that I needed to make some adjustments to play the way the gaffer and my team-mates wanted me to play. It may not have seemed like a big thing but for me, that assist for Sadio mattered because it ticked all of the boxes – it had precision, it had substance, it gave us a chance to score and it was effective for the team.

Most importantly of all, it got me on the board in my personal duel with Trent as our annual assists challenge continued. I say that with tongue pressed firmly in cheek. Both of us are a bit wary that our in-house competition has become such a big thing. It has only ever been a friendly rivalry that's designed to spur one another on for the good of the team. If Trent got fifty assists and I got none but the team won a trophy then no-one would be happier than me. I would have to listen to him going on about it for the rest of my days, of course, but I could cope with that. (I think I could anyway).

When Trent first came on the scene, he wouldn't say boo to a goose. He was quiet. Ben Woodburn and him were an inseparable wee pair so we called them 'the pups'. Trent never really came out of his shell at first. But since then we have seen his character growing and growing. When I first met him, he was also one of the most respectful young lads I've ever met. The respect he has for every other player that is even slightly older than him is incredible.

He is such a bad loser, though. He loses his head all the time. I'm always next door to him when we stay in a hotel and I sometimes have to bang my wall because he's shouting at his PlayStation after losing a game on FIFA or whatever. It doesn't matter what he's doing, he's ridiculously competitive and that shows on the pitch.

So we are both competitive people and our 'rivalry' has benefited the team. In the first season of our assists challenge, he beat the previous record and then I joined him in that achievement. We have both become attacking outlets and, as a result, some teams now set up with five at the back when they play us, maybe to try and stop Trent and myself. We have had to learn that, when that happens, we might have to take ourselves out of the game to a degree and instead try to create space for others. The great thing about this team is if an opponent focuses on one or two of us, we have more than enough quality in other areas to play differently. This showed in our results. Not many teams have found a way to stop us from playing over the previous year or so.

One of the few who did were Napoli; our 1-0 defeat in the Champions League group stages in 2018 representing a rare occasion when we hadn't done ourselves justice. Heading back there this season, we all felt we had a point to prove but although we performed much better than twelve months earlier, the outcome was still the same and for the second year in a row, I had my own reasons for regret.

What most people don't know is that on the morning of the game, I wasn't going to be playing. I went for a fitness test and my knee was double the size. I'd picked up a knock against Newcastle when I went in for the challenge that led to our equaliser and it turned out that I'd tweaked a ligament. I went into the test thinking I would struggle to run but I had a couple of painkillers beforehand and when I ran, it felt okay. I did a few movements with the ball and that felt okay too. I knew I wasn't one hundred per cent but I felt I could function so I made myself available and the manager picked me. I'm not one to miss games through injury if I can possibly help it and I also had the assurance of the physios telling me that it wasn't the type of knock that would get too much worse if I played. The only sign anything was wrong was that I played with tape on my knee but, other than that, it was business as usual as far as myself and everyone else was concerned.

Like most players, I'm usually able to put knocks to the back of my mind as soon as the game starts. That was the case in Napoli and it definitely didn't play a part in my involvement in the incident which turned the match in their favour when a penalty was awarded against me for a foul on José Callejón.

When I look back on it, I can see why the penalty was given. I stupidly left my leg out in the box and the Spanish Michael Phelps did a magnificent job of diving over it. So I view it as a poor decision by me in that split second. I gave Callejón an opportunity and he took full advantage of it. But I still don't think it was a penalty. It may have looked like one to the referee – and, again, I can see why – but there wasn't anything like enough contact. There was no point in blaming anyone else, though. I took responsibility and when I walked into the dressing room afterwards I apologised to the lads straight away because, for me, that was the right thing to do.

I went over to Milly and said sorry to him but he stopped me in my tracks. "Don't you ever say that again," he said. "You can get lost if you think you are going to say that and get away with it." I took a bit of comfort from that because Milly is someone who we all look up to, so for him to say that he didn't want me to take responsibility for our defeat was a big help in terms of getting over my mistake.

At least I wasn't alone on that front. For the first time arguably since he had been with us, Virgil made a mistake that led to a goal. Virg is the best centre-back in the world and will be remembered as one of the best to have ever played the game but the reality of what we do is that defenders will make mistakes – although not too often in his case. When we do, there is a risk that it will cost a goal.

On this occasion, he was trying to get us playing our way out because the clock was ticking down but he got caught and Napoli scored a second. It didn't really matter in terms of the result because it just meant the game ended 2-0 instead of 1-0. Besides, the type of team we are means we will always be prepared to stick to the principles of how we play, even when the risks become greater.

That has worked for us on countless occasions so just because it didn't pay off in Napoli doesn't stop it from being the right approach. We want Virg to look to use the ball in those situations and the fact that this was the first time in 18 months or so that it cost us speaks volumes for him and his quality. Put it this way, no-one would have been pointing fingers at him and that wasn't just because of his size.

Some mistakes create a bigger stir than others, of course, and in the hours after that game I made one that led to newspaper headlines and a controversy almost as big as the one over Napoli's penalty. Twitter had been bugging me for a while. As a platform, it should be one of the best ways of bringing society together and allowing people to interact but in my experience, and I don't think I'm alone in this, it becomes unnecessarily negative and sometimes vindictive far too easily. I hadn't suffered anywhere near as much as certain others on this front because things had been going so well for Liverpool for quite some time and, more often than not, the comments were positive and complimentary.

There had been a bit of stick and some of it veered into abuse but it had also given me an opportunity to engage with fans, like a young Liverpool fan called Alfie Radford who had donated his pocket money to the food banks outside Anfield. When I read about that on Twitter I sent him a letter and a signed Firmino shirt because the food banks are a cause that is very important to me. I also believe that when kids do something like this, it should be acknowledged. That is Twitter at its very best and I still love that element of it. If it was like this all the time, imagine the force for good it could be and how much difference it could make to society. Unfortunately, it isn't like that often enough.

The turning point for me came when I was away with Scotland and I saw what some of the lads have to put up with. I was already at the stage where I was becoming less and less active on there, mainly because I didn't want to spend hours and hours on my phone as much as anything else, but I was also aware of inviting negativity into my life. I'm not the type of person who looks for the approval of others when things are going well, so being on there started to feel a bit pointless for me.

That feeling intensified ahead of the Belgium game when some of the lads were showing me the stick they were getting on Twitter, including from some ex-pros. As captain, I am protective of the whole squad and I accept that criticism is absolutely valid, especially during a week as disappointing as that one. Yet, some of the stuff I was seeing went well beyond what is reasonable. I made my mind up there and then to come off Twitter. I didn't actually do anything about it at that point because I was just trying to put anything negative out of my mind ahead of such a massive game. It was only after the Napoli game that I deleted it. I hadn't even looked at what was being said on there. I just got rid of it and that's when all hell started to break loose.

I had thought that by deactivating the account it would just mean that I couldn't go on it. It wasn't something I had given a great deal of thought to. I hadn't realised that people would be getting notifications and that my disappearance would get almost as much attention as Lord Lucan's.

The theory was that I'd got rid of Twitter because of criticism relating to my performance against Napoli but I can honestly say that, to this day, I have no idea what was being said about me on there, never mind reacted to it. The worst thing was, I had made my move just before I got on a plane at Naples airport so, while I was flying over Europe with no phone access, I was totally oblivious to the storm rumbling.

Just like Mo and Sadio at Burnley, that then became a bigger story than the game itself and all because of my failure to understand technology and how it works. I've since gone back onto Twitter, mainly because I believe that as a footballer I have a responsibility to engage with supporters in whichever ways are possible but I'm disciplined enough not to look at the notifications unless someone close to me brings something to my attention that I really need to see.

The idea of using a social media tool as some sort of weather vane makes no sense anyway. Fortunately, I'm busy during games but if you were to go through some Twitter feeds while matches were on you would see some unbelievable lurches in opinion. Maybe it's just that the ebb and flow of football isn't suitable for these platforms but it's probably more down to the fact that we can all get incredibly emotional when we are watching a match and the difference is that we can now tweet our thoughts rather than just keeping them to ourselves.

I can only imagine what was being said when we ended September with back-to-back away league wins at Chelsea and Sheffield United. It goes without saying that the victories were more than welcome but it's probably also true that the results were better than the performances. But I would much rather get a win without being at our best than lose having played fantastically well. Winning isn't just about performance, it never has been and never will be. Obviously, playing well improves your chances of taking three points but it is just important that you have the mental strength to cope when games become more testing against opponents who are making life difficult for you. Chelsea and Sheffield United both did that but we found a way and that's what it is all about, especially when you have aspirations to achieve something special.

The second half at Chelsea was particularly tough. They have some really good young players and there were times towards the end of the game when we were hanging on a bit. This probably influences the way people view that fixture. It created a narrative that we had been dominated and were maybe a bit fortunate when the reality was that we had been the better side in the first half and actually took a 2-0 lead. There was a spell after Trent scored our second with a brilliant free-kick when it looked like we could run away with it but, credit to Chelsea, they responded well, got a goal back through Kanté and we had to see the game out.

We probably hadn't been helped by Man City beating Watford 8-0 and rightly being widely praised for the way they played. It meant our performance was always going to be judged less favourably but we got the exact same three points for six less goals in what I would argue was a far tougher fixture. It also meant we had clocked up fifteen wins on the spin which wasn't too shabby for a team having its form questioned.

That is not to say we weren't working as hard as ever on the training ground to reach our best levels. The culture of this club is that you should always be looking for ways to improve and you should always strive for more. But you also have to be realistic to recognise that there will be peaks and troughs, not just throughout the season, but sometimes in the same game. It is how you handle those extremes and everything in between that matters. Digging in is a big part of that and there were times at Bramall Lane when we really had to go back to basics, getting our blocks in, making tackles, going with runners, picking up second balls and just battling in general.

As their results since then have underlined, Sheffield United away is a tough game. We weren't at our most eye-catching and our football was never particularly free flowing but there was another team on the pitch and they made it as difficult as possible for us to play well and they should get credit for that.

Despite that, we never lost belief we could find a way to win. The gaffer had to make a couple of substitutions for that to happen, but we got the result that we were looking for. Divock coming on was key because we went to two up top and that made their back three a bit more narrow which, in turn, made it harder for them to jump out to their wingers. That allowed us to dominate territory and possession a bit more and that was how we were able to get our goal.

I'm sure Gini would admit it wasn't the greatest strike of his career but unfortunately for Dean Henderson he made a mistake. We were all delighted for Gini who does so much unseen work for us. He is a player who has the trust of all of us but his role in the team means others are more likely to get the limelight than he is, so it was great – and wholly deserved – that he should have a moment like this when his contribution mattered more than anyone else's.

We know the result could have been different. Three minutes before Gini's goal, I'd managed to block an effort from John Fleck when a goal looked likely and they had other chances. Was it our greatest performance of the season? No. Did we feel comfortable? No. But we also felt that the least we were going to get was a draw which wouldn't have been bad, especially as we had won all of our previous league games.

The problem was, we had gone into the season viewing every point as a prisoner effectively and we knew any slips would create additional pressure – that was the prism through fixtures like this were viewed. I know it won't have been an easy watch from the away end but we have shown enough times that we are capable of grabbing a late goal, so I suppose the fans just have to trust us. As the gaffer said afterwards, it was never 'a clicking day' but it was a good day. Another one.

ROBBO

FINDING
A WAY

ELEVEN millimetres. It is 0.4333 inches. A thumbnail. Half the width of a pound coin. It isn't much bigger than the space between words on this page. It is also, perhaps, the distance that was the difference between us winning the league title and being runners-up in 2018/19. Don't tell me size doesn't matter. I say 'perhaps' because I don't believe an entire season can be reduced to a single moment. Football isn't a perfect science, one incident does not guarantee another. Human beings dictate the outcome of every passage of play, every game and every title race. So reducing an entire campaign to a single instance that didn't go your way doesn't really make sense. It would also make you go mad.

That eleven millimetres, though, is a constant reminder of how miniscule the gap between success and failure can be and how champions have to take full advantage of small margins and make the most of big moments. That was the challenge for us going into 2019/20, we had to make sure that when the big moments did arrive, we not only ensured that more went in our favour, we also capitalised on them to the full.

Not every team responds to that kind of setback with a resolve to go again and to be even better. Some fade away, broken by the experience or happy to have come so close and maybe even willing to use their misfortune as an excuse rather than an inspiration.

Fortunately, we are not built that way. Even if there had been those amongst us who were wary of another title challenge for fear of getting hurt – and I can assure you the opposite was actually true – I can say without fear of contradiction that the gaffer and his staff would not have allowed such feelings to emerge for any more than a fleeting moment. That is why one of the themes of pre-season was preparing us to suffer. There could be no feeling sorry for ourselves or resting on our laurels because we had gone toe to toe with Manchester City, a team rightly regarded as one of the best English football has seen. We had to be mentally stronger so that even more games could be bent to our will. Anything else would have meant that we would fall away and be known forever as a team that came ever so close. None us wanted that. No-one wants to be remembered for eleven millimetres.

It is for these reasons that, in the years to come, our game against Leicester City at Anfield will be viewed as one of the pivotal fixtures of our campaign. We knew beforehand that this would be a massive test against a side that had been going from strength to strength under Brendan Rodgers. What we didn't know was that we would be taken to the extreme.

This was an occasion for the kind of big characters that you need when the tension is ratcheted up and the margin for error becomes smaller and smaller. The gaffer had said before the game that Leicester would be our toughest opponent of the season so far and he wasn't wrong.

We were the better side for most of the game but we were unable to add to Sadio's first half goal and that meant Leicester were never out of it. When James Maddison equalised with ten minutes remaining, I think the expectation of most people would have been that we were destined for a draw which would have brought our seventeen-game winning streak in the league to an end.

We could have settled for a point. We could have decided to conserve our energy in the knowledge that we would still be in an incredibly strong position at the top of the league and that less exacting opponents would lie ahead. When you have fallen short by a single point having accumulated ninety-seven and when you've seen the difference that eleven millimetres can make, you can't afford to settle, though. You have an obligation to yourself and your team to keep on going, to keep pursuing the win that would add another two points to your total. Going one better in this game could help us to go one better over the course of this season – that was how we had to look at it.

That was the reason why we were the ones on the attack deep into stoppage time. It is also why Divock was trying to make things happen in the Leicester half as the clock ticked down. Just by being positive and refusing to accept our fate, individually and collectively, we put Leicester on the back foot when they just wanted to see out time.

That caused Marc Albrighton to make a mistake under pressure. He nicked the ball off Divock's toe but then there was a communication breakdown between him and Kasper Schmeichel. This was one of those situations that happens in the blink of an eye but somehow also seems to be unfolding in slow motion. Sadio picks up the ball and Albrighton makes a clumsy challenge, catching his shin in a desperate attempt to make a tackle.

"Penalty," I shout and 50,000 other people join in. Thankfully, the only person who matters at that moment agrees and Chris Kavanagh, the referee, points to the spot.

The Leicester players go mad, as most players would have done out of sheer competitiveness, surrounding him and making it clear that he's got it wrong. It is absolute bedlam on and off the pitch. I look across to my right and spot the only two people inside Anfield who aren't caught up in the emotion. While everyone around them are losing their heads, Henderson and Milner are keeping theirs. While everyone is focusing on the referee, Hendo calmly picks the ball up and passes it to Milly. This couldn't be a bigger moment and fortunately for us we couldn't have a bigger character to deal with it.

The only problem is he has to wait. The referee might have made his decision but the Video Assistant Referee has to decide whether or not Kavanagh has made the right call. This was the first time VAR had been used to check a penalty award in a league game at Anfield and it just added to the suspense.

For me, it was on the softer side of penalty awards but there was definitely contact. People like to say 'I've seen them given' and this was definitely one of those where everyone has 'seen them given'. Whether it's soft or not is irrelevant, it is a foul and the referee was right to give it. Like anyone else, I had my heart in my mouth a bit when VAR got involved but having seen the contact from where I was, I thought it would take something ridiculous for the decision to be overturned. Thankfully it wasn't.

Milly ended up having to wait over a minute before he could take the penalty but he stayed calm and composed. As soon as he picked up the ball there was only one thing in my mind – goal. There was no doubt, no steeling myself for possible disappointment and definitely no fear. I know how hard Milly practises for every scenario. He has the kind of mindset that allows him to deal with pressure in a way not too many others can. He takes the responsibility of being Liverpool's penalty taker so seriously, like every other responsibility he has. He practises endlessly and also does his homework on keepers. So whenever he picks the ball up and has a go from twelve yards out, I fully believe he will score. The law of averages means everyone misses at some point and that is an occupational hazard if you are a penalty taker but my confidence in Milly couldn't be any greater. This isn't to take anything away from any of the other lads because we have some brilliant strikers of the ball – and I'm sure they feel the same way anyway – but there is no-one who I would rather have taking a stoppage time penalty to win a game than him.

I was around five yards away from the box and in my mind I was getting ready to celebrate. I watched his run-up and I just knew. This was a sliding doors moment, just like the one at the Etihad nine months earlier when we went within those eleven millimetres of taking a crucial lead only for John Stones to intervene and change the course of history.

This time, fate was in our hands, or rather Milly's right foot. We had the opportunity not just to win this game but also to lay down a massive marker for the season. Leicester were our main rivals along with Man City and dropping points to them at home would have been a blow to us and given a lift to them. A late penalty wouldn't just matter in terms of the outcome of this game, it would also be symbolic of our intentions and our mentality. None of this affected Milly, of course. He just went through his usual routine like he was taking part in a practice session at Melwood. All of this pressure on one player and he doesn't even blink. Schmeichel is sent the wrong way, the ball hits the back of the net and Anfield erupts again. This felt huge.

It must have been enormous because even the hero of the hour got excited. Actually, the perception of Milly outside the dressing room is the opposite of who he is. He plays up to all the 'Boring Milly' stuff but he couldn't be further from it. I'm from a slightly younger generation but he is someone who I related to from the word go because of his sense of humour, his personality and also his approach to football. He is cut from old school cloth and I think I am too, so it made sense that we hit it off to such an extent that he has become one of my mentors, along with Hendo. I think Milly actually liked me before he even met me, simply because I am a left-back and my arrival meant he was less likely to have to play there!

The danger with Milly is that we focus so much on his mentality that we overlook his technique and his quality. That happens to both him and Hendo. Milly has played at the highest level for so many years. He has played for Leeds. He has played for Newcastle. He has played for Villa. He has played for City. You don't play for clubs like those and have a career like Milly has had unless you are hugely talented. You certainly don't have a medal collection like he has either. His performance has been elite level from the moment he made his debut and the fact that he has maintained the same standards well into his thirties is incredible. A career like his doesn't just happen because he has a strong mentality, it happens because he also has unbelievable ability. The combination of those qualities allowed him to convert from twelve yards in the most pressurised situation and it gave us a priceless win.

The emotion – a powerful mix of relief and elation – poured out of me. I just bellowed "yeeerrrrsssssss!" at the top of my voice and went to give Virg a big hug.

Just as I set off, Ayoze Pérez walked across me and must have thought I was shouting at him because the next thing he's shoving me in the back. At first I thought it must be one of the lads knocking into me in the midst of our celebrations but when I turned around I saw it was Pérez, which took me by surprise.

I watched the incident back afterwards and I can see why he thought I might have been screaming at him but I genuinely wasn't. I couldn't have cared less about anyone apart from my team-mates at a time like that. It is about enjoying the moment, not picking fights. I've got a lot of respect for the Leicester players and I had no interest in upsetting them, but things got a bit out of control which can happen in the heat of the moment.

Ayoze obviously wanted to make it public on the pitch. I was happy to talk to him in the tunnel but he was too angry for that. Afterwards, Brendan Rodgers accused me of starting it all but I'd hope that if he took another look he would understand what actually did happen. It was something over nothing and the next time we played, Ayoze and myself gave each other a high five and that was it, all done and dusted.

Inside I was a bit gutted, though.

I was thinking 'why me?' because I knew everyone would jump on that spat and make it bigger than it actually was. My biggest problem is sometimes I act like a fan on the pitch. That's not something I can shake off but it's also something that I wouldn't want to shake off because it's important for all supporters that they have players who they can identify with and that we also identify with them.

I share their passion and sometimes that means I can get a bit carried away and caught up in things that some players might avoid. There will be those who argue that I could tone it down a bit and I respect that but it isn't something I force and it isn't me trying to be someone that I'm not. It is totally authentic and if a psychologist ever studied me I'm sure they would say that the same emotions are the reason for some of my strengths as a player. The last thing I would want to do would be to detract from my identity as a footballer by trying to keep a lid on my passion when it has served me so well. I wouldn't be doing myself justice if that happened and I would also be letting down my manager, my team-mates and our supporters.

Besides, I saw a few of the Leicester lads at Trent's 21st in London that night and we were all able to laugh about it. They were understandably disappointed about the result and the way we had won it but as players they know stuff like this is almost always a storm in a teacup and it doesn't diminish our respect for one another.

In football, something that helps you one week can go against you the next. Like all clubs, we had moments when VAR seemed like a great idea and others when it felt it was the worst thing to happen to football for years. To be fair, these kind of changes are never going to be an instant success. There have to be teething problems because we are introducing technology into a process which has only ever been overseen by referees and assistant referees previously. There are also new protocols to be followed so it's far from being straightforward, especially as we also have to allow for an element of human error from officials as they get used to it. My hope is that it will get better and more consistent in the seasons to come. If that does happen then situations like the one we encountered in our next game, at Old Trafford of all places, will be much less likely to happen.

Games against Manchester United are our biggest of the season. History and stature dictates that. In recent seasons, clashes with Man City have been more decisive and more significant but United is the one that our supporters and the rest of the football world views as the big one in English football.

As players we are no different. We might not get caught in the hype but we don't need anyone to remind us about how much these fixtures matter. It is a fantastic rivalry. There is a healthy respect between the two clubs but, on matchday, you would rather run down the M62 naked than see your opponent given any kind of unfair advantage.

Unfortunately, this was how it turned out for us with United getting a decision in their favour which I would argue was one of the worst of the season. It wasn't their fault, of course, they just did what professionals should do by playing to the whistle and making the most of their good fortune by scoring a goal. But it shouldn't have been allowed to stand.

We were on the wrong end of another VAR decision in that game when Sadio had a goal disallowed for handball. At first,

I celebrated with him but he told me straight away that the ball had struck his hand, so I knew that wouldn't be allowed to stand. That rule can be quite harsh but it was made clear at the start of the season so we couldn't have any complaints about that one. The foul on Divock in the build-up to United's goal was another case entirely, though.

There are decisions that you disagree with but you can see why they are given – the penalty I gave away in Naples would be a good example – and then there are ones that baffle you for as long as you live. The foul on Divock definitely falls into the latter category.

I actually played the ball into Divock's feet and I was about to go for the return when Victor Lindelöf brought him down. Again, no issues with Lindelöf. It wasn't a big offence, not worth a booking or anything like that, but it was a bog-standard foul, the kind that happens on multiple occasions during every game. I think even the United players were expecting the whistle to blow.

I looked at Martin Atkinson and I think he went to blow but then had second thoughts. Maybe he gambled, thinking it was unlikely to lead to a goal and if it did then VAR would come into play but United did score and, like Leicester a couple of weeks earlier, we went nuts. When the review started I was convinced the decision would be overturned and that the game would restart with a free-kick to us in United's half. I was even thinking about what we might do with it because it was in my area of the pitch. Then the verdict came through and the crowd went wild. I didn't even need to look at the scoreboard.

My heart just sank. We had basically fallen foul of one of VAR's grey areas – officials know VAR can and does intervene and so don't always whistle but the threshold that is set for overturning decisions means VAR doesn't always intervene. I reckon even Sir Alex Ferguson himself would admit that this one was a foul. Through gritted teeth, obviously.

After going behind, we struggled to get any real fluency going forward. United were digging in, sitting deep and getting numbers behind the ball and having been given a goal, they had something to hold on to. Usually, we are able to come up with the answers ourselves and the gaffer gives us the freedom to express ourselves in the belief that we will eventually find a way to break down stubborn opponents. But as the match wore on, it became increasingly clear that this wasn't going to be one of those games, so the gaffer turned to the bench as he searched for solutions.

The changes he made turned out to be inspired with all three of our substitutes making an impact, none more so than Adam, who grabbed a late equaliser to silence the crowd and earn us a point. If ever a goal symbolised our squad mentality it would be that one. There was no better representative of this Liverpool than Adam because he symbolised everything that we stand for. He may not have played as much as he would have wanted over the last couple of years but when he did he always made a contribution and even when he didn't his influence on all of the players was massive.

I know there have been times when injuries have taken their toll on him as an individual but he has always put that personal disappointment behind him and put the rest of us before himself – that speaks volumes for him. Most importantly, though, when he was on the pitch he delivered in one way or another.

Adam is the type who doesn't just want the ball, he absolutely demands it. Even when he has a man on his back he will show to feet to give you an outlet and he has the ability to keep the ball under pressure or move it on quickly, depending on what the situation demands. These qualities are a Godsend, none more so than late in matches when you're either looking to protect a result or get back into a game. What he does for the team probably isn't as eye-catching as what some of the other lads do but it is absolutely priceless and I've lost count of the number of times when I've come off the pitch thinking he's done a brilliant job for us.

At Old Trafford, he came off the bench not long after Ox and they both made a big contribution. This is what I mean about squad mentality. If you aren't starting it's totally natural for players to be disappointed because we're all desperate to be in the team but when Adam and Ox arrived on the pitch that day, they were determined to make the most of the time they had. It was the same when Naby came on later in the game. All three of them got on the ball and looked to make things happen. Without those substitutions we probably wouldn't have got anything out of that game.

It was my ball to find Adam at the back post and when he hit the back of the net it was quite emotional for those of us who are closest to him. We know what he has been through and we also knew how much a goal of such importance would mean to him.

Before I came to Liverpool he was arguably the main man here, I certainly recognised his importance to the team when I was at Hull, so to see him struggling with injuries and having setbacks was incredibly tough. Scoring a massive goal at a place like Old Trafford gave him a lift but it also boosted us, too, and not just because we had been staring defeat in the face.

This underlined our refusal to give in and our mental strength under pressure but, just as importantly, it highlighted yet again that we aren't just a team, we are a squad and one that is full of individuals who are ready and able to do their bit whenever opportunities arise. The fact that it was Adam who made the difference made it even more special and I would go as far to say that it made a draw feel like a win.

We remained top of the league, we had prevented our fiercest rivals from ending our unbeaten run and none of us had expected to win every game, so a point at Old Trafford in those circumstances was nothing to be overly disappointed about. The reality was that we left there feeling a little bit more unbeatable having pulled a positive result out of the bag so late on, having not been at our best.

That didn't stop questions from being raised about why we hadn't taken all three points. To me, this is a bit disrespectful to United and what they stand for. They are still a massive club, they are still a good team, they are still our biggest rivals and it is still a huge derby. The post-match perception focused on where we had fallen short but it was well over the top. I looked at the league table and it showed that we were six points clear. We could even have nicked it at the end when Ox hit one that went just wide. If that had gone in, no-one would have said anything, so the fact that a draw at Old Trafford prompted so much negativity just showed how high the expectations of us had become.

One of the accusations that came our way centred on our preparations and whether we were guilty of over-estimating United. Maybe we are aware of this particular perception and that makes us desperate to put it to bed, whereas at other venues we just go and play our game without any of those thoughts. That's possibly the only difference but other than that we just treat it as another game. I can't say how Liverpool players of the past went into this fixture but we stick to our normal routine and don't do anything out of the ordinary.

When we go to Goodison, the challenge is quite similar in the sense that United and Everton are our two biggest rivals and we've been doing well for the last couple of seasons, so this puts the onus on them to try to stop us from achieving our objectives. It was the same when United were top dogs under Sir Alex, winning lots of trophies and dominating the league, but they would expect to be challenged at Anfield even if Liverpool were not doing so well.

Motivation is such a big factor in these games and, particularly when you look at Liverpool and United, the determination not to roll over for one another at home is also huge because the fans simply would not allow it. Over the last couple of seasons, United have raised their game against us at Old Trafford and we've probably not played to our absolute maximum and that's meant we haven't been able to win those matches – but we haven't lost either.

If you'd said to me when I signed for Liverpool that we'd have two seasons in which we only conceded one goal at Old Trafford (and that should have been disallowed) I would have bitten your hand off. As a club, we've also only lost one of our last ten fixtures against them. The narrative now is that if we draw away to United it's a bad result for us, which shows how far we've come. If it stays like that for as long as I'm at Liverpool I won't be complaining because it will mean we're doing well and we're also lifting expectations.

People only expect more of you when you consistently come up with the goods and we were developing a reputation for delivering almost as often as DHL. All manner of challenges were coming our way but the big characters we have allowed us to meet them more often than not. Tottenham at home – the first time we had met since the Champions League final – was another huge test and we made it even bigger.

Having scored after a minute in Madrid we decided to give them that goal back in the first minute at Anfield. There was definitely a feeling of shock around the ground when that happened. We knocked off and Harry Kane took advantage. What followed restored normality, though, with Hendo and Mo scoring in the second half to give us a hard fought, but fully deserved, win.

The gaffer told us that this was one of the most complete performances he'd had since being at the club. He also said that the best thing about it was that you could not see the influence of the Spurs goal. We put it behind us, kept going for the ninety-plus minutes, controlled the game, created all the big chances, never wavered or settled for a point after drawing level and thankfully we got the result that we wanted. This was a performance of champions.

There was a relentlessness about us built upon a refusal to accept defeat or things going against us and the best thing of all was it seemed to be a culture throughout the whole club.

Most of the regular starters were given the night off when we played Arsenal at home in the Carabao Cup but the one thing that didn't change was the team's attitude. For once, I got to watch as a fan and I know why people will have been fearing the worst when we went 3-1 down and then 4-2 down.

We had a very young team out there and it would have been easy for the boys to accept their fate in the knowledge that this competition wasn't our main priority. But having trained with these lads I knew they had the character to back up their talent so it didn't surprise me that they kept on going, getting themselves back into the game twice and demonstrating why the gaffer had shown so much faith in them.

Even I didn't fancy our chances, though, when the game entered the 94th minute and we were 5-4 down. Heroic failure looked inevitable until Divock came up with an unbelievable scissor kick to take the tie to penalties. As soon as the ball hit the net, I think everyone in the ground knew that there would only be one winner and, knowing Curtis Jones, he will have had more belief than anyone else that this would be our night. Not many teenagers have as much confidence as he does and not even a penalty to win the tie in front of the Kop could faze him. Even much more seasoned professionals have blinked when faced with that kind of situation but whatever pressure existed, Curtis didn't feel and he scored comfortably to take us through. In this case, the margins couldn't have been much smaller but once again the boys had found a way to win.

It wasn't just domestically either. It was the same in the Champions League as we came out on the right side of a seven goal thriller in our first home game in that competition since the miracle against Barcelona. The Red Bull Salzburg game will live long in the memory for various reasons, the main one being that we threw a three goal lead away before snatching victory.

On top of that, Takumi Minamino, Erling Haaland and a number of other Salzburg players left a lasting impression on supporters and players alike with eye-catching individual performances, while Mo once again underlined his status as one of European football's most reliable match-winners by scoring the decisive goal.

There was even rarity value, too, as I scored my first ever Champions League goal. Having waited so long for the big moment to arrive I was particularly pleased that it was a good one, not that I would have been disappointed if it had gone in off my backside or from a miskick.

It wasn't until I saw the goal back afterwards that I fully appreciated it from a team perspective. I knew I had started the move by bringing the ball inside and knocking it inside Taki, of all people, but the rest became a blur because it happened so fast, so I needed to look at it on TV. The first thing that struck me was how brilliant Hendo's ball to Trent was. As an overlapping full-back, you couldn't ask for any better. Passes like that don't just expose the opposition, they leave them wide open in a way that means only a poor final ball or a bad miss will get them off the hook.

Given it was Trent on the receiving end there was never much chance of the delivery falling short from that kind of position but I'd imagine my goalscoring record, if it can be described as such, meant Salzburg still had hope of a reprieve. Trent laid it on a plate, though, and Clarkston's most ruthless finisher did the rest.

It was the kind of goal that might have looked relatively easy but it wasn't. It was in the Champions League against a good opponent and it required every one of us to get every element right, on and off the ball, or else it wouldn't have been possible. When you have moving parts it is easy for an attack to break down when a pass is just slightly off and that's without even taking into account the other team are set up to stop you, so it does bring extra satisfaction when a move like that pays off. Personally, it was special for me because it was my first in the Champions League.

Most importantly, it was the kind of move that we work on as a team. We work on getting bodies in the box, no matter who you are or what position you play. As long as the protection is right and we're not left wide open for the counter, we have license to get forward. It's all about sensing the moment and having a structure that allows calculated risks to be taken. If I was getting into the box regularly, I'm sure opponents would look at the space I would be leaving and seeing it as something for them to exploit. But if all of the necessary requirements are in play, I can bomb on and look to get involved at the business end.

On this occasion, we didn't have too many in the box so I thought I would follow the attack and it paid off. After the game Pep Lijnders said it was the perfect goal for him because it involved one full-back creating for the other, so he was buzzing about that. He still talks about it to this day which isn't a bad thing for Trent and myself because it means we've left a lasting impression on the assistant manager, although he might start asking why we don't do it more often!

All of the analysis beforehand suggested Salzburg would not be changing the way they play. They had a clear philosophy and a commitment to play a certain way, so the expectation was that they would be sticking to it. We were expecting them to play out from the back, to press us as high as they could which was going to be dangerous to us from a defensive point of view but we also knew that if we were able to break their press we would be able to create chances.

That was certainly how it turned out during that first half. Everything clicked for us. Our passing was solid, our pressing was really effective and our finishing was good, all of which combined to make it a top performance. I didn't need a re-run to tell me that. I could feel that while we were out on the pitch. The problem was, I've got no doubt the Salzburg players felt exactly the same way during the 20 minute period either side of half-time when they came back from 3-0 down to get back on level terms.

Before then, we had been in total control and it looked like we could score almost at will but even during that period we were still wary of the threat Salzburg carried because they are the kind of team that is capable of catching fire and when they do, they can cause a fair bit of damage. So I wouldn't say complacency was an issue for us. It was more a case of them getting back into the game and us not dealing with that well. There's no question that they would have been difficult for any team to handle during that spell with the likes of Taki and Haaland displaying their talent. There are times when you have to hold your hands up and say 'well done'. The bravery that they played with at 3-0 down is not something that you see often and they were rewarded for that.

Thankfully, Mo got us off the hook with a typically well-taken finish which allowed us to get off to a winning start. Salzburg had made a big impression, though, and one player in particular had caught the eye. This would not be the last that we saw of Takumi Minamino at Anfield.

The trend for that entire period was for us to find a way, whether that meant scraping through on penalties, grabbing a last gasp equaliser, scoring a late winner or coming back after being behind. The only game that went against type was Genk away in the Champions League when we won comfortably but the theme was still about responding to adversity.

Ox scored his first goals since coming back from an injury that could have threatened his career. They were both brilliant strikes too, the second one especially, and while no-one needed to be reminded of his ability it was brilliant to see him produce again at the highest level after everything he had been through. It was yet another big contribution from a top player and this boded well for the team as a whole.

This was a season when we would all need to step up to the plate in various ways and increasingly the signs were that this was happening. Like Milly against Leicester, Adam away to United and the regular contributions from so many others, individuals were taking the opportunities that came their way and in doing so they were benefitting the team. An extremely high standard was being set, now all we had to do was maintain it. That might be easier said than done but we weren't about to start taking things easy.

Those eleven millimetres were all the incentive we needed.

06

HOPE IN
OUR HEARTS

EVERY season has turning points, sliding doors moments when one team takes control of its own destiny and its closest rival suffers as a result. When they go for you, it feels like a shot in the arm and an adrenaline rush rolled into one. Everything opens up and everything seems possible. When they go against you, it feels like a kick in the bollocks and not just any old kick in the bollocks. You feel sore and tender for days afterwards and even the gentlest reminder brings the pain rushing back, making you flinch and sub-consciously cover up.

When Vincent Kompany scored that goal to all but guarantee the title for Man City in May 2019, the pain was instant. They knew what it meant and so did we. Their gain was our loss and, unlike earlier turning points, this one was almost certain to prove decisive. I would be a liar if I said Kompany's goal didn't cause suffering but it also did something else – it demonstrated to everyone at Liverpool that if we wanted to win the league we would need to turn the tables. Not only would we have to step up our performance levels and improve on a consistency which had earned us ninety-seven points – an incredible total but not good enough – we would have to find different ways of winning games, especially the ones when it looked like victory was getting away from us. To be blunt, we had to do some bollock-kicking of our own.

Thankfully, we were not starting from scratch. Digging deep to find a way to win was already a big part of our make-up and there had been no better illustration of this than forty-eight hours prior to Kompany's heroics when big Divock struck at the death to give us an incredible victory over Newcastle.

Looking back, that was a goal which didn't prove decisive in terms of that season's title race but it did a hell of a lot more than give us three points at St. James' Park. That single moment informed everything that followed, giving us even more belief and, just as importantly, letting every team that plays us know that we will always keep going until the very end. Think of any great team and this is a quality they always have. We knew we had it ourselves but we needed to make it count more often because that was what was demanded by the standard that City had set.

So, when we found ourselves 1-0 down at Villa Park with eighty-seven minutes gone, we needed a miracle. We needed someone to do a Kompany by popping up out of nowhere to score a goal. Actually, that's wrong. We needed two people to do it. This was early November and our six point lead at the top was about to be halved. Worse still, City were coming to Anfield the following weekend and would have the chance to wipe out our advantage altogether. It would be ridiculous to say the title was on the line in early November but momentum was. Everything was in place for another sliding doors moment which made what followed as crucial as it was dramatic.

We hadn't been at our best and we knew it. In the first half, we had struggled to find any kind of rhythm and Aston Villa took advantage with a cheap goal from a setpiece that probably summed up where we were at. It wasn't that we were bad. We should have been on level terms only for one of the season's most ridiculous VAR decisions to cost Bobby an equaliser. We just couldn't make things go our way.

We allowed frustration to settle in a little bit too early as well because we were trying to force our way back into the game. I was probably as guilty of that as anyone, especially during the first half when I spent far too much time chirping away at Sadio while he was doing the same to me. It never went as far as being a falling out on the pitch but we definitely let one another know that we weren't happy with each other. He wasn't doing what I wanted him to do and I wasn't doing what he wanted me to do. It was as simple as that. We have a brilliant relationship in the main but when things aren't going well, it's inevitable that there will be a bit of tension and on that day it was between Sadio and myself. We kissed and made up at half-time – but I knew there were bigger problems to solve at the interval. We definitely needed the manager to put things right with our performance. And he did just that.

The gaffer is really animated in the ninety minutes but I've never really seen him animated at half-time. He never comes in shouting and bawling, it's always very tactical and if we're not doing well he shows us two or three clips from the first half and talks about how he wants to approach the second half.

Pete Krawietz picks the clips after consulting with Harrison and Mark who are up in the stand videoing it all. Pete has a notepad on the bench and he picks two or three, max, because we haven't got time for six or seven. The gaffer uses the time to speak to us without disruption and it is all about finding whatever tweaks we need to make improvements. He did ask us a loaded question at half-time against Villa, though. He pointed out that we were wearing our white kit and asked whether we were worried about getting it dirty. Point taken.

One thing that we hadn't been aware of during the break was that City were losing as well. This was a rare occasion when we were both kicking off at three o'clock on a Saturday afternoon and whereas usually we would be watching one another over the weekend, this was a proper head to head and that gave it the feel of a six pointer at two different venues.

At about 4.45pm, it looked like there would be a six point swing in City's favour as they went 2-1 up with a late Kyle Walker goal. Not that we knew what was going on at the Etihad. We had enough on our plate at Villa Park. Our ten-month unbeaten league run was on the line and so was the momentum which had built from the start of the season. Worst of all, we were at risk of having our advantage at the top wiped out altogether.

Then, out of nowhere, the turning point came and it couldn't have come from a more unexpected source – the head of Andrew Henry Robertson.

Up to that day, I'd done most things as a professional footballer. I had been relegated. I had won the Champions League. I had been released as a kid. I had been injured. I'd had good games and I'd had bad games. One of the few things that was missing from my CV was a headed goal. That changed in an instant and so did the course of a game that had been getting away from us. The finish itself wasn't anything special but the fact that I was attacking the six yard box in open play so late in the game spoke volumes for both our growing desperation and our willingness to commit bodies forward from all positions.

The ball in from Sadio couldn't have been better. It had a lovely in-swinging drift that allowed me to watch it all the way onto my head. All Tom Heaton could do was shuffle across his goal line in the knowledge that if he came out, I would be getting there before him. The funny thing was that even though I hadn't scored a header before then, I knew I was scoring before I made any kind of contact with the ball. I couldn't explain why that was the case, it was just an incredible feeling of inevitability and that was followed by a sense of indescribable euphoria when the ball crashed into the net. A bad defeat had suddenly been transformed into a decent point. But we didn't see it that way. We wanted more.

I sprinted away from their goal, leaving someone else to retrieve the ball which deserves to be a collectors' item given what had just happened, and headed back to the halfway line. The most natural thing in the world would have been to race to the away end at the side of our goal because absolute bedlam had just broken out but, for once, we had to leave our fans to get on with it without us. From where I was, it didn't look like they needed any help with their celebrations anyway.

While the supporters were doing their job, we had a heightened desire to do ours to the absolute maximum. At the moment when the game re-started, I can tell you exactly what every single Liverpool player was thinking – *go and win it*. It was that collectivism that had brought us back into the game and now it was fuelling our desire to turn defeat into victory.

At moments like that, you sense opportunity and you smell blood. All of a sudden, it felt like the pitch was on a slope and everyone on it was drawn towards the Villa goal.

Their players were understandably rocked by what had just happened having come so close to winning the game. All they could do was hang on in the hope that we would run out of time. For them, the clock was ticking far too slowly while for us, it was racing. The key was to remain calm and keep on playing our football. Doing that had brought us back into the game and now it would give us the best chance of winning it. That calmness under pressure is easily overlooked when a game ends in a dramatic frenzy but without it we wouldn't have even drawn level.

In that long spell when we were behind we stuck to our principles, getting on the ball, looking for space and waiting for opportunities to come. We didn't try to force the issue or change the fundamentals of the way we play and one of the key factors in that was the way Hendo and Adam allowed us to dominate. That midfield control grew as the game wore on, allowing us to monopolize possession and create chances that we hadn't been able to take until my goal. It might have been the excitement caused by scoring in such unexpected circumstances but there was a moment when I believed with all my heart that I was going to be the match winner, too.

As we headed towards the last minute of stoppage time, we were awarded a free-kick in a central area on the edge of the Villa box. It was perfect for a right footer or a left footer so the gaffer told Trent and myself to stand over it and put doubt in Tom Heaton's mind. I sensed this was a certain goal, no matter who took it. That is what momentum does, it makes you feel unstoppable. In my head, I was whipping the ball over the wall and into the top corner before wheeling away to celebrate. Then I caught myself on and realised that I was stood next to one of the best free-kick takers around. 'Go on Trent,' I thought. 'Make yourself the hero'.

The Villa wall stood strong and his effort deflected for a corner. Trent didn't flicker. One of his greatest strengths is remaining calm and he just trotted over to take control of the setpiece. It was the 94th minute and he was still thinking as lucidly as you would in the first. Despite the physical fatigue that everyone on the pitch was feeling, he was alert enough to recall something that had been highlighted in the pre-match analysis.

Villa would sometimes leave a gap at the near post when defending corners and the feeling was that if we could get someone into that area we might be able to take advantage. It is the kind of situation that all teams look at before every game but to exploit it you need a lot of things to come together at once. The delivery has to be perfect, the opposition has to act in the way expected and you need a player to not only attack the ball, but to have the quality to score.

In the heat of that moment, at the end of a draining Premier League match against a stubborn opponent, we ticked every box. Trent's corner was perfect, Sadio attacked the ball, getting across his man and meeting it with a perfect header that gave Heaton no chance. I saw a picture afterwards that showed just how brave Sadio had been, diving in despite knowing he was likely to get booted in the head. That is him all over – a brilliant combination of bravery, strength, skill and desire.

I wouldn't ever want to change what I do and being part of a team that always keeps going no matter what is something really special but when the ball hit the net I would have given anything to be in the away end. I saw the videos of the celebrations afterwards and it looked unbelievable in there. For our supporters, it wasn't just a late winner, it felt bigger than that. That's why they went nuts. People have said to me since that the reason they went so mad was that it felt like a title-winning moment, even though it was only early November.

As players, we can't get drawn in to thinking like that. We have to take the view that there is still a long, long way to go. There are still far too many points to play for to start believing it could be our year. If the supporters want to dream and even start feeling their dreams might be about to come true, that's great and we wouldn't be doing our jobs if we didn't give them opportunities to get excited about what might lie ahead.

Our feelings in the dressing room were dominated by what we had avoided – defeat; dropping points; allowing City to close the gap; putting additional pressure on ahead of the reigning champions' visit to Anfield; a kick in the bollocks. Not that any of us were totally free of pain. Games like that take it out of you, emotionally and physically, and it's rare that you come off the pitch without some sort of ache or strain. In my case, I had an ankle problem that was really bugging me. If truth be known, I had come close to missing the game and it took an incredible amount of effort, expertise and, most of all, trust to get me out there.

Much of the credit for that must go to Lee Nobes, our head physio. Since joining us from City, Lee has been one of the unsung heroes behind what we achieve on the pitch. We are fortunate at Liverpool to have so many world class coaches, medical professionals, fitness experts, masseurs, analysts, kit men and various other staff and they all do everything in their power to give us the best possible chance of performing at our best. As players, we can't ask for any more. If there is a culture of excellence around us off the pitch, we have the best possible opportunity to achieve a similar standard on the pitch.

When it comes to making sure we're physically ready to give our best and, when necessary, feel confident enough in our bodies to play even when not one hundred per cent, Lee is top class. I've got a great relationship with him and I trust him absolutely because I know he will never take any unnecessary risks and will always do the right thing in any given situation.

In the days leading up to Villa away, my right ankle had blown up and it wasn't just a case of struggling when I was striking the ball or putting weight on it, I was waking up in the morning and the pain would hit me straight away. I was becoming increasingly concerned that I wouldn't be able to play and I wasn't the only one. The manager was also expecting me to be unavailable and I didn't like that.

I always want to play. I don't like the thought of missing out on games and I will do anything to avoid doing so. If there is a chance that I can get out there and give it a go I will take it and, as the Villa game drew closer, that became my target. I knew I wasn't right and being one hundred per cent fit wasn't even close to being a possibility but I was determined to at least try.

First, though, I had to convince two people that this was a good idea: one was the manager, who has to act in the best interests of the team, and the other was myself as – although I was desperate to play – I had to be sure that I wouldn't be exposing myself to greater risk.

This is where Lee comes into his own. He gave me all the reassurance I could have wished for. Although he told me I was going to be in pain and my ankle wouldn't feel right, he made it clear that there was no risk of further damage being done to my joint. This was all I needed to hear. I have absolute trust in Lee's judgement and if he says I'm good to go, I'm good to go. It is as simple as that. Lee hadn't hedged his bets or covered himself, he had given me the green light, so I went to see the gaffer and told him I was ready to play. Even then, Jürgen could have turned around and said he didn't want to take the risk, especially seeing as it was only early November and there was still a long way to go, but just as I had been convinced by Lee's assurance, the manager was persuaded by mine.

I have sometimes wondered what might have happened had I not been able to get out there because obviously I was involved in the turning point of the game but I'd like to think that someone else would have popped up and made the difference, because that's what we're all about. As it was, I was just grateful and relieved that when the chance came, it arrived at my head rather than my right foot. Even at the best of times my right foot isn't too reliable, never mind when I'm struggling with it. Crucially, winning that game in the manner that we did meant that we went into our next fixture against City on a massive high.

In the days leading up to their visit to Anfield, the rivalry was being stoked up like we were two heavyweights fighting for the championship of the world. Given what had happened in the previous season, the hype was inevitable but it's important to point out that there was no trash talk.

The fact that we have the same objectives and want the same prizes might make us rivals but it doesn't mean we lack respect for one another. If anything, the opposite is true. We know just how hard it is to consistently win games in the Premier League and City had done that better than anyone for a few years, so you have to admire that.

The reason why their standards are so high is that they have a great manager and a brilliant squad of players. I know the media were asking questions of them and wondering whether their standards had dropped but we didn't look at it that way. We saw them as the most significant barrier between us and the Holy Grail and there was no chance of any of us taking our latest encounter for granted, even though there were plenty of people who were making us strong favourites. I did my best to switch off from all that, especially the talk about us being home and hosed for the league title if we won. That kind of speculation is no good for anyone, especially when it's so early in the season and there is still so much football to be played. It's even less helpful when your opponent has as much quality as City. So I deliberately found myself switching off from all of the conjecture and focusing instead on anything that would enhance my focus. Central to that was the knowledge that City had pipped us to the title six months earlier and the feeling of what might have been.

I don't usually like to dwell on near misses. I'm naturally a positive person and looking back on times when you've just fallen short isn't always helpful but there are times when it can heighten your motivation and this was one of them. I didn't need any reminders of how I felt when Kompany scored against Leicester and I doubt it would have been useful to dredge those feelings back up but I did cast my mind back to the day when City sealed the title and we fell agonisingly short. We were at home to Wolves and City were away to Brighton and just thinking about that ninety-minute period made the hairs stand up on the back of my neck. I can't recall another occasion in my life when I have experienced such an incredible mix of excitement, elation, pain and suffering in such a short space of time.

For all too brief a moment, everything seemed possible. We were 1-0 up and City were 1-0 down. On television they would have been showing the league table as it stood and, at that exact time, we were top on the last day of the season. Out on the pitch it felt absolutely surreal because a surge of electricity went around Anfield which brought the supporters to their feet and we knew something big was going on.

We went into the dressing room at half-time and all I was thinking was: 'What the hell is going on?' The gaffer gave an unbelievable half-time speech. He said: "Look, I'm not going to lie to you, it is 1-1 now, City have equalised. We can't control what's going on there, we need to focus on us because once we scored the first goal we started being shaky and we can't afford that."

The second half was strange because the crowd went flat and so did we. Everyone in the ground knew that City were running away with it at Brighton. When Sadio scored our second it was probably the least celebrated goal of the season. It felt more like a late consolation in a 5-1 loss than the second in a 2-0 win.

On top of that, the Wolves supporters were celebrating the City score, really rubbing it in, even though their own team was on its way to defeat. I had no problem with that, though. I've been there as a fan with Celtic and that's part and parcel of being a football supporter. If you don't want stuff like that to happen as a player you have to make sure that you're the ones celebrating while another team is on the receiving end. That was our challenge and fortunately, we have a crowd that lifts us at times like that.

I had already been substituted late on when our supporters did something that I truly believe was a key moment in the success that we went on to enjoy at home and abroad. Just as we were all consumed by disappointment, Anfield erupted. Every fan who was able to was on their feet. 'We shall not, we shall not be moved. We shall not, we shall not be moved. Just like a team that's gonna win the European Cup we shall not be moved.' Wow. This was hairs on the back of your neck, tingling down your spine and tears in your eyes stuff. This was the crowd celebrating the team, showing incredible faith in us at a moment of despair and also reminding us that although one big trophy had eluded us there was another still to play for. I believe that was a massive step towards us becoming European champions.

The lads walked off that pitch after the final whistle and to a man we all thought: 'Now we need to go and win the Champions League'. We needed to win it for ourselves, for our families, for the club, for every single fan who had given us that kind of incredible support. We had put everything into the Premier League and fallen just short but no sooner had that reality set in and the supporters were turning their attentions to what was still possible.

In hindsight, it wasn't just a step towards winning the Champions League, it was also a step towards winning the Premier League. That moment when Brighton scored and everything seemed possible changed something in all of us.

We all saw what winning the title would mean to people. It wasn't that we didn't know that the league was the Holy Grail at Liverpool or that we hadn't heard supporters talking about how special it would be for them, but this was the first time we had seen and heard that desire being demonstrated with so much passion that it reached into your soul and shook you.

I have a responsibility to keep my focus on what's happening on the pitch but it was impossible not to look at the crowd while this was going on. I tried to tell the supporters in the Sir Kenny Dalglish Stand to keep calm because I knew how important it was for all of us to concentrate on our game but their excitement was off the scale and this was something that all of the players carried with us from that day on. We all knew that if we went on to win the league, Anfield would go off in a way that would be beyond our imagination.

In itself, that was an added motivation for us. Who wouldn't want to be part of that? Who wouldn't want to experience the biggest collective euphoria seen at a football ground in this country for many, many years, possibly ever? I know I did but I also knew City would not just hand their title over to us and that when they took us on at Anfield they would see it as their chance to remind us why they were champions. It may not have been a title decider, it was far too early for that, but games in November do not come any bigger.

At least we knew what to expect. As we lined up defending the Kop, City were about to kick off and I thought to myself, 'they might not let us see the ball for a minute or so here'. The next thing, they'd smashed the ball deep into our half and pressed us back. We hadn't known what to expect after all. This was a a statement of intent. The message couldn't have been clearer – City were coming for us. They were going to be aggressive, get in our faces and make life uncomfortable.

As an approach, it certainly took us by surprise and we spent most of the early minutes camped around our own box as they came for us in a big way. Our play was rushed and we were not able to gain any kind of control.

Credit to Pep Guardiola for adapting and catching us unawares. Everyone in the world has an expectation of how City will play because it is so well established and so effective but here we were dealing with them being direct and aggressive. I suppose it was a compliment to us that he changed their approach at the outset. We were penned back by opponents playing like men possessed. At one stage, even big Virgil sliced one high into the air and there can be no greater indication of how much pressure we were coming under than that. City must have thought they had us on the ropes and if they did they were entitled to.

They also thought that they had a penalty when the ball struck Trent's hand but Michael Oliver waved play on and we were able to get out. I knocked the ball up the line to Sadio and all I was thinking was: 'Get us up the pitch and give us a breather'. It was a relief just knowing that we had a few seconds' respite because there aren't many in the game who are better than Sadio when it comes to keeping hold of the ball and turning defence into attack.

Sadio is also a killer. He senses vulnerability and exploits it. Subconsciously, he will have seen that City's early dominance had created a weakness because they had committed so many players into our half. With every step he advanced he will have been thinking a chance could follow. That's why he didn't stop, put his foot on the ball and wait for the game to catch up with him. He kept going and put the ball into the box.

At first, his calculated risk didn't look likely to pay off as City had got enough players back to be able to clear but because they had been turned around and we had turned defence into attack in next to no time, the clearance that followed was panicked. On top of that, City hadn't been given the opportunity to regain their shape and Fabinho collected the ball in plenty of space in front of their box. The big fella took a touch to get the ball out of his feet and then *bang!* Claudio Bravo saw the shot but he couldn't get anywhere near it.

The Anfield roof came off but for once I wasn't in tune with the mood in the stadium. While everyone else went nuts, I fully expected the goal to be ruled out. It wasn't that I thought Trent had handled, I actually felt the referee had made the right call, but I knew the ball had struck his hand and given the way the laws were being interpreted in the first few months of the season, I anticipated our goal being chalked off and City being awarded a penalty at the other end. This was going to be a kick in the bollocks and a possible turning point of the kind I'd never experienced before but at least I was ready for it.

All eyes were on Michael Oliver and I was steeling myself for him to do that TV screen sign with his hands to indicate that VAR had intervened. But it didn't happen. Instead, he pointed to the centre circle, ordered City to kick off and all hell broke loose.

If roles had been reversed I would have reacted in exactly the same way that they did but I wasn't about to sympathise. For me, it was a legitimate goal and the only injustice would have been if it had been disallowed. But, at the same time, I understood why the City players were so angry. It isn't often that a penalty appeal at one end is followed by a goal at the other, so I can only imagine how tough it was to take. I also recognised that out of nowhere we had given ourselves a foothold in the game without having taken control. Now we needed to lift our performance or else the lead would be short-lived.

That, though, is one of the best things about this Liverpool team. When it comes to sensing the moment and reacting accordingly, we definitely have a knack of reacting to events. This is something that has stood us in good stead. At times, it has felt like a switch has been flicked and out of nowhere we are all over opponents without warning, playing football which is a level above what we had previously been producing. When it is like that our supporters respond accordingly, turning the stadium into a bear pit. We feed off each other. It's one of the main reasons why Anfield has become a fortress for us. It must be horrible for teams who have to play us when it is like that. Even City, with their incredible array of talent, have found it difficult to cope at times, although we would be the first to admit that they were the ones causing us problems up until Fab's goal. That was the catalyst for what followed and within a matter of minutes we found ourselves 2-0 up.

The goal that increased our advantage was one of the best I have been involved in. If you wanted to pick some sequences of play that capture what this team is about, this would have to feature on the highlights reel and I'm not saying that because I was involved.

Trent started it all off with a trademark cross-field ball that opened up the entire left flank for me and a perfect counter-attacking opportunity for the team. There aren't many players in the world who can play that kind of pass but Trent does it pretty much every game. The difference this time was that he pulled it off with his left foot. Part of me wanted to stop and applaud but there was a ball to chase down. I took one touch, looked up and spotted Mo making a run, so I whipped it in straight away with my left foot as City's defence tried to scramble back into my position. The ball bounced once in the area before Mo made perfect contact with his head, sending it into the far corner and giving Bravo no chance.

From Trent's left boot to Mo's head there were a total of four touches and a move which went from one side of the pitch to the other and almost back again was done and dusted in seconds. It was only when I watched it back afterwards that I realised what a special goal it was. In the days that followed, a lot of people on social media were comparing it to Terry McDermott's famous goal against Spurs. I wouldn't go quite that far but it was a goal that was totally in keeping with the best traditions of this club and also with the style of play that Jürgen demands from us.

The scoreline wasn't a fair reflection of the game to that point but we couldn't have cared less. In the previous season we had only taken one point from our two games against City and we knew we had to change that record.

That message was reinforced at half-time, too, because we all knew how big this opportunity was and there was no way we could afford to relax. We couldn't even do that after Sadio put us 3-0 up. City kept putting us under pressure and got a goal back from Bernardo Silva. The final fifteen minutes was tough as they had a lot of the ball but we dug in to make it eleven wins from our first twelve games. Most importantly, the victory allowed us to open up a nine point lead over City and plenty, including José Mourinho, were saying that kind of gap was too big and the title was ours to lose. José knows more about winning titles than I do but this was November 10th! There were still seventy-eight more points to play for, so none of us were getting caught up in that kind of talk.

That isn't to say that we weren't well aware of the opportunity that was opening up for us, because we were.

There were so many good signs: the way that we had coped without Alisson while he was unavailable, the fact that goals were being shared around with so many players chipping in at vital moments, the number of times we had found a way to win without being at our absolute best, a sense of belief that grew with each and every unbeaten game. Not everything was great, though. My ankle problem flared up again, leaving me hobbling as I returned to the dressing room after the game.

I was worried I would be a doubt for Scotland's forthcoming Euro 2020 qualifiers against Cyprus and Kazakhstan. I hate missing any games and I'm always desperate to play for my country so I think everyone could sense my concern, even though I was delighted with the result. If there is one thing that footballers are selfish about, it is definitely their fitness. If we're not right in any way it occupies our mind like it's the world's biggest problem when the reality is, more often than not, it's just a minor occupational hazard and it will be sorted sooner rather than later.

That's just the mindset of competitive sport – if you are part of a team having worked so hard to get there, the last thing you want to do is miss games. All of us know that there are much, much bigger issues in the world but when you are in the bubble that elite sport creates, it is pretty much inevitable that your own physical wellbeing dominates your thoughts, especially when you have an injury.

So I was definitely feeling sorry for myself but that changed in an instant when I saw a man in a wheelchair being brought into the dressing room area. I knew who it was straight away without needing to be told and seeing him stopped me in my tracks. It was Sean Cox.

We hadn't met before but I knew a lot about him because, like everyone associated with Liverpool, I had followed his story ever since he was attacked outside Anfield and almost killed by Ultras shortly before our Champions League semi-final first leg against AS Roma in April 2018.

The fact that he was back at the stadium at all was a miracle. In the hours and days after he was brutally assaulted we were getting regular updates on his condition so we knew that there were grave fears that he would not pull through. As a Roman Catholic I prayed for Sean but, given how bad his condition was at the time, I also feared the worst. This was an ordinary bloke with a wife and kids who had been left at death's door having come to see us play football. I wouldn't even want to consider the mentality of those who left him in such a state because they don't deserve our thoughts but the fact that one of our own had been left fighting for his life hit all of us hard.

That night should have been a joyous occasion and at first it was. We had beaten Roma 5-2 and although there was still a second leg to come, we knew we had put ourselves in with a great chance of reaching the final, so there was a lot of excitement as well as a resolve to finish the job in Rome.

At that point we were oblivious to what had happened to Sean. We were obviously playing when the news started to emerge but it didn't take long for us to work out that something was wrong after we came off the pitch.

At first, I couldn't put my finger on it. People around the club who we see after games were congratulating us and saying the right things but I could tell something wasn't right. It was only when Milly and myself got summoned to do a post-match drugs test that we found out what had happened. The club doctor, Andy Massey, had been kept informed and he told us that one of our supporters was in a really bad way. The two of us were stunned. We didn't know his name or where he was from but we both got that terrible feeling that you only experience when one of your own is in danger. At that point, the result was absolutely secondary.

Usually, on my drive home after a match, I will go over the game in my head and call family to talk about it but this time I just sat there in silence, wondering how something so bad could happen. When I got back I sent texts to a few people at the club asking them to keep me informed and they all said they would but they also said things didn't look good.

Usually when you have a big win in a massive game, Melwood is buzzing the next day but this time it wasn't. The headlines were bleak – *Liverpool fan fights for life* – and the mood was sombre. We didn't even have a name for the victim at that stage, all we knew was that he had travelled over from Ireland with his brother and they had both been attacked. It was a waiting game; waiting to find out who he was and waiting to find out how he was.

Eventually, that information started to come through. He was called Sean Cox and he was in intensive care at Aintree Hospital. A member of the club staff was going to the hospital to check on the family and to offer them our support so we were able to get condition updates more regularly from then on. There wasn't any particularly good news but neither did we receive the news that we were all fearing. A few days after it happened, Sean's son, Jack, was brought to Melwood. As soon as I saw him I realised he was only a bit younger than me and then I was told it was his 21st birthday. That stopped me in my tracks. The poor kid. I couldn't count the number of times my dad had gone off to see Celtic when we were little and there was never a thought that he might not come home. I couldn't imagine what Jack was going through. None of us could.

Trent and myself sat down with him on the grass while the other lads went through a specific routine and we just spoke like young men. We listened to Jack and it was clear how much he loved his dad. We also talked a bit about football and tried to lighten the mood as much as we could in the circumstances, but both of us knew full well that he was going through a terrible experience that nothing could have prepared him for. I gave him a hug when he was leaving and hoped that he would have a lot of better days ahead given how difficult his 21st birthday had been.

From that day on we kept getting updates, little milestones which suggested that, slowly but surely, things were going in the right direction. We were in Kiev, the day before the Champions League final against Real Madrid, when we found out Sean was being flown back to Dublin and that gave all of us a massive boost. We knew the road ahead was still going to be long and arduous but this was definitely progress, especially given how bad the initial progress had been.

A few weeks earlier we had paraded a banner made by fans in support of Sean after we had reached the final. We were all desperate for any kind of good news, so this was more than welcome. Later that year, Gini and myself unfurled the same banner following a pre-season friendly against Napoli in Dublin and took it to the part of the ground where Sean's family were sitting. This was about showing solidarity but, behind the scenes, the club and ourselves were offering more practical support which hopefully helped the Cox family.

Our supporters were different class as well, with fundraisers being held, donations being made and a bucket collection organised by Spirit Of Shankly raising almost £30,000 in coins and notes. The LFC Foundation then matched that amount. It felt like everyone in Liverpool and many more besides were finding ways to support the family and that feeling grew still further when Everton's Séamus Coleman made a donation in aid of his fellow Irishman. Liverpool reminds me of Glasgow in this way. When it really matters, people really pull together for a cause and will always look out for one another. I just wished that, in this case, it hadn't been necessary.

There was a long-standing open invitation from the club for Sean to attend a game at Anfield whenever he was well enough to do so and that moment arrived when we played City. Seeing him afterwards gave all of us even more of a lift than the result, particularly as he was in such good form. Hendo was wearing a watch and Sean tried to take it off his wrist as a joke while the pair of them embraced. I loved that. He had a twinkle in his eye and his smile let us know how happy he was to be back at Anfield, even though it was clear that his injuries had taken a heavy toll. I have been asked what the highlight of the 2019/20 season was and this would have to be right up there. We all had an emotional involvement and there was no bigger win throughout the entirety of the campaign than having Sean back with us.

Meeting Sean had three big effects on me – it gave me a massive admiration for his family for everything they were doing for him, it added to my determination to do everything I possibly could to bring success to our supporters and it reminded me that, in the grand scheme of things, minor injuries aren't a big deal no matter how much they nag away.

I headed off to international duty as desperate as ever to play for my country but I knew I was a major doubt. I was checked over by the physio when I arrived and it was decided that I wasn't in a good enough condition for the fixtures against Cyprus and Kazakhstan. I was devastated but, in my heart of hearts, I'd already known what the outcome would be. The boys won both games anyway so they obviously didn't need me!

Back on Merseyside, I was also having to sit out training as we prepared for the trip to Crystal Palace. As the week wore on, so the expectation grew that I would miss out on that game too.

While this was happening, I have to admit that some of the context I'd gained from meeting Sean was lost. The fear of missing out affected my mood. Palace away is always a tough game at a venue that puts all visiting teams to the test and it's the kind of fixture that I love playing in. The physios and medical staff didn't give up on me, though, and by the Friday I was given the green light to train. Again, I wasn't one hundred per cent but I was out there, having a go and by doing that, I knew I was giving the manager a decision to make. I declared myself fit and he gave me the nod. Game on.

As usual, Selhurst Park didn't bring out the best in us. I don't think it brings out the best in anyone except Palace. Our football didn't flow and we struggled for rhythm. It quickly became a case of digging in and staying in the game by making sure we won our individual battles. Sadio gave us the lead early in the second half only for Wilfried Zaha to equalise. A draw down there is almost always a good result, particularly when you're not at your best, but the fear of making a hostage of points drove us on.

With five minutes to go, Bobby scored the winner and it felt huge. Like Villa away, these are the games where league titles are won. It doesn't get much harder than Palace away straight after the international break but we had just about come through it.

The difficult opponents kept coming and after a 1-1 home draw with Napoli at Anfield in the Champions League, we had another home game against Brighton. Unlike most of our fixtures during that period, the game seemed to be pretty comfortable – until Alisson got sent off. A couple of towering headers from Virgil had put us in control but the first thing Adrian had to do after coming on was pick the ball out of the net, as Lewis Dunk scored from a free-kick. All of a sudden we were facing the Alamo and it really did seem like we could feel the tension rising with every second. The sound of the final whistle unleashed an enormous sense of relief in the stands and out on the pitch.

We hadn't made life easy for ourselves but, once again, we had come through. The schedule had been relentless but we had strengthened our position at the top of the table which was so important because we were about to enter a phase that had the potential to undermine much of the good work we had done.

TAKING ON THE WORLD

TEN games in four different competitions over thirty days, a Merseyside derby, a six thousand mile round trip to the Middle East, a do or die Champions League tie in Austria, a bid to become world champions for the first time and Christmas Day itself – it's safe to say the festive period of 2019 was like no other any of us had ever experienced.

Describing it has hectic probably doesn't do it justice and if any of us had stopped to think about it any stage we could easily have lost our way amid the madness of it all. Instead, the demands actually heightened our focus and the determination we had to achieve all of our objectives. The treadmill was at maximum speed and we had no choice but to keep going at full pelt. Had we looked for excuses, accepted the odd bad result along the way or started to feel sorry for ourselves at any point, this was a schedule that had the potential to derail us. The feeling outside the club was that our standards would inevitably drop but we never saw it that way. For us, it was an opportunity to dominate England, show our authority in Europe and, as the great Bill Shankly put it, conquer the bloody world.

It was incredibly demanding but we knew that was what the squad was there for and it was also what we had prepared for in pre-season. Yes, all of us were going to be tested like never before but we knew that if we did everything right through December in terms of preparing properly, recovering properly and just looking after our bodies really well, we would be able to cope. A lot of people outside were saying it was good that we had a lead at the top of the league going into December. They thought we would slip up due to the amount of games and the travelling but our mentality was exactly the same; we love playing football games, we love winning and the more the merrier. That mentality allowed us to come through with flying colours, winning nine out of ten games. The only defeat came as a result of impossible scheduling that forced the club to choose between two competitions.

Our form leading up to this period was a massive help. At the start of the season, we had been playing well and winning games but people were questioning why we weren't keeping clean sheets. Yet, by this stage, we could feel ourselves getting right in the groove. We had beaten Man City fairly comfortably, we had come from behind against Aston Villa, we were putting in some very good performances and confidence was sky high.

When you play at a club like this and everything is going in the right direction, you do kind of feel invincible and you go into every game expecting to win. There is a danger that comes with that, though, because you can start to rely on that feeling a wee bit and that is when you are likely to slip up. Our priority was ensuring that our attitude was at one hundred per cent as any drop-off would have put us at risk. It was up to us to maintain our momentum and our standards. This was where the experienced lads in the squad came into their own. They kept us going but, having said that, I can honestly say that over the entire month I didn't go into a single game thinking we would drop points. I knew we could and I recognised that every one of our opponents would cause us problems yet our belief was so high that we expected to win every game.

We weren't given a gentle start. Whatever our record might suggest, Everton at Anfield is one of our toughest games of the season. I'm not even from Merseyside but it is one of the first matches I look for when the fixtures come out because I know how much derby games mean to everyone involved. How could I not, given I grew up in Glasgow, enduring and enjoying Old Firm games? There are more than two teams in Glasgow but when the big two collide the outcome either lifts your soul and makes you feel all-powerful or saps your spirit and you end up not wanting to leave the house. Derby day was everything in Glasgow. If you win it, you had bragging rights until the next one and I have some family members who were Rangers fans so there is no escaping the rivalry.

Before the away allocations started getting cut, Rangers used to get a lot of tickets for Parkhead and I genuinely hated going up the stadium steps and seeing their fans all there. Not because I hated them – they were just supporters going to the match like we were – I just hated the feeling of absolute dread it stirred in me. The fear of losing these games is so big it consumes you. The thought that at some point in the game they could score a goal or, worse, grab a winner is something that keeps you up at night and it feels ten times worse when you actually get into the ground. There were times when I actually thought to myself that it might be better if I could be knocked out and told the result once the game had finished rather than put myself through that kind of agony.

I definitely wished I hadn't been there when Ugo Ehiogu won the game for Rangers with an unbelievable overhead kick in March 2007 but there we were, sat in our usual seats in the Family Stand watching the Rangers fans go absolutely nuts. That day was a coming of age in more ways than one. It was my 13th birthday and I'm not superstitious but maybe I should have been after that. The only saving grace was I could only turn thirteen once in my life. I've never had a worse or more painful birthday, put it that way.

I went to bed that night thinking that I hated the Celtic players for letting us down. I didn't really, most of them were heroes and I adored them, but I would have given anything to avoid feeling as gutted as I did and, at that moment of total despair, I wasn't convinced that they cared as much for Celtic as I did. How could they if they'd allowed Rangers to beat us on our turf on my birthday?

It was similar when I was in the away end at Ibrox and they beat us 3-0. I was raging. So I know how the mind of a football fan works because I have been one – and I still am one. Like any fan, I've thought I am the best manager in the world and if only such and such had played – as I'd wanted – the result would have been different. I have laid in bed wondering why the players aren't willing to die for the shirt like I would. Football creates this kind of irrational passion in all of us. It was only when I got a bit older and the penny dropped that players always care, always want to win and never set out to lose deliberately. When I realised that, I was able to get a little bit of peace in myself.

On the flip side, there was nothing better than seeing your team win a derby. I was at Ibrox two days after Christmas in 2008 when Scott McDonald scored the winner and the feeling was better than anything I had experienced 48 hours earlier.

I'd managed to get a ticket through my uncle who went home and away with Celtic every week and I went with him and my cousin. When the goal went in, our end erupted, it really was bedlam. That's still my favourite experience as a Celtic fan because of the feelings it provoked immediately after we scored. Euphoria wouldn't even do it justice. If everyone in our end had been drugs tested at that exact moment we would have all failed because there's no way anyone could have explained the chemical surge that we were all experiencing.

This was very much a natural high, though, and it was all too fleeting. Beforehand, I was gripped by fear of losing and afterwards I was consumed by the possibility of not winning. I don't care what anyone says, you don't *enjoy* an Old Firm or Merseyside derby. It just isn't possible. If you were looking at it logically, you would question why anyone ever puts themselves through it but, thankfully, we're not logical and this means that in the aftermath we get to revel in our victories as if we've just triumphed in a battle for life itself. I used to love nothing better than going to the golf course where I was a member after an Old Firm win and giving it out to the Rangers fans and I've no doubt they felt exactly the same way when roles were reversed.

So I know what it means. I had received a top class education in the pride and passion of derby matches. Even though I grew up two hundred miles away from Liverpool, the single fixture that I was probably best prepared for was the one against Everton. The two clubs might be a wee bit apart at the minute with Liverpool fighting for trophies and Everton finding their feet again under Carlo Ancelotti but none of that makes a difference when the derby comes around. We also know that just like our supporters, their fans want to be the ones with the bragging rights so they go can go into work the next day and make fun of their peers. That's what happens in Glasgow and it also happens down here so much of my motivation comes from that.

There is a different feeling derby week and you don't need a calendar or a fixture list to know that the game is around the corner. When I was a supporter, I would wonder if the players felt the anticipation in the same way that we did and, in my case, I definitely do. One of the main reasons for that is Paul Small, a masseur at Liverpool.

When I first joined I was told that Smally is a Liverpool institution and I still don't know whether that's a good thing or not because so is The Grafton. As well as being an institution, he is also an Evertonian, so when derby week comes around the banter flies. He tries to take the mickey out of us and we take it back – that's what it's like in this city. It is a friendlier derby than the Old Firm. The passion during the game is definitely off the scale, just as it is in Glasgow, but you can go for a few pints with your Everton mate after the game and, for me, Smally represents that side of things. He obviously works for Liverpool and is as committed to the cause as any of us but he usually has his snood over his eyes during the derby. He knows better than anyone else what lies in store for him in the days afterwards if we win.

Smally is a big part of what we do. I love going in to see him for a massage because I know the time will fly when I'm in with him. He will be treating me but it is also just two mates having a bit of banter. I took to him on day one and since then I can't think a day will have passed without us winding one another up. He is a massive Steven Gerrard lover and I'm a massive Celtic lover so we have plenty of conversations about that. He likes to get in my head about Rangers v Celtic so I flip it by making it about Liverpool v Everton.

I have massive respect for all the years he's worked at Liverpool and the contribution he has made to the club, but I genuinely think there's part of him that wants Everton to win the derby. I think he wants the lads he treats to do well and wants us to do well as a team and as a club but genuinely, in that week, he wouldn't be human if he didn't have a fleeting moment when he wondered what it would be like if Everton won. I know if I worked for Rangers, I couldn't not want Celtic to win either. You can't just turn that passion on and off. It's what makes you who you are.

We both go a wee bit quieter the day before the game because he obviously wants to get a result at Anfield and we want to get the job done. I'm always partly worried that Everton might get a result and then everything I've said to him in the build-up backfires and he can hit me hard the next day. Thankfully, Smally hasn't had as much chance to have a go at us after recent derbies but, like a lot of people, he probably felt Everton's chances of being top dogs had increased when our line-up was confirmed for the latest instalment.

I remember reading after the game that when our team was named, people were questioning it, Liverpool fans included. The gaffer made five changes with one of them being forced on us because Ali was banned, so Adrian came back in. But we were well used to rotation at this time of year so it didn't cause anything like the same stir inside the dressing room as it did outside. The lads coming in were raring to go. I had seen them in training so I knew they were all ready. To name a couple, Shaq and Divock were both more than ready that night and they got a flying start with three goals between them in the first half hour. Everton hung on in there and although we went in 4-2 up at half-time we were a bit disappointed because we could have been out of sight. We were more controlled in the second half and Gini topped off a great night with a goal in the ninetieth minute.

The gaffer rang the changes once again for our trip to Bournemouth, just the seven this time around, but the end result was the same as we won by a three goal margin for the second game running. We kept a clean sheet too – our first in fourteen games – and although we had known it was coming, it was still nice to get one under our belts.

That was significant for us, although probably not as memorable as the celebration that followed Ox scoring the opener. Before the game Ox and Trent had agreed to do some daft dance together if either of them scored but Trent started on the bench and when Ox raced over to him ready to cut some moves Trent just stood there with his arms stretched out.

That was probably our only false move all afternoon as we ended up being as dominant as we had been in any game all season. The last twenty to twenty-five minutes felt a bit like a training match because we were keeping the ball so well with Hendo pulling the strings in midfield. This was a reflection of our confidence and control rather than anything negative about Bournemouth. We were right on our game, creating chances, dominating possession, limiting their opportunities and just generally making the right decisions at the right time.

Naby and Mo got our other goals and once the game was in the bag, the gaffer took me off and replaced me with Curtis for the last fifteen minutes. He joked that he was giving me a rest – a whole quarter of an hour! I would only have moaned if it had been any longer than that, though, and I got to enjoy watching Curtis underline the growing strength in depth that we had. The lads coming into the team had all had to wait for their chance, but they were all shining and that gave us the confidence to think that if we did have to keep making changes in every single game we could do so. These lads were more than ready. Sometimes it takes a while to get up to match speed but they were all raring to go. Everyone was stepping up to the plate, everything was falling into place and we were all firing.

It needed to be like that, too, because we had given ourselves no margin for error in the Champions League and we knew that if we lost to Red Bull Salzburg we could go out of the competition at the group stage. They were Europe's hype team at the time and I don't mean that disrespectfully. There was a lot of excitement about them because of the quality of their players, their style of football and the amount of goals they were scoring. So there was a lot of noise around the game and it felt like, in certain quarters at least, there was an eagerness to see the holders put in their place by the upstarts. That definitely helped our focus and we went over there and showed why we were champions of Europe.

They started really well and in the first fifteen minutes we had to soak up a bit of pressure, which we did really well. We didn't panic and then Naby scored against his former club before Mo put us in command with an unbelievable goal. I still don't know to this day how he put that shot in from such a tight angle.

Even at 2-0 up, none of us thought it was job done, though. The game at Anfield had taught us how dangerous Red Bull could be if they are given a sniff and we all had vivid memories of virtually their whole team running away to the away end when they made it 3-3. A lot had been made about the difference that Erling Haaland had made that night and the goals he was scoring in general, which was fair enough because he is an excellent player and their entire front three would be a handful for any team. But this was a game where Virgil really came into his own. He stood up to that threat, faced it down and dominated his area of the pitch.

Knowing him as I do, he will have been thinking about keeping a clean sheet and showing not only Haaland but also Taki and Hwang Hee-chan that they would be getting no change out of him. It was one of his best performances of the season and that's why he is the best in the world – because he can perform to an unbelievably high level, week in and week out. We had got the job done and gone through to the last 16, which was all that mattered. When you look at that qualifying group, it might have seemed comfortable for us on paper when it was drawn but it was far from being so in reality and we were delighted to come through it.

I had a bit of a tight hamstring so the gaffer put me on the bench as a precaution for our next game at home to Watford. Ideally, he probably wanted to leave me there to remove any risk of the injury worsening before we headed off to Qatar for the Club World Cup but Watford made life really difficult for us and I was brought on after an hour.

We were 1-0 up thanks to another goal from Mo but even though Watford had not won in the league for over a month, they played with real confidence and belief. We had thought this could happen beforehand because it was Nigel Pearson's first official game in charge and we were anticipating a bit of a bounce. Other than that, we didn't really know what to expect because although we were aware that Watford had good players and that Pearson is a good manager, it was difficult to find out how he would set them up – he hadn't been in charge long enough for there to be a big body of analysis.

Our analysis lads are really good and they managed to root out some Leicester games that he had been in charge of which helped but there was still an element of the unknown. Watford were good that day – how well they played shouldn't be under-estimated – and had they took the chances they created, the result might have been different. As it was, we ground it out, Mo making the points safe with his second goal late on.

I shot straight home to see Rachel and the kids afterwards because I knew this would be the last night I would be home for a week. We were flying to Qatar the following morning. Like any family, we would prefer to be together in the week before Christmas because it is such a special time, especially now that we have kids. Rachel never gives me a hard time because she knows it's my job but that doesn't make it any easier. It was Aria's first Christmas and, as a dad, you want to be around to enjoy those moments. She was eleven months old and Rocco was two and a half years old, so it was all going on.

I missed Rocco's nativity at nursery but he didn't really have a part because he was so young. He just did 'the wheels on the bus' and then sat on Rachel's knee. We managed to visit Santa as a family before I went, though, because we knew I probably wouldn't have time when I got back from Qatar so it was all pretty intense, trying to get everything ready for Christmas at the same time as preparing for a big trip. It goes without saying that you do feel guilty as a dad when you go away at a time like that but there were twenty-five lads in a similar boat and we're all well aware that there are people who have to make much bigger sacrifices in their jobs. We were going to try to win the Club World Cup and if everyone was good in Qatar and at home, Father Christmas would be arriving the following week. Even at the age of twenty-six things don't get much more exciting than that!

It was all still a bit weird. I'm definitely not used to having to pack my Factor 50 in the middle of December but what made it really strange was the reaction to us going. I spoke to Ali about it and he said in Brazil, and South America in general, the Club World Cup is as big as it gets. He told me that if Flamengo won it, there would be a parade every bit as big as the one we had enjoyed after winning the Champions League and that supporters would be doing anything they could to raise the money to travel. That stopped me in my tracks, not because I thought there was anything outrageous about that, I just couldn't get my head around the contrast with the way our participation was being treated in England.

Whereas it felt like Flamengo had a nation and maybe even an entire continent behind them, we were being asked whether or not we should take part with some suggesting we should be prioritising our Carabao Cup quarter-final against Aston Villa. I've got nothing whatsoever against the Carabao Cup and if the scheduling had been more helpful I would have loved to have played in that game. But if it is a straight choice between that and trying to win the Club World Cup for the first time, it isn't a very difficult decision. Our disappointment was that as a club we had been put in a position in which we had to choose and that's something which should be looked at for future years.

As soon as we knew we would be going to Qatar, we wanted to come back with two things – a gold badge on our shirts and a trophy to go on the wall at Melwood. We were not travelling all that way just to take part. We were going to win.

I'd bought one of those portable PlayStations to take with me because we were going to be away for eight days and I thought I'd get a good use out of it in my hotel room. It definitely had the feeling of going to an international tournament because usually when we go on trips during the season we're back home after a day or two. I even took adapters with me, just in case. I am quite OCD so I pack the night before, even when we go to hotels for one night. I bring all my stuff and know what I need and when I need it.

Usually we know what to expect when we get to our destination because the Champions League has well established procedures that we are all used to following, but Qatar was a trip to the unknown in lots of ways.

I was one of the few who had been there previously as an under-13 player with Celtic so I was expecting the same good organisation and facilities. When we landed, we got the feeling straight away that it was a similar set-up to a World Cup. The protocols and the welcome we got, everything like that, gave it a big tournament feel. We were already determined not to waste our own time and effort by coming back empty-handed and the sense that this was a major competition only added to that feeling.

Virgil, in particular, was hell-bent on us becoming champions of the world. All he kept talking about was getting that gold badge on our shirt. We had seen Real Madrid wearing it and it looked great on an all-white strip. More than that, though, it symbolised greatness.

I looked at the list of previous winners – Real, Barcelona, Bayern Munich, Inter Milan, Manchester United – and Liverpool weren't on it. That was strange for us because we're used to following in the footsteps of the great Liverpool teams of the past and this was a rare opportunity to create new history. We were desperate to show that we were world champions. The gold badge meant everything. It was the same in the Champions League, it was a real motivation to turn the sleeve badge from a number five into a six. When we did that, it meant so much. I didn't know what the trophy looked like but I knew what the badge looked like and I wanted it. It's iconic.

Our focus couldn't have been greater but we also needed to keep an eye on events back home with the youngsters playing at Villa in the cup and the Premier League carrying on in our absence. Missing a round of fixtures in the league wasn't ideal but the way the fixtures fell couldn't have been better for us with our two closest challengers, City and Leicester, playing each other. That gave us a bit of comfort as we knew at least one of them was going to drop points. In this respect it couldn't have worked out more favourably for us – we focused on winning all our games before heading to Qatar, we then got to spend some time together in a warmer climate while fighting for another trophy and we knew only one of our domestic rivals could make ground on us. We also had confidence that we would be able to pick up where we had left off, regardless of the concerns that others may have had on that front.

At one point, the gaffer had asked all the lads if we wanted to go. It was kind of up in the air because of the issues with fixture congestion. But we all said that we didn't know if we would play in a Club World Cup again and he had the same opinion. That's why we went to Qatar and the young lads played the game against Aston Villa. It wasn't ideal but ultimately we were forced to choose between the two competitions.

We couldn't even watch all of the Carabao Cup tie. We all wanted to, but the time difference was a killer. Our semi-final against Monterrey was the following evening and we had training in the morning so we were only able to watch the first half in our hotel rooms before going to sleep.

By the time I put my head on my pillow, the boys were 4-0 down but if ever a half-time scoreline failed to reflect events on the pitch this was it. In the first fifteen minutes, especially, they were incredible. The confidence they played with and the quality they showed – I don't think many people were expecting them to perform to that kind of level but they did. Harvey Elliott was showcasing his skills which came as no surprise to us having trained with him. All of the boys stepped up but, of course, young lads make mistakes and that's what killed them on the night. You look at any Liverpool team and everyone at the club would agree that in normal circumstances we shouldn't be beaten by five goals but this result was the exception that proved the rule. Every one of those lads stood up to it massively and they shared an experience that none of them will ever forget.

The reaction of the Liverpool fans during and after the game spoke volumes about how well the team had done. Our supporters appreciate effort and desire and they also recognise good football, so to hear them singing throughout provided a better indication of the performance than the result did. It might not have been the first team but it was a team that did Liverpool proud and that's all anyone can ever ask.

In terms of playing to their level, the boys probably did a better job than we did in our semi-final against Monterrey. I'm not one for excuses but we found the conditions tough that night. It was hot at pitch level, the playing surface was sticky and I definitely felt lethargic out there, which isn't like me at all. Our preparations hadn't been straightforward either. Monterrey had won the CONCACAF Champions League and were clearly a decent side but we didn't know a great deal about them. Clips of them in action were harder to find than footage of a Nigel Pearson Watford team.

On top of that, we only had one fit centre-back available with Virgil being ruled out through illness, Dejan nursing a knock and Fabinho and Joel back in Merseyside as they recovered from injuries. It was going to be Joe Gomez plus one. Joe is an incredible talent – his only flaw is he is English! – but it's definitely not ideal to go into a game of such importance with him as the only recognised centre-back. The gaffer didn't have too many options and it was one of those situations in which whatever he did wasn't going to be perfect. It was a case of make do and mend and, ultimately, he decided to play Hendo there which, given his strength in the air, reading of the game and ability to communicate, was definitely the best we could have done in the circumstances. Yes, we were losing Hendo from midfield but we had options there and, anyway, this was an emergency and who better to respond than the captain?

So, while Virgil was locked away in his hotel room, I had Hendo next to me which made it easier for him to shout at me than usual! I look up to him massively but this was a game where he needed me to help him out, for once. It was also important that I played my natural game as much as possible without overthinking the fact I had a midfielder alongside me. It was about finding a balance. Five minutes in and I went to press on the outside, which was pretty normal for me. When Virgil is there, he will just move across and Joe will follow suit. Hendo just stayed where he was. The next time I was in earshot he said: "Robbo, don't do that again." I wanted to laugh but he would have killed me if I had, so I just said: "Okay, Hendo, no problem" and from that point I tailored my game accordingly.

I don't know what he was worried about. He did amazingly well, putting in an unbelievable performance while playing out of position in an all-or-nothing game. The cards we had been dealt were not the ones we would have wanted and we had issues in midfield, too, with Gini also being poorly and Fabinho unavailable. But we had to make the most of the resources we had available to us or we could forget all about getting that gold badge on our shirts.

I had expected Monterrey to have good footwork and a high technical level but I also thought that maybe we would outrun them. The one player I knew was Rogelio Funes Mori and that was only because he is the brother of Ramiro, the former Everton defender. When I saw him I genuinely thought it was the Funes Mori I knew, but obviously this brother can finish because he scored to cancel out Naby's opener. Anyone who hadn't expected our semi-final to be a contest quickly found out that it would be. We knew Monterrey were there on merit and it was the same as the other teams over there. We showed Monterrey the ultimate respect and they ended up proving what a good side they are. They played very well. We couldn't have asked for a bigger test in our opening fixture.

We probably put a bit more pressure on ourselves for that game than pretty much any other during the entire season. We knew we had put ourselves on the line by going out to Qatar in the first place with sections of the media questioning our decision and accusing us of disrespecting the League Cup.

This was a trophy that our club had never won before but in the back of our minds we were also aware of the criticism that would come our way if we didn't even make it to the final. So there was definitely pressure and we felt it. We didn't want to look like mugs and, had we ended up having to take part in the third/fourth place play-off game, that's exactly what would have happened. The problem was, Monterrey were not about to roll over for us just because we might get a bit of a hard time if we lost so we had to find a way to win. It was clear from the outset that it wasn't going to be easy.

I don't think it was a coincidence that the solutions to the problems we were facing were found on the bench. Trent and Bobby both came on late in the game with fresh legs and fresh minds and that made all the difference. We had been on top and just about the better side, but signs of a winning goal were few and far between so the gaffer made a brilliant call in making the changes when he did.

Sometimes any change of personnel can make a difference but it's not often a manager can introduce players of their quality. Their impact on the game was clear from the moment they arrived on the pitch. The way the pair of them combined for the last gasp goal that took us through to the final said everything about their ability.

At first, I thought it was a good goal – a decent cross by Trent and a pretty standard near post finish by Bobby. I wouldn't have cared if it had been a mishit via a deflection with a mistake by the keeper thrown in for good measure, but it was only when I got back to the dressing room and watched a replay that I realised I had underestimated how good a goal it was.

It was a pass rather than a cross from Trent; the kind of pinpoint delivery that very few players in the world are capable of, especially when the tension is so high. I actually apologised to Trent for not giving him the respect he deserved because I had thought it was just a standard knock into the area when it was anything but. On top of that, Bobby's run across his man was unbelievable. He timed it absolutely perfectly and while the finish wasn't anything out of the ordinary, his movement was and that made everything that followed pretty straight-forward for a player of his quality. Most importantly of all, they had combined to ensure that we avoided extra time which might have been a problem given Monterrey had been in Qatar for longer than we had. We had achieved our first objective by reaching the final. Now we just had to win it.

In comparison with other finals we have been involved in, we were wrestling with what this one meant, to an extent. It definitely felt like we would be playing this final for ourselves in some ways. The Champions League finals in Madrid and Kiev were all about Liverpool fans. They were everywhere. Even those who hadn't managed to make it out there were making a massive deal of it at home. The distance involved, the timing and the fact that the Club World Cup isn't as big a deal in England as it is in South America, meant this was always likely to be an occasion where the Brazilian supporters held sway and that was how it proved. A few thousand fans made it from Liverpool which is unbelievable when you take everything into account, especially the cost a week or so before

Christmas. But they were not as visible as usual and although we were still playing for them, it did feel different.

To be fair, the number of Flamengo supporters probably helped us because they made it feel like a big occasion. We were staying at the St. Regis in Doha and the hotel opposite had a rooftop bar that their fans took over, singing, dancing, playing drums and generally making themselves seen and heard. That was the moment it really hit home to me just how big a fight we would be going into. It was clear that it meant everything to them and I fully expected the Flamengo players to feed off that kind of passion. It would be impossible not to.

The gaffer reinforced that point in our pre-match meeting at the hotel. He told us that Flamengo were representing Brazil and we had to represent ourselves, our club and our city because no-one else in England was really interested in the competition. He was looking to create a siege mentality. For once, we wouldn't be able to rely on our fans out-numbering the opposition and making the stadium feel like home.

Jürgen also made reference to 2005 when Rafa Benitez's team had lost the final to Sao Paolo. And he reminded us that Liverpool had never previously won the competition. That struck a chord with me. We have an incredibly history in Europe but to be in the Club World Cup you have to win the Champions League, which is so hard to do, so chances like this don't come around often. There was definitely a desire to put the record straight but there was also a feeling that we would need to bring our A-game to do so.

From a personal perspective, I knew I was right as soon as the game kicked off and that was a big boost. I felt much more energised than I had against Monterrey and any lingering after-effects caused by the travelling had thankfully gone.

Mo must have felt even better because every time he touched the ball he got a massive cheer. That was actually one of the times when I realised how much weight he must carry on his shoulders. People had come from all over the Middle East just to see the Egyptian King. No-one – apart from my family – comes to watch me play, even when I'm playing in Glasgow!

The way the game went meant this wasn't a night for individuals to shine, though. It was hugely competitive and everyone had their hands full with their own personal duels. Space was at a premium and no-one was prepared to give an inch. This kind of encounter suits me but it's harder for the flair players.

Sadio, in particular, was coming in for some rough treatment and it was clear from very early on that Flamengo were targeting him. In some ways, there can be no greater sign of respect than an opponent singling you out in that way but as well as the physical attention, the Brazilians were also looking to wind him up. As brilliant as he is, Sadio is only human and I could see it getting to him. I couldn't blame him either. Flamengo's right-back, Rafinha, was getting away with absolute murder against him, none more so than when he blatantly pulled Sadio back and Sadio ended up getting booked for throwing him to the ground. I could see all this going on and I just wanted to get my arm around Sadio to get him into the dressing room at half-time, so we could sort it all out. Like anyone else, Sadio can lose his head a wee bit and the fact that he had been booked concerned me because it was pretty obvious that Flamengo were trying to get him sent off.

As we approached the break, I knew how important it was to get him back inside so that the gaffer could get to work on him because he is unbelievable in situations like that. The way

I looked at it, we had fifteen minutes to get one of our best players back in the right frame of mind and if we could do that, it would be a big blow for Flamengo who had spent the entire first half trying to get at him. The one thing we knew we couldn't afford was for Sadio to get sent off early in the second half. Dealing with this problem was going to be every bit as important as anything we had to deal with on the pitch.

First, we had to get him inside. I headed over to him, more to protect him than anything else, but Rafinha was hovering just trying to get inside his head and I wasn't having that. "I'll get him, don't worry," I told Sadio. It was mainly for effect. Rafinha was in earshot and I wanted him to hear it but I also needed Sadio to know that I had his back. As a team we support each other in every way and given I play ninety-five per cent of my games with him in front of me, I have a particularly strong bond with him on the pitch. We protect one another in different ways. This was my turn to be there for him.

I didn't know there was a camera in my face at the time. I don't know why they zoomed in on us, possibly because Sadio had just been booked and the director was seeing the same possibilities that we were. In that instant, I started to go viral. I didn't know it until well after the game but the footage was all over social media before I'd even got back into the dressing room. I had thought nothing of it at the time. The only thing that mattered to me was that Sadio heard exactly what I was saying. It wasn't a message for the world. It was one for Sadio with the added bonus that Rafinha would hear it too. I needed both of them to know that they weren't going to kick him off the park. We are a team and we would not stand for that.

I respected the fact that this was probably the biggest game in the careers of many of the Flamengo players. I even admired their physical approach up to a point but once it went beyond that, we had a duty to ourselves to stand up to it. That was all I did. As with Mo and Sadio at Burnley, the fact that it was broadcast meant that it all got blown out of proportion. I didn't want the attention that came my way afterwards but the main thing was that Sadio went out in the second half, kept his cool and played a very good game. Job done.

Before kick-off, Jürgen had told us to "come back as heroes" but Flamengo were too good and too tough to allow that to happen without a real battle and they took us into extra time. This was definitely the equivalent of being back in the hotel pool in Évian. The question was: how much were we prepared to endure in order to get the best possible result? I might not have had my head under water this time but I still wasn't breathing easily as the combination of a muggy night in Qatar and thirty additional minutes took their toll.

Like us, everyone in Brazil was praying for a hero and they got one, but not in the manner they were hoping for. With time running out, Bobby Firmino, the boy from Maceió, won the game for us with the kind of clear-headed finish that is only possible so late in a match if you have unbelievable quality and composure. And who picked him out in the box? Sadio. Sticking together had paid off – again.

After the final whistle went I was determined to have a conversation with Flamengo's full-back – but not Rafinha. The two of us did exchange a couple of pleasantries on the pitch but it was the other full-back, Filipe Luís, who I wanted to catch up with. Along with the likes of Patrice Evra, Ashley Cole and Jackie McNamara and Tom Boyd at Celtic, Luis was one of the players in my position who I had really looked up to. I watched him a lot when he was with Atlético Madrid and loved everything about him. I went over to him, commiserated about the result and was about to congratulate him for the unbelievable career he has had when he interrupted. "You're the best left-back in the world," he said. Wow.

That meant everything and I spoke to Ali about Filipe afterwards as he's one of his best friends in Brazil. He told me what a great guy he is. It meant a lot to get that respect from someone who has done it at the highest level for so many years. What he said surprised me – which might say something about me. You never let yourself believe anything like that, never, but coming from someone like him it was massive. Filipe has no reason to say it, other than he means it.

I'd had it in my head that I wanted to say something to him after the game. I didn't care if he didn't say anything back but he came to me first and said what he did. I respected him so much as a player and a professional and I didn't think he would be playing in Europe again, so I wanted to say what a fantastic career he had had. It just so happened that he got his words out first. There was definitely a mutual respect between us. That was probably my favourite moment of that entire trip. It was the ultimate compliment. I had looked up to him. He played for Brazil and become one of the very best in our position in the modern era and we had a moment like that together. It's unfortunate that people pick up on the moment I'd had with Rafinha earlier on and not something like that. But I'm also glad there wasn't a TV camera around to pick up that conversation. I'm not great with compliments at the best of times so I definitely wouldn't want something like that broadcast to the watching world.

I'm not going to lie and say that getting our hands on the trophy meant as much as winning the European Cup six months earlier but it was still special. Liverpool were champions of the world for the first time, we had earned the right to wear those beautiful gold badges and the entire trip had been made worthwhile.

We were shattered, though, and this was reflected in the dressing room afterwards with a scene of total exhaustion unfolding for ten minutes or so after we first got back in there. If you didn't know us, you would have been forgiven for thinking we weren't really that bothered about winning the competition – when the opposite was true. We just had nothing left.

Some of the lads were doing media duties and I was one of the last to get in there myself because I had been told one of our travelling fans had learned that his father had passed away back in Liverpool, so I went out to pass on our condolences to him. I could see how much it meant to him that we had won and all I could do was let him know that he was in our thoughts. Supporters like that are there for us at all times so it is right we are there for them when it is possible to do so, especially when we are so far away from home and someone has suffered a personal tragedy.

I got back into the dressing room and it was quiet, which suited me at that point. Most of us were on our phones, replying to congratulatory messages from friends and family and checking how the kids were, when the door burst open. I looked up and there were Pep Lijnders and Andreas Kornmayer charging in with the trophy while singing 'Allez Allez Allez'. The place erupted. This was exactly what was needed. It gave us some energy again and within seconds, every single one of us was bouncing around. Sometimes the players are that focused on what has just happened that it needs someone to get the party going. We ended up jumping up and down on the tables. There was non-stop singing for the next five minutes. You can't put a value on moments like that, they are so precious.

It was definitely different winning a trophy in mid-season. Instead of kicking back, enjoying the moment and making the most of it, by the time we left the Khalifa International Stadium we were already in recovery mode because we were only four days away from another game which had the potential to define our season.

In the time between, we also had another 3,000 mile flight, Christmas Day and a trip to the Midlands to face Leicester City on Boxing Day. Because the lads were in a rhythm and their focus was so strong, our minds switched straight away to what comes next, rather than dwelling on what had just happened.

The contrast with Madrid couldn't have been greater. There, we went back to the team hotel and partied all night. In Doha, we got off the team bus at the St. Regis to be greeted by some pyrotechnics and a private room that was set up for us to enjoy ourselves. That was never going to happen – even though it was a lovely touch by the hotel. There were beers laid out on a table but we all headed for the pasta station instead. We were all trying to get food into our bodies because we knew this would help our preparations for Leicester. I had Spaghetti Bolognese at two o'clock in the morning!

Another thing in the back of our minds was that we wanted to get back home for Christmas in the best shape that we could be, having been away for over a week. There was a moment when I was a wee bit tempted to celebrate but it passed as soon as it arrived. I nursed one beer along with Adam and we stayed up for a couple of hours with Hendo and Milly who are both teetotal. The only reason we stayed up was because we don't sleep after games due to the adrenaline. There was no partying, I had one bottle of lager. It wasn't how I envisaged the aftermath of a trophy win but we had too much to play for and even though they had lost to City, Leicester were still seen as one of our biggest rivals for the title. The party could wait.

Before we travelled back to Merseyside, the gaffer told us that he was changing our plans for the trip to Leicester. In normal circumstances we would stay in a hotel the night before an away game but he'd decided it would be more beneficial for us if we were in our own beds, having spent so much time in hotels. He also brought forward training on Christmas Eve and Christmas Day, which meant a great deal to us.

It may only seem a small thing but when you travel on Christmas Day or train at 4pm, you're still thinking about it in the morning in terms of 'when do I have to start getting ready to leave' and so on. It meant I could watch the kids open their presents early in the morning, then go in to Melwood to train before heading home to spend the day with my family. It was everything we could've asked for. Not many people see that side of things but everyone can appreciate why it would be so important to us.

It also underlined how much the gaffer trusts us. If he'd thought the lads were going to go and have a couple of red wines or beers with their dinner and not take it seriously then he would have put us in a hotel and rightly so. The choice he made was yet another example of why we have such a good relationship with him.

There were fourteen of us at my house for Christmas dinner, including my parents, Rachel's mum and dad and my brother and his wife. They were all able to indulge a bit more than I could and if anyone had walked into the room when dinner was served they would have been able to spot my plate a mile off. My meal looked very different to all the rest. I had ONE paltry pig in a single blanket. It killed me. One is never enough! My brother took full advantage of the situation by scooping as many of them up as he could. I also had no gravy because it is quite heavy. I had limited roast potatoes, a Yorkshire pudding so small it breached trade descriptions and a few slices of turkey. Our guests were able to enjoy a drink so I became the host, topping up glasses and making sure everyone was well looked after.

I have to admit it wasn't easy watching my dad and brother getting merry while I was totally sober. All I could do was drink juice with the kids. But when it comes down to it, I know that the time will come when I can let my hair down and I also fully recognise what is at stake and the responsibilities that come with the job. For us, Christmas isn't as enjoyable as it is for others and that's fine. I get comfort and enjoyment out of my family having a good time rather than from me drinking. I also realise that we are fortunate in lots of other respects, so I won't be complaining – except when it comes to pigs in blankets.

I have to confess that I did allow myself one small indulgence on Christmas night. When the chocolate cake got brought out I couldn't resist. I only had a small slice, it was actually more of a sliver than a slice, while everyone else had big wedges that could have been used as doorstops, but it tasted great.

The following day we got on the plane to Leicester and it felt like I was going to confession with Hendo being the priest. As soon as he asked me what I'd had to eat on Christmas

Day I told him. I was waiting for him to instruct me to recite ten Hail Marys as penance but luckily Trent waded in and admitted he'd had a bit of cake too. Suddenly there were two of us and that made it a bit trickier. Hendo just looked at the pair of us and said: "You two better play well today. While you two were tucking into chocolate cake I was having Spaghetti Bolognese." The pressure was on, although given the way Trent went on to play I would be tempted to give him chocolate cake every day of the week and twice on Sundays if he wants it.

Trent was on fire that night. We all were but his performance was incredible for any full-back, never mind one who had only just turned twenty-one. I genuinely knew within the first five minutes that we were right on it and, as good as Leicester are, I didn't see how they would be able to deal with us if we maintained that level.

If you look in the opening five minutes, we won the ball back three of four times ... Sadio had a big chance ... Mo had a good chance ... we weren't letting them settle and that set the tone for everything that followed. The only time I had any concern was when we approached the half-hour mark without having made our dominance tell in terms of the scoreline but then Bobby popped up with a well-taken header from Trent's cross and our control increased. We just had their number that day which was no reflection on them because we knew as well as anyone that they could and probably should have taken a draw at Anfield but we were right at it and I think our freshness would have surprised anyone, given we were not long back from Qatar.

A display like that doesn't happen often. If you have seven or eight players who are on their game that is usually enough but on that day nobody had a bad performance. Trent gets the headlines – and quite rightly so – because he was phenomenal and it was the most complete individual performance that I'd seen him play, along with the Barcelona game at Anfield. If anything, Leicester was probably of a higher standard because absolutely everything he did was spot on, from his defending to his crossing, and he even scored a brilliant goal. It was phenomenal to see a young player performing to that level but not one of us were found wanting on the night.

The only one who was a bit quiet was Alisson and that was because he hadn't had much to do. We had produced some great team performances up that point and the way we played against Spurs, Arsenal and City at Anfield showed what we are capable of but people definitely started thinking a bit differently about us after we won at Leicester. It wasn't so much the result, although winning 4-0 away to a title rival is obviously worthy of note; it was more the dominance that we showed and the way that we handled the physical and mental challenges we were facing.

There was talk that the title race was over but we didn't get involved with that. There was no way we were about to start thinking it was in the bag on Boxing Day when there were still twenty games for us to play.

There was a big psychological boost, though, because it felt like we had blown our nearest rivals away. I always believed Manchester City would finish second and take over Leicester and that's how it turned out but at that moment Leicester were the team closest to us and no-one had been expecting us to deal with them so emphatically.

There had been a lot of nonsense spoken before the game about us being tired and maybe being there for the taking but the reality couldn't have been further from the truth. I think that kind of talk wound us up a bit because we did feel disrespected by it. Leicester are a good team and we know that they could beat anyone on their day but it would have had nothing to do with our mentality or our preparations if we had lost. We weren't tired and we showed that from the very first moment.

Eight matches down, two to go.

The finishing line wasn't in sight because we still had another four and half months of the season left but there was definitely a feeling of being in the final stretch of our most testing period of the campaign. Not that the fixture list was getting any easier. Wolves and Sheffield United were next up and while both games were at home we fully expected to be tested.

For me, Wolves are the most underrated team in the league. They are so good. They have quality all over the park and, no matter what the situation is, they are always one of the toughest opponents we play all season.

They play five at the back which is different, and their wing-backs are fantastic. I never look forward to playing against Matt Doherty, in particular. He is a fantastic player and we always have a good battles. Then they have Adama Traore who is always a big danger. He is one of the fastest and strongest wingers you will ever play against. I played against him in the Championship and his end product wasn't there. He would probably admit that himself but now, in terms of goals and assists, he's tearing teams apart. Thankfully, he didn't start at Anfield because they had played Man City a few days earlier and the team was freshened up a bit. I wouldn't say I was relieved to see him on the bench because I knew he would be coming on at some point and I was also aware that Wolves would have quality in every position regardless.

If anything, the fact that Traore wasn't starting gave me more to worry about because I realised that if he was introduced with half an hour or so to go, I would probably be a bit tired by then whereas he would be fresh.

In the back of my mind, I knew I needed to try and save a bit of energy just in case but that wasn't easy as Wolves still had the likes of Pedro Neto and Jonny buzzing about, making life difficult for us.

There wasn't much between the two sides and the outcome hinged on a couple of VAR calls in the first half that both went our way. They were both the right decision. The ball struck Adam's shoulder before Sadio scored for us and Jonny was just offside when Neto thought he had an equaliser. After such a resounding win at Leicester, this was an afternoon of fine margins. It was easy to see why Wolves had managed to get some big results against big teams. They've not managed that against us yet and hopefully that continues but they are definitely one of the hardest teams we face.

Sheffield United was made slightly easier by the fact that we got an early goal. George Baldock was unlucky to slip as we both chased Virgil's long ball and Mo was on hand to put my cross away.

Whereas at Bramall Lane, United had been able to frustrate us for a long time, this time around they were the ones chasing the game after only five minutes and this worked in our favour. We were able to keep possession and make them run around and that made it a lot more comfortable for us.

Like Wolves, they are such a hard team to play against with their teamwork being of such a high standard but we pride ourselves on this as well and Sadio's second half goal put us out of sight.

The result was significant in lots of ways as the win took us 13 points clear at the top of the table with a game in hand and it also meant we had gone an entire calendar year without losing a league match. Whatever was coming our way, we were finding a way to deal with it.

DOUBTERS AND BELIEVERS

I ALWAYS want to play. I don't think I will ever be the type who feels so confident in my status as a regular that I can take being rested with a pinch of salt because I expect to come straight back into the team. If I'm out of the side, I view it as an opportunity for my replacement, especially at a club like Liverpool where there is so much quality throughout the squad.

So the winter months can be a bit of a double-edged sword for me. I know the gaffer views the schedule as a particular challenge and quite rightly so because the games come unbelievably thick and fast but whereas he will be looking for opportunities to rest and rotate, I will be experiencing fear of missing out.

The logic of a footballer is very straightforward – if we perform well in one game, we expect to play in the next. Managers have to see the bigger picture, though. There are times when they have to be cruel to be kind and they also have to take care of an entire squad, not just certain individuals. The culture of the squad at Liverpool is such that we all respect his decisions and also each other's right to play. Not that this makes it any easier when you get told that you're being given the day off, especially when the game you're missing is a Merseyside derby in the third round of the FA Cup.

I knew before we played Sheffield United that I probably wouldn't be involved against Everton. The gaffer always wants to rotate for the FA Cup because it is an opportunity for him to rest those of us who need it while giving game time to the other lads as well. The fact that it was a derby meant we weren't totally sure about what he was going to do, though. We had a rough idea that there would be changes but with Everton being our opponents I think most people had an expectation that the core of the team would remain the same with a bit of tinkering around the edges.

In the event, only Milly and Joe Gomez survived from the Sheffield United game. I know there was a fair bit of surprise when our team was named and Everton probably thought this was their best chance of winning at Anfield but we were still quietly confident.

In situations like this it's harder for supporters because, understandably, they view it through the prism of regular starters making way for squad players but I train with and against these lads day in and day out so I fully expected them to make a game of it. The widespread perception was that the gaffer had taken a major risk and I've no doubt that there were quite a few who were already preparing to accuse him of dis-respecting the FA Cup but, as the ensuing ninety minutes showed, they were the ones guilty of disrespect.

The likes of Curtis Jones, Neco Williams, Nathaniel Phillips, Harvey Elliott and Pedro Chirivella may not have been household names when the game kicked off but what should have been taken into account was that they are all considered good enough to train with the reigning European champions on a daily basis. That simply doesn't happen if they lack quality or don't have the right attitude. Even if any of them were lacking attitude – and none of them were – it would have been knocked out of them pretty quickly because of the culture we have at Liverpool. Lads who have come up from Kirkby to Melwood have the quality to train with us and yes, they might have to fill out physically or get better technically but they are all good enough to train with us and get thrown in to play. That's why, when these FA Cup games come about, we are able to make these changes. Not many fans at Anfield would have known too much about Curtis Jones before the game but they knew who he was afterwards and we knew he could do it on this kind of stage regardless.

I actually wasn't supposed to be at the ground but, like the other lads who had been rested, I couldn't resist going. We all trained at Melwood before the game while the matchday squad was preparing at the team hotel. The gaffer had told us we didn't have to be at Anfield because of the number of games we had played and the amount of travelling we had done but every single one of us wanted to support the lads. They sometimes sit in the stands and watch us, so we wanted to return the favour. That shows the togetherness and mentality of the squad. We could have stayed in our homes – we'd not spent a lot of time with our families – but every single one of us went to back the team, and rightly so. In my case, that meant watching from my box with Trent. I think, between us, we made almost as much noise as the Kop. He's usually laid back so it was interesting to see him as a Liverpool fan on derby day, jumping up and down and shouting and screaming with the best of them.

We both fancied our chances and one of the reasons for that was Milly was out there. His experience and know-how was going to be vital, especially when we came under pressure, and he underlined his value early on with a piece of typically obstinate defending that probably prevented Everton from scoring. It came at a personal cost to himself, though, as his efforts caused him an injury and he had to limp off. I think if I had been on the bench I would have gone on. I don't think the gaffer would've avoided it, regardless of how many games I'd played. But that is why he makes these decisions, to take that urge, that temptation, out of the equation because things like that can happen. Milly got injured in the first ten minutes and I would have then played eighty minutes – that's not a rest. Even if I had been on the bench and not been required I still would have been mentally tuned in, which defeats the object of being rested in lots of ways. As it was, Yasser Larouci came on and he was phenomenal. As a left-back, I loved seeing how well he played having been given a platform to perform, and it was clear that the crowd loved everything that he and the other young lads did too.

Adam Lallana definitely didn't fall into the category of 'up and coming young player' but he set the tone for everything the team did in that game. His was one of the best individual performances of the entire season and the most important thing was how selfless he was. He allowed the youngsters to display their ability by getting through so much of the dirty work, none more so than Curtis who was able to do what he does in the knowledge that he had a senior pro backing him up all the way. Curtis might have grabbed the headlines – and rightly so given he scored the winner with an absolute worldie – but Adam was unbelievable that day.

I'm not sure Curtis's goal needs any more discussion given it was the most talked about at Melwood in many years. Not by the rest of us, by the man himself! Every time he mentioned it, the strike got better. He was either a little bit further out or the angle was even more against him. Obviously we didn't build him up because he was doing that all by himself but we all knew it was a brilliant goal. We just didn't want him to keep on telling us! Curtis is a very good finisher but to hit the top corner from that position was incredible, especially in his first start at Anfield. As soon as the ball left his boot, it looked like it had goal written all over it, it was a fantastic strike. Trent and I went wild. It was a massive goal for the team and for the supporters but we also knew how much it would mean to Curtis as a local lad and a Liverpool fan.

On top of that, the quality of the finish illustrated why the team selected should not have been underestimated. You don't score goals like that at elite level unless you have talent and, having seen Curtis develop over the last couple of years, I can safely say that nobody should have any doubts about his ability. He also has real belief in himself. Sometimes, with young players, this can be seen as a bit of a negative because they'll walk onto the pitch with a bit of a strut that gives away their self-confidence and people can get the wrong impression. I'm cut from different cloth and I always feel the need to prove myself but the likes of Curtis have great faith in themselves and this shouldn't be knocked out of them especially as, in his case, his attitude is spot on. His development as a person and a player has impressed all of us.

Curtis is similar to Trent in the sense that there's added pressure being a local lad. You've got all your mates and family hoping you do well and, while this is definitely a positive, it also brings a bit more of a burden because you are so desperate to make them happy. You might also have some negative influences around you too when you play for your hometown club, so it's not always easy.

Trent is a unique individual who takes everything on his shoulders and absorbs all of these kinds of pressures but not everybody is like that.

Curtis, I believe, can be.

I think he will play for Liverpool. We have an unbelievable midfield at the moment but Curtis has already established himself as part of that scene, as an option, and I believe he will go on to play for Liverpool on a consistent basis. His game has come on so much in recent years and he's improved by listening to the manager and the lads and taking everything on board. There's no doubt in my mind that he has a big future ahead of him if he keeps on doing that.

Having missed out against Everton, I was due to come back into the team in our next game away to Spurs. But twenty-four hours beforehand, I came close to pulling out of the travelling party. This time it was me asking the gaffer whether I should play because Rachel had been rushed into hospital.

It was a bolt from the blue. She was getting pain in her chest, just below her shoulder, and her temperature dropped suddenly. I'm in the fortunate position of having access to the club's medical staff and, after Doctor Sarah Massey assessed Rachel, she told us that we needed to get her to hospital as soon as possible.

We headed straight over to Chester, calling Rachel's mum on the way to let her know what was happening. She drove down from Scotland to be with her. There was a concern Rachel might have sepsis. They put her on antibiotics straight away and further treatment was required, but not until the next morning. Obviously, this gave me a massive dilemma, so I went in to see Jürgen after training. This time it was me raising the possibility of missing a game. "Look gaffer," I said. "If she gets any worse, I don't think I can go to be honest."

There was no point dressing it up any other way. The manager deserves that kind of honesty at the very least but also Rachel is the mother of my kids and the person I love, so I needed to be honest with myself too. She had told me to go to work but just as she was thinking of me, I was thinking of her. If there had been any kind of deterioration in her condition I would have pulled out of the squad, no question, but the doctors were brilliant with her. It wasn't long before she stabilised, which came as a massive relief to all of us.

I had an agreement with Jürgen that if the situation escalated at any point then I would leave. That, for me, shows why the gaffer's man-management and understanding of people's circumstances at any given time are so good. He told me he would have to make a decision on the team at some point, but that he would give me as long as he possibly could. He also made it clear that if there were any setbacks overnight, there would be a plane ready to go. But once I knew Rachel was on antibiotics and reacting well it eased my concerns. I was also in touch with her mum, which was a massive help in terms of putting my mind at rest. So I was able to sleep relatively easily in the knowledge that she was safe in hospital, responding well to treatment and her mum was with her. I had to get in touch with my mum and dad and they came down to look after the kids, which was also a big help. Rachel wanted me to stay with the team and although she was probably high on whatever drugs she was getting, it was clear that she wanted me to stay and do my job.

This didn't stop me from feeling guilty. During the ninety minutes I was fully concentrated on the game, but part of me thought I shouldn't be there. Playing the match itself wasn't my issue because I knew Rachel was reacting well and the problem was being dealt with. I had known before the warm-up that things were okay because she sent me a message before the game, saying she was fine and wishing me good luck. I was able to go into the match with no major worries about her care or well-being but, of course, the person I love and share my life with was still in hospital so I'd have to be a bit strange if I was able to play football without thinking about her.

Yet, in a weird sense, when these things happen, football also becomes my getaway. For ninety minutes, I can concentrate on something else. Previously in my career I've played a couple of days after somebody has died but in the moment, football is a release. Going into the Spurs game I was fine mentally because I knew Rachel was fine, everything had been sorted and she was better for it. Also, the doctors had decided that she would be okay to go home that night.

I suppose these are the things that people out of the first team bubble don't see. They watch us playing football and judge us on how well we play but they don't necessarily know about the health issues, injury problems or family concerns that may be bothering us. We are no different to anyone else in that respect. If we have babies and they are teething, we will almost certainly be tired. If a loved one is poorly, we will be worried. As professionals, we do everything in our power to leave our personal lives behind us when we go onto the pitch but we are also human beings with all the same frailties as any other person.

When we played Man City away last season, the game was actually on Rachel's due date. There were rumours swirling around beforehand suggesting I was going to miss out because she had gone into labour, but there was no sign of the baby at that stage so I had no hesitation in playing. The baby didn't end up arriving for another seven days either so imagine if I'd been sat on the sofa watching one of our biggest games of the season while Rachel was at home! There's no question I would have missed the Spurs game if necessary because her health was at stake and that wasn't nice – but thankfully it didn't come to that.

The game was tough in itself. We were very good at times during the first half and should have gone in more than 1-0 up because we had a couple of chances to add to a well-taken goal by Bobby. But the longer the game went on, the more Spurs came into it and we ended up hanging on a bit towards the end.

They missed a couple of great opportunities and, as had been the case in the Champions League final, Alisson stood strong for us. It wasn't a vintage performance and Hendo was quick to tell us afterwards that we needed to be better but we also know that seeing games like that out would only improve our chances of taking what we wanted from the season.

There was a lot of focus afterwards on us making the best start to a campaign in the history of Europe's five big leagues, but we were not about to be distracted by that. Records are nice and good ones can only ever be helpful but the only thing we were interested in was winning our own league. I'm pretty sure that will have been the main topic of conversation on the team night out that took place in London that night, as the lads enjoyed a rare opportunity to let their hair down. It was for me, anyway, because while they had a meal together and enjoyed themselves I was on my way back to Merseyside to be with Rachel. The gaffer also had to get back for an appearance and he kindly offered to give me a lift on his flight with some other staff members, so we were able to spend a bit of time discussing our objectives and how we would go about achieving them.

By the time I got home, the kids were asleep and Rachel was settled, so the day had worked out well for all of us. Rachel was okay, the team had picked up three points at a difficult venue and we were another step closer to our target. The only downside was me having to miss the team night out, but I'm sure the lads coped just fine without me.

For the first time since the start of the season we had more than a week to prepare for our next fixture, a luxury that had been unimaginable during December, when it seemed like we were either playing games or travelling to and from games every other day.

With Manchester United being our next opponents, the lengthy build-up only added to the buzz around Melwood. But although I could feel the sense of anticipation building, I didn't want to get too involved in it.

I was in the canteen a couple of days beforehand and a few of us were talking about what the atmosphere was going to be like. I shouted over to Tony Barrett to see what he thought and he said if we won it would definitely be the day when 'And Now You're Gonna Believe Us' erupted at Anfield. I didn't like that. "It's too early for that," I said. "They need to wait until it's almost in the bag. That's the time, not mid-January."

I got the enthusiasm and, if I was a fan, my mindset would have been exactly the same. But as a player, all I could focus on was the need to keep things ticking over without getting too excited. I also knew that, in some quarters, the song could be used as a stick to beat the club with the moment we suffered any kind of setback. This had happened previously and I didn't want it to happen again. On top of that, I knew United would like nothing better than to derail us, so I was determined not to get caught up in the expectation that was growing on a daily basis.

The problem with this approach was that I was also part of a team which was creating so much excitement. It was now three months since we had dropped points to anyone and that was our away game against United. If the fans were daring to dream, it was us who were allowing them to and as long as we carried on fulfilling our end of the bargain, everything else – including my own neuroses – would be academic.

In this respect, the first hour of the game went as well as we could have hoped. Virgil gave us the lead from another of his Nike Air Virgil leaps and, for long spells, we were as dominant as I have known us be in this fixture. There was even a period at the start of the second half when it seemed like we had them penned into their own half for almost ten minutes. Our pressing was relentless and we were able to win the ball back almost as soon as we lost it. Chances were created and while none were taken, the pressure was incessant.

This is where our style of play, the manager's approach and the passion of the Anfield crowd combines so powerfully. The energy that is created by shooting towards the Kop at times like that also plays a part and should not be underestimated.

When I was younger, all of Celtic's goals seemed to happen towards the same end where our most passionate supporters were, so I'm sure there must be a science behind it all. It's like being in a Sunday League game and shooting downhill with the wind at your back. That's genuinely what it feels like. You know that any time you get close the anticipation increases, the supporters make more noise and we're inspired to push even harder. It's little things like when we win a corner in front of the Kop end – the cheer is noticeably louder than when the same happens at the Anfield Road end. I can remember thinking that if we got a second goal during that spell the roof would have come off, but although Hendo hit a post and others came close it just wouldn't come.

All that was missing was that second goal and the fact that it hadn't happened allowed United to grow in confidence. The gaffer is really good at using half-time to calm us down, getting us to re-focus and showing us what we need to do better but we all knew that, unless we increased our lead, United would have a period when they came on strong. That's just the nature of the rivalry. At least we were prepared for it and we actually dealt with their attacks pretty well – with the exception of a decent chance that Anthony Martial fired over.

After that, I never felt like we needed another goal to secure the points but, my God, did I want one, just to get the job done. It's at times like this when Mo comes into his own. Big players exist for big moments and ever since he joined us, Mo has had an incredible knack of coming up with the goods when we need it most. A lot of that comes down to his own ability to sense when opponents are vulnerable. At times he recognises that even before they do and by the time they do realise, it is usually too late.

As they pressed us back towards our own goal and forced a late corner, United should have been able to feel pretty safe but as soon as Ali caught the loose ball they were in trouble. Mo was already peeling off towards the halfway line in the knowledge that one of the best distributors in the game had the ability to pick him out. Ali's kick was perfect and from the moment the ball bounced into Mo's path, everything else seemed inevitable.

Mo is one of the ultimate professionals, he is in the gym constantly, working on his physique. In that passage of play, all his hard work paid off. Daniel James is one of the quickest players in the league but Mo held him off and was able to slot home. The next thing, Ali is sprinting by me and I thought 'I better get a shift on here!' It was a fantastic moment. We'd seen Pepe Reina celebrating at the Kop end after assisting a goal against United and, now Ali had done the same, he was determined to mark it in similar fashion. In that moment we knew we had beaten them. Games against United are always tough and this one had been no different but in the seconds after that goal went in, it felt like there was a surge of electricity going around the ground.

Then, it started. 'And now you're gonna believe us. And now you're gonna believe us. And now you're gonna believe us – we're gonna win the league.' Over and over again, louder and louder, a chant suddenly became a declaration. This wasn't hope, it wasn't even a statement of intent, this was the Anfield crowd telling everyone who was willing to listen and plenty more besides that their team was going to be champions.

I have to confess, though, that for a split second after it started I just thought: 'Please don't'. But then the hairs on the back of my neck stood up and immediately I understood. Two seconds later, I was joining in. The emotions that this one song stirred are indescribable. The only thing that has ever come close is when everyone in the ground sings 'You'll Never Walk Alone' on big European nights, but this was on another level again. The genie was well and truly out of the bottle and all we could do was go with it. It felt like an approval from the fans and a sign of good times to come. That day they wanted to sing that song to their rivals. The way it made me feel, the shockwaves it sent through my body when they started singing it, I thought then that we would go on and do it. I still get shivers thinking about that. That was the moment when we thought: We aren't letting these people down.

At that point, I think I went from thinking we *could* become champions to believing we *would* become champions. Of course, we couldn't come out and say it and none of us would, but there's no question that everything felt right. There was a definite shift and in hindsight it had probably been building for a bit before the United game, I just hadn't been ready to acknowledge what the supporters already knew. Over a period of time, everything was moving in the direction of this being a special season and that we were going to run away with it. It's easy to say that now it's happened but I honestly felt that way at the time. When our crowd sung that song as emphatically as they did we had to believe it, of course we did. If you said you didn't believe it, you'd be lying.

Actually, there may have been one exception. During this period, Hendo was so focused and so driven that I don't think he could have got caught up in the excitement if someone had knocked at his door with the Premier League trophy and told him it was done. To say he was in the zone would be one of the understatements of the season.

We all have our own game faces but throughout January it seemed like he had his on every day. I had visions of him taking the kids to the park on his days off glaring at strangers, screaming at passers-by to get their act together and wondering why random dogs weren't obeying his instructions! At Melwood, his influence was absolute. He literally didn't have to say anything. He could have remained silent because the example he was setting on the training pitch and in games was so powerful that words were no longer required.

From playing out of position against Monterrey in mid-December, right through the first couple of months of the new year, he was so outstanding that all the rest of us could do was try to live up to the standards he was setting. He got us through some of those games with a combination of strength of character and individual talent none more so than Wolves away where he scored the opening goal, kept us going after they equalised and then drove us on to get the three points, supplying the pass for Bobby's winner.

None of this came as a surprise to anyone who has been fortunate enough to share a dressing room with him. We know the man and we know the player, so the doubts that have been raised about Hendo externally have always been a source of bemusement to us. I would agree with those who believe the football he played during this period was the best of his career, but the bar was already high on this front. He just took it to another level, showing just why he is captain of this club by keeping us all together and being our leading force.

Over Christmas and into January, his performances were exceptional and even when we were not at our best as a team, Hendo made sure we never stopped pushing to be as good as we could be on any given day and made sure we got over the line on occasions when doing so was a big challenge. He was putting in nine and ten out of ten performances every single game and we all responded to that. You can't hide or accept an off day when your captain is delivering to that level and that's why he finally started getting the recognition he deserved.

Hendo has always been questioned since he took the armband off Steven Gerrard. Stevie isn't an easy person to follow, of course he isn't, and Hendo understood that more than anyone. But he deserved to be judged fairly and on his own merits rather than constantly being compared to a Liverpool legend. It was only when everybody started seeing Jordan Henderson as Jordan Henderson – not as the guy who had taken over the captaincy from Steven Gerrard – that this started to happen.

Nobody will replace Stevie as a Liverpool player given everything he achieved and what he stood for, but Hendo is now established as another winning Liverpool captain and deservedly gets the respect that goes with that status. He had led us to the Champions League and now he was striving towards something that had never previously been accomplished in the Premier League era. Momentum then started to build about him being player of the year and that gave all of us a good feeling because not only was it richly deserved, we could also see him growing with that recognition.

I'll readily admit to being biased about this as I'm really close to Hendo and I look up to him. He has also had a huge influence on me in the way I try to captain Scotland. I look at Hendo every day and try to pick things up from him, especially the way he tries to keep improving. I'm not exaggerating when I say he goes into every game like it's a cup final and his entire approach has rubbed off on the rest of us, improving the squad probably without even noticing it and definitely without giving himself the credit he deserves.

It goes without saying that the gaffer is obviously the one who puts the squad together but, in terms of setting standards within the dressing room, Hendo and Milly are also big factors in why we are successful. Despite all of this and regardless of the belated recognition that has come his way, I still feel Hendo deserves greater credit for his actual ability. So much so that when I retire, I will look back and say he was one of the most underrated players I ever played with. Take away his leadership qualities, his work-rate and his effort – because that is all there to be seen and is now widely acknowledged – his footballing quality is good enough to be the captain of Liverpool Football Club and good enough to play in midfield for one of the great Liverpool teams. He nearly got sold to Fulham at one stage and might have been in and out of the team earlier on his career at Anfield. But his quality has always been there for all to see and hopefully now it is being appreciated more. If anyone still harbours any doubts about him they should watch the entirety of our victory at Molineux. This was a captain and a player at the peak of his powers.

There was another teamsheet without my name on it when we played Shrewsbury Town away in the fourth round of the FA Cup. This was our 37th game of the season and we were still not out of January, so the gaffer understandably took the opportunity to mix things up again. As against Everton, Curtis enhanced his own reputation with another well-taken goal and I started to feel a bit more comfortable in my own armchair when Donald Love scored an own goal to put us 2-0 up. Then Jason Cummings came on and caused mayhem. I know him from the Scotland set-up and I knew he could be a nuisance on the pitch, so I wasn't particularly surprised to see him giving us problems. He scored twice to earn Shrewsbury a replay at Anfield and, in fairness, it was the kind of FA Cup story that everyone loves – except when you are on the wrong end of it. I sent Cummings a message afterwards telling him he'd done us no favours because the last thing we needed with our schedule was another game. It was his day, though. No-one could begrudge him that.

Another Scotland mate lay in wait for me in our next game away to West Ham. Along with the lads at Liverpool, Robert Snodgrass is the person I'm closest to in football. I was up against him, I love that, and we had another good battle with neither of us wanting to let the other one get the upper hand.

As a team, we had a collective determination not to allow any points to slip through our fingers on this occasion. In the corresponding fixture twelve months earlier, we only managed a draw on the back of dropping another two points at home to Leicester. Realistically, they were the two games which caused us to fall short of Manchester City that season. You can often accept draws but we looked at our results from those two games and two points out of six isn't championship winning material.

Going back to West Ham was big for us for that reason – we wanted and needed to right that particular wrong. The fact that it was also our game in hand meant it was an opportunity to take another big step and we managed to achieve all of our objectives with a 2-0 win. We were efficient rather than brilliant with Mo and Ox making the difference. This was a night when our collective sense of purpose was at least as important as our ability as a team. David Moyes said afterwards that we were "as good as there's been around" which was a big compliment, especially coming from someone who has managed Everton and Man United.

I also got to spend some time with Snodgrass after the game, so I was asking him how it was going under Moyes because he had not long been in charge. But Snoddy was only interested in filling my head about us being champions. I already believed that was going to turn out to be true but there was no way I was telling him that!

The two of us have a relationship where we basically give each other stick. We're also a good double act when it comes to dishing it out to others, but there's also an emotional side. We won the Champions League the day after his wedding and he was one of the first people I FaceTimed after the final. He was in a nightclub somewhere with his mates – I don't know how his missus allowed that but fair play – and it was really important to me that I was able to speak to him. This time around, we were able to talk in person. He was saying there was no chance anybody would catch us.

Snoddy is like a bigger brother to me. When I came down to Hull, I was more of a boy than a man and he took me under his wing, him and his family, so it was brilliant for me to hear him talking about me as a possible champion. He is still someone I look up to and it meant a lot to see that he was proud of what I was achieving with Liverpool.

Then he put me back in my place. "Would you be able to

get me Salah's shirt?" And there was me thinking he was just being nice!

That was the only thing that West Ham took off us on the night, though, so I could live with getting him Mo's shirt. As long as his prediction about the title race turned out right, I could live with a lot of things.

DEFENDING THE FAITH

FROM the moment I joined Liverpool, we were the ones doing the hunting. Chasing and harrying on the pitch, stalking those domestic rivals who were picking up silverware and pursuing European giants in a quest for Champions League glory.

Then, all of a sudden, this changed. The hunter became the hunted. We were the European Cup holders and everyone wanted our crown. We were the unbeaten Premier League leaders and everyone wanted our scalp. From being insurgents, our rise to the top meant we now had to get used to being in power, with every team that we came up against wanting to overthrow us. We weren't just there to be shot at, we were walking onto the pitch with targets on our back. Not that any of us were complaining. This was exactly where we wanted to be. We just had to get used to it.

This was definitely a new challenge but it goes hand in hand with being successful and, seeing as the shoe had been on the other foot for so long, we could hardly complain. Being a Celtic fan, I had witnessed it myself in Scotland. Whether it was Celtic or Rangers, everyone else wants to see them fall flat on their face. The great Liverpool sides had it in the 1980s and the same went for Manchester United under Sir Alex Ferguson. It just goes with the territory. It wasn't as if anyone had ever made things easy for us previously, but the motivation to beat any team increases when they are in the ascendancy. Manchester City had it and now it was our turn.

Results do not always reflect just how difficult the opposition has made it for you and there was no better example of that throughout the course of the season than our 4-0 win over Southampton. They came to Anfield in early February and caused us no end of problems, in the first half especially. Everyone at Liverpool loves Danny Ings but we didn't want him to come back to haunt us. He obviously had other ideas and that opening forty-five minutes was as testing as almost any we have had at home in the last couple of years.

Southampton certainly put their stamp on the game and if they had taken some of their chances when they were on top, the outcome might have been different. We rode our luck a bit, particularly when Ingsy had a penalty shout turned down, but we managed to come through the storm and from the moment Ox scored straight after the interval, we took control.

They were entitled to feel hard done by and afterwards the gaffer was spot on when he said that we were not even close to being perfect, but if you can win 4-0 against a good opponent without hitting top gear you must be doing something right. Most importantly, it put a bit more pressure on City who

Off the mark:
Scoring my first Champions League goal (*below*) in the 4-3 thriller against Red Bull Salzburg at Anfield. (*Right*) celebrating with Trent and Hendo

When the going gets tough . . . Putting in the graft behind the scenes. At Liverpool, we pride ourselves on our work ethic

Late late show: On the run during the 2-1 win over Leicester at Anfield in October. James Maddison's late goal levelled the score but Milly kept his cool to convert a 95th minute penalty

Making a point: (*Above*) Adam pops up at the back post to convert my cross and get us a precious point at Old Trafford against Manchester United. Adam always delivered during his time at the club

Game faces: (*Left*) Arriving for the Champions League group game at Genk with Virgil which we won 4-1 before returning home and beating Spurs 2-1 at Anfield a few days later

Villa thriller: We were 1-0 down and facing defeat at Villa Park. Our equaliser came from an unlikely source – my head! We weren't satisfied with a point and when Sadio scored a late winner it completed a remarkable comeback in a game I nearly missed with an ankle problem

Standing together:
(Left) Lining up ahead of the Manchester City game at Anfield in November. *(Below)* tussling for the ball with City's Kyle Walker

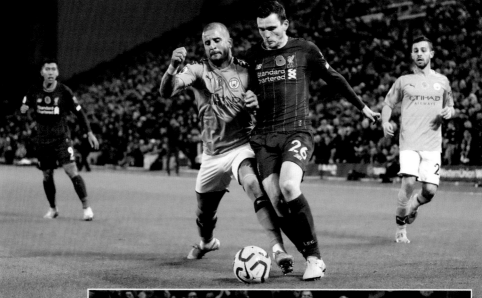

Victory cry:
(Right) Letting it all out after Sadio had scored our third goal as we headed for a vital 3-1 win over our main title challengers

You'll never walk alone: Behind the scenes at Anfield before our game against Brighton with the club's impressive wall of honour as a backdrop. Liverpool's history can't help but inspire you

Red family: Parading a banner with Gini in support of Sean Cox at the pre-season game in Dublin against Napoli in August 2018. It was amazing to see Sean and his family at Anfield for the City game

Small comfort: Milly gets in on the joke as we take a picture of masseur Paul Small trying to get a crafty sleep on a plane journey home. Smally is a Liverpool institution

Anfield passion: (*Above*) I love playing in front of our supporters. I understand the emotions because I'm a fan myself. (*Left*) head to head with Tom Davies during our 5-2 win over Everton in a busy December – everyone wants to win a derby!

Champions of the world: All smiles with Trent and Milly after we had beaten Flamengo 1-0 in the FIFA Club World Cup final in Qatar. With a big game coming up against Leicester, my post-match celebrations amounted to a plate of Spaghetti Bolognese at two in the morning!

Golden feeling: Celebrating becoming champions of the world by lifting the FIFA Club World Cup trophy in Qatar. We all voted in favour of going to the tournament – we wanted to make history for Liverpool and get that famous gold badge on our shirts

had to go to Spurs the following day. We knew from recent experience it wouldn't be an easy game for them. That's how it turned out with Spurs winning which meant we were able to go into the winter break and enjoy it a bit more.

We needed a break by then. It had been a long, hard slog and some of the lads had trips booked to places like Dubai and the Maldives, where they would be able to recharge their batteries and get a bit of sun on their backs. Me? I went back to Clarkston. Don't get me wrong, those sunshine destinations do interest me regardless of how much Factor 50 I might need, but I also enjoy going home. Mentally it helps me because I am able to forget that I am a footballer and escape the limelight. At that time, it was exactly what I needed.

While I was up there, I bumped into people in the street who I went to school with and families I have known since I was a kid. That is my comfort. It's just people I know asking after me. In some cases, they might be proud of me because I'm a lad from their area and I'm playing for one of the biggest clubs in the world. But they also know that I'm the same Andy Robertson who they've always known and that makes it easier for me to relax and be myself.

We have a wee flat up there, five minutes away from my mum and dad's, so I can catch up with family and also spend time with my pals. I could have been on a beach somewhere tropical but Scotland gives me something that I can't get anywhere else, even in the first week of February.

Staying in the UK meant I was able to follow the latest controversy with great interest too. By taking time out during our allotted winter break, we somehow ended up on the wrong end of a situation that wasn't of our making.

As soon as our FA Cup replay against Shrewsbury was

scheduled for this period, the club started to come under pressure regarding team selection – even though the players had long since been told they would be off and had made arrangements accordingly. It was all a bit bizarre.

Most other leagues have winter breaks and when that happens no football takes place. Yet here we were having to play a cup tie during ours! In my view, you either have a winter break and shut football down with nobody playing or you don't have one. It doesn't make sense if games are going to be added. It's unfair on those teams it happens to. Southampton and Tottenham also had a replay so they didn't really have a break. How is that fair? Either you get rid of FA Cup replays so this doesn't happen or the winter break is accepted as a complete shutdown with replays happening at another time.

We got told at the start of the season that a winter break was coming in and we'd have a week off in February, so to have that week taken away from us definitely wasn't consistent with the reasons for the break. The gaffer is a great believer in having a winter break so he stuck to his guns, telling us to take our time off as planned and giving Neil Critchley and a young squad the opportunity to gain some experience and maybe even create a bit of cup magic at Anfield.

I gave my box to Harvey Elliott and Curtis Jones for the night, so their families could enjoy the occasion a bit more. I wished them both good luck and told them to get the job done, which they did despite all the negativity that had surrounded the gaffer's decision to go with such a young team.

It meant a lot to all of the senior players because we see these young lads coming through and they push us all the time. For them to get the green light to play together in front of a full house at Anfield was an incredible experience for them.

Watching them grow into that game and do what they did was amazing because although they all have massive talent, this was a big step up against players who were physically stronger and more experienced. They all did remarkably well on the night and seeing how much pleasure they took from such a hard-earned win gave a massive boost to everyone at the club. The impact this had on all of us should not be underestimated, particularly given the added bonus of the first team players actually being able to enjoy our winter break.

Norwich away was one of our most memorable trips of the season. The result in itself was something to remember as our 17th win in a row left us needing just five more victories to secure the title with twelve fixtures remaining.

The way the three points were earned will also live long in the memories of all who were there. Sadio went through his full repertoire of skill, strength, speed of thought and top class finishing to get the goal that took us over the line.

It wasn't even the best of balls that set him up, it was just a hoof up the park by Hendo! Seriously, it was a great pass but Sadio still had a lot to do when he received the ball and I'm sure Hendo would agree that, in this case, the run made the pass. For Sadio to bring the ball down on his chest, spin away from his marker, turn and finish with his left foot was incredible. That's why he's one of the best players in the world for me. How many other players could have scored a goal like that? Not many.

I know from experience how difficult he is to deal with because I see it in training on a daily basis. He can do the unexpected, he can beat you with his upper body strength, he can go past you with skill or fly past you with speed. As well as having that kind of talent, he has also become a lot more consistent. When he first joined Liverpool, Sadio was already really good but he has become even better because his level of consistency has improved so much. Against Norwich, people maybe didn't think there was a chance when the ball was in the air, so for him to turn that situation into a goal – and a decisive one at that – was incredible.

What really made the trip unforgettable, though, was the flight home. It was a tough day weather-wise and we had a run in with Storm Dennis.

We got onto the plane at Norwich Airport and we were already braced for a rocky ride because the wind was picking up and the forecast wasn't ideal, to say the least. Then the pilot let us know we should be prepared for a bit of turbulence and I could see the concern growing on a few faces.

Flying doesn't bother me. When it does get a bit bumpy, I usually go for gallows humour – but I was definitely a wee bit jumpy this time. I looked across at Kev Guy from the club staff and he was just staring out of the window. His face was as white as chalk.

There was a sense of apprehension and some of the lads and staff said they would prefer to travel by road. The gaffer made it clear that he would never force anyone to fly in a situation like that and nobody would be judged if they decided to get off. It briefly crossed my mind to jump in a car but I came down on the side of a bumpy one-hour flight ahead of a five-hour drive. A few did get off and the last one was given a big cheer just to ensure he knew we had seen him as he tried to creep off the plane.

When we set off on the runway we got shunted to the left before we took off and, at that point, the thought of spending five hours in a car didn't seem so bad after all. Once we got up in the air it was alright and coming into John Lennon Airport it was a wee bit side to side but we made it back safely. It was one of the bumpier flights but you trust the professionals and the landing was perfect. The whole flight clapped when we landed, which I'm usually against, but I didn't mind that time.

Less than 48 hours later, we were back on another plane and facing up to another storm which wasn't great for anyone, especially the lads who'd swerved the flight back from Norwich. The weather wasn't our biggest concern, though. That was provided by Atlético Madrid, our opponents in the last sixteen of the Champions League.

When the draw was made, I thought they were one of the most difficult opponents we could have got. Diego Simeone has eleven guys who basically go to war for their manager. It's incredible to watch as a neutral but we had to come up against it. We knew they would make life as difficult for us as they possibly could. In some ways, they have similar traits to us. All eleven players work so hard for the team, they have an identity built on intensity and they use the passion of their fans to their advantage.

We were going back to the Wanda Metropolitano, the place where we had won the European Cup eight months earlier, but we knew this would be no heroes' return. We would be treated as champions in one respect and one respect only – Atlético would be stopping at nothing to knock us off our throne. Whatever emotion the venue stirred and whatever memories we had of our previous visit had to be parked. We couldn't have been handed a tougher tie and there would be no opportunity for reminiscences.

The last thing we needed was to concede an early goal. Not

only would that play right into Simeone's hands, it would suit Atlético's tactical approach by giving them a lead to hang on to. It would also give an extra edge to an atmosphere that had been fermenting since well before kick-off.

Four minutes in and they had what they wanted and we were faced with a situation we had been determined to avoid. I could look for excuses. The goal was scrappy with the bounce of the ball favouring them and the throw-in that led to the corner should have gone our way, but we have to look at ourselves. We needed to defend that situation better and we didn't. From that point on, they retreated back in the knowledge they had something to hold on to. The game became more about Atlético preventing us from getting the equaliser than about them going in search of a second goal.

It felt like they were desperate to beat us. That's a compliment, not a criticism. There was a hunger in the stadium that you don't experience all too often and it was shared by the Atlético players and supporters. They are a big club, they have spent a lot of money, have a fantastic manager and they showed the kind of desire to give us a bloody nose that you would normally associate with a lesser light. They are always full of passion but it did feel like they were hell-bent on beating the champions. We could feel the passion of their fans.

They sat back and, to be fair, they did a better job than most in terms of stopping us from creating. They only had one more shot on target but we had none. We could've been more creative and put a bit more of a mark on the game but the early goal killed us because they were happy with 1-0. We could tell that from very early on. It became a night of frustration because we knew that an away goal would change the dynamic of the tie, but we never really came close to getting one.

I was definitely annoyed. The result and our performance were bugging me and so were some of their antics. They are a team who are hard in the challenge, and that's definitely above board, but when we did it to them they tended to roll about for the next couple of minutes to try and disrupt the rhythm. You come up against teams who you know will waste time and we had to be better dealing with it than we were that night.

Walking off that pitch, it felt like they thought they were through – the celebrations were bigger than you would expect after a one goal win in the first leg – and I think we all wanted to remind them that they still had to come to Anfield.

That was the message from Virgil and myself when we did a TV interview after the game and I know the gaffer said similar in his press conference. We know the power of Anfield, we know how the fans react on those nights, what we're like on those nights and, as far as we were concerned, this tie was far from over. From my point of view, it was important to front up after a defeat, particularly as it gave me the chance to start setting the tone for the second leg. I wanted to get the fans ready because we were going to need them probably more than we needed them against Roma or games like that.

At the point when that interview took place I could have probably played the game at Anfield there and then. We were all fired up. Looking back on it now, I probably did set myself up for a fall a wee bit and rival fans will have been desperate for me to fall flat on my face but I would always rather show faith in my team-mates and my club than shy away just because I might end up getting a bit of stick. I don't think I said anything wrong, it was just a basic statement that we would be ready for them at Anfield and they would need to be ready too. As it turned out, they were ready. That's the way it goes sometimes.

It might have looked like I am a bad loser when viewers were watching that interview but I'm actually not. Getting beat definitely hurts and probably even more so at Liverpool. The way we have gone about our business over the last few years, it doesn't happen that often and you get used to the winning feeling. The reaction when we lost to Man City at the start of 2019 probably sums up our attitude to defeat. Losing stung us and everyone couldn't wait to get back out on the pitch so that we could put it behind us. We then went over a year without losing another league game. Also, in the back of our minds we know that there will be those who are waiting for the opportunity for us to slip up so that they can have a pop and in its own way that serves as a motivation. So I don't like getting beat but I wouldn't say I am a sore loser. I can accept defeat, especially when we get beaten by a better team on the day. The difference with Atlético was I had allowed myself to become frustrated at some of their antics and I let it show.

In most walks of life, if you get a knock at work, you don't get a load of cameras put in front of you and asked to explain what's gone wrong and how you're going to put it right. For us, it's a different life in this respect and it can be difficult but I would like to think I'm getting better at it. With Scotland, unfortunately the last couple of years have not been as good as we have wanted it to be and being captain puts me at the heart of this, publicly and privately. I've had to front up more often than not and while I'll carry on doing that no matter what, I would give anything for the subject matter to change because that would mean we are winning more regularly.

The defeat to Atlético was only the third time I had been on the losing side for Liverpool in over a year – and one of those was the loss at Barcelona that didn't prevent us from reaching the Champions League final – so it did feel like a bit of a shock to the system. That's the way it had to be, though. If it doesn't feel that way, the likelihood is that you're either on the way to developing a losing habit or else you have one already.

For all the words that are spoken, the best place to respond is on the pitch. The only problem with that is opponents can scent blood when a team which is riding high has had a bit of a setback and, because we are all just human beings, there are times when the confidence that has been built up over an unbeaten run takes a bit of a knock.

That made our next game crucial and although West Ham turned up at Anfield fighting for their lives, we started well with Gini giving us an early lead from Trent's cross. Anyone expecting a straightforward night after we scored would have been disappointed, though, as West Ham fought back to go 2-1 in front. They made life really difficult for us and credit to them for that but, despite never really being particularly fluent, we kept ourselves in the game through a combination of our desire not to lose for the second game in succession and our ability to create chances. This made a welcome return after going missing in Madrid. I managed to set up the equaliser for Mo and Sadio went on to grab the winner thanks to Trent getting his second assist of the game.

There were a few themes that developed afterwards which I didn't quite disagree with, but I did think they took the focus away from other areas. One stemmed from a statistic which showed that I had clocked up more assists than any other Premier League defender since 2014. Yes, I was proud of that record and the twenty-seven assists I'd had in that time was a good number but I would be the first to admit that I am helped massively by having so many players around me who are desperate to score.

My final ball and my composure have got better, largely due to the help I've received from the gaffer and his assistants. I'm definitely much prouder of my improvement as a defender, though, and this doesn't get anything like as much attention because the spotlight shines much brighter on the goals we score than the ones we prevent.

The gaffer actually questioned my defending openly not long after I arrived at Liverpool, saying there were never doubts about me going forward but there were questions about me at the other end of the field. I never had any problem with that whatsoever. Not only did I know it was an area I needed to improve, I also knew he would help me to improve.

I worked hard every day to get better and I think it shows in my game but, for whatever reason, my assists get more attention. I'm not complaining, it's nice to have a good reputation for anything, but my primary focus will always be on the bread and butter of my job, with everything else being a nice bonus rather than the other way around.

The perfect example of how many others view it differently came after our draw at Old Trafford. My assist got a lot of attention but I would be the first to admit that it wasn't even a great cross. It was just a ball into an area where there were a bunch of bodies and Adam made sense of it all by arriving at the back post to stick it away. From my point of view, it might have been one of the worst crosses I put in all season but it was into the right area, at the right time, and it paid off. I also got an 'assist' later in the season for a five-yard pass to Fabinho and he banged one in from thirty yards.

This is one of the reasons why I take more pride in the

defensive part of the game. I know I've become a better defender than I was when I was at Hull or Dundee United and I would get some criticism, most of it justified, for the way I defended one versus one. Some of my best moments in a Liverpool shirt have been when I was defending – putting my body on the line in the Champions League final in Kiev when Ronaldo was through on goal; big tackles in big games; throwing myself in front of an open goal against Spurs; big blocks away to Sheffield United; working back to prevent Barcelona from getting a fourth goal at the Nou Camp that could have ended the tie. I take more pride from those moments than I do from the assists. Don't get me wrong, I love setting up goals and I get a really good feeling when I do, but first and foremost I want to be one of the hardest defenders that wingers come up against.

Being a good defender now, you don't get as much respect as may have been the case previously. Gary Neville is probably one of the best full-backs of his era and I know he was great at overlapping and linking up with David Beckham but it was his defending that made him stand out more than anything else. Nowadays, full-backs don't seem to be respected as much for their defensive qualities but at the same time, if they show any weaknesses defensively it will be highlighted and used as a stick to beat them with. It's a strange situation. From my perspective, I could put in five poor crosses, one finds Bobby, he scores and everyone else say that's Robbo's 23rd assist or whatever; but I could keep a winger quiet for eighty-five minutes, he gets past me once, sets up a goal and I'm torturing myself. That's because I view myself as a defender first.

I know it's difficult because everyone wants to see goals and for that to happen you need assists but Trent and myself are defenders and, more than anything else, we want a clean sheet. We want to be the best defenders we can be and if we get an assist on top of that then great, because that is part of our game. Sheffield United away was the perfect example. I reckon in most people's eyes I won't have had a good game that day because I didn't do a great deal with the ball. But in my opinion it was one of my most important performances of the season because I made a couple of vital blocks, one from a shot that was almost certainly going in, we kept a clean sheet and took three points. I always look first to the basics of my game and that means how well I defended. If we have kept a clean sheet and I have helped that in any way then I have had a good game. If we get a clean sheet and I get an assist then we've had a very good game as a team.

The other theme I took issue with after West Ham was the idea that we were somehow a lucky team.

I would be the first to admit that we had a bit of fortune in that game. Lukasz Fabianski will probably look at a couple of the goals we scored and think he should have done better but this is what happens when players and teams are put under pressure.

When you're a kid you get told that 'if you don't buy a ticket, you won't win the lottery' and the amount of attacking pressure we put opponents under means we buy more tickets than most. It's not rocket science. It's the same with the number of late goals we score too. More often than not, if the scores are level, we will be the ones pushing forward in search of a winner. We won't be sitting back in the knowledge that one minor slip, one deflection or one piece of brilliance by an opposition player might cost us. We do everything we can to make something happen and we get our rewards for this.

It wasn't luck when Manchester United kept scoring in stoppage time under Sir Alex Ferguson. 'Fergie Time' was a reality because United forced teams to crumble. Physically and mentally, they kept going until the pressure told. The more this kind of thing happens for any team, the more you know it's not down to luck. It's about talent. It's about determination.

We have seen a number of goalkeepers make mistakes against us. Hugo Lloris would be a good example. He is a top goalkeeper, a World Cup winner capable of making unbelievable saves. But we forced him to make an error towards the end of the 2018/19 season that was totally out of character for him and it allowed us to score a 90th minute winner. It was the kind of save he would normally expect to make ninety-nine times out of one hundred but this was the Kop end at Anfield with Liverpool pushing for a late goal and Tottenham having to strain every sinew to keep us out. Something had to give and it did. That's no reflection on Lloris or Spurs who gave everything they had but on the day we were not going to be denied. So when people suggest we are lucky in those situations I point out that our relentlessness forces mistakes. Every player is human and our job is to expose their frailties. The more pressure we can apply, the more likely it is to happen.

The only problem is, as much as we try to do that, others are trying to do the same to us and the target on our backs seemed to be bigger than ever as we headed towards spring. Having won eighteen successive games, it was inevitable that rival teams would become increasingly determined to knock us out of our stride. I've been on the other side of that coin as a member of the Hull team which gave Liverpool a bloody nose with a 2-0 win at the KC Stadium in the season before I moved to Anfield.

In the dressing room before that game, none of the Hull players were kidding ourselves that we had as much quality as Liverpool so we had to set out to disrupt their normal way of playing and make life as difficult for them as we possibly could. That's why the idea of easy games in the Premier League is such a nonsense. Every team is capable of having their day. Norwich ended up getting relegated but they also managed to defeat Man City and gave us a proper test at Carrow Road. Aston Villa were also minutes away from beating us.

That's why we took nothing for granted when we visited Vicarage Road to face a Watford team which had gone five games without a win. All of the performance indicators pointed towards an away win but we definitely sensed danger. Watford were in the relegation zone but they have a good squad, they had got to the FA Cup final the season before and we knew they would be able to take our game as a free hit.

Ultimately, they took their free hit and smashed it out of the park. Fair play to Watford for that. They played to their best level and we didn't reach ours. We had zero complaints about the result and no matter how much a 3-0 defeat hurt after being unbeaten for so long, we just had to take our medicine. I've been asked a few times when I knew it wasn't going to be our day and I always say the same thing – the first minute.

It's an exaggeration, of course, but there was never a sense that we had Watford where we wanted them. I had a chance before they scored which I probably should have done better with but then we started to give bad goals away and it doesn't matter what your record is, if you do that you're going to lose games. Us being unbeaten counted for nothing to Watford and nor should it have. If anything, they used that to raise their own game.

Having said that, even after we went 2-0 down I still believed we could get something out of it. We just needed to get one goal and we would have a great chance of getting a draw. As soon as they scored a third, I knew we were done. I know there was a lot of focus on us going through the season unbeaten and becoming the new Invincibles but that wasn't on our minds at that point. If we lose a game heavily, the last thing on our minds initially is that it might have cost us a record.

It actually hadn't crossed my mind that we might go through an entire season without losing.

I know there was a lot of talk about that happening and it's probably quite boring to hear but all of us were taking it game by game. I never actually thought we would go unbeaten because there are so many variables at play. If it had been a thought that I was entertaining, I would have been cracking jokes about it. I had been winding Hendo up about lifting the Premier League trophy since January and telling him it was in the bag because I knew he'd bite but I never did the same with our unbeaten record. Even in my disappointment, I felt enormously proud of the lads for managing to go unbeaten for such a long time.

Walking off that pitch, I could see what it meant to beat Liverpool and that showed how far we had come because, for a long time, Liverpool had maybe been a bit hit and miss. If you got them when they were having a good day you would be in trouble but, equally, if they weren't quite at it, teams were able to take points off them.

The reaction to us losing told its own story. Gary Neville was popping champagne corks, Arsenal put a celebratory tweet out and plenty of others – who had had little to say since the start of the season – found their voices. So many were desperate for Liverpool to lose that I saw it as a badge of honour. If someone is desperate for you to lose (apart from Everton and United who naturally want us to lose every week) then we must be doing something right, so I took some pride from that. Anyway, the main thing was that we ensured we would be the ones drinking champagne at the end of the season.

The result had stung enough without Watford's club mascot getting in on the act but there he was celebrating in front of our fans and gesturing to them as we were applauding them for their support. I didn't say anything. What would you say to an adult dressed as in insect anyway? I just stared him down.

Besides, I had gone out of my way to be respectful to the Watford lads, telling them that with performances like that they were definitely staying up and there was a fair bit of mutual respect going on, so I didn't want to spoil that by falling out with a six foot tall hornet. We lost to a team that deserved to win that day, one hundred per cent. They had whipped their crowd up, so good luck to them. I definitely could have locked horns with their mascot but next time I see him I'll shake his wing and we'll kiss and make up!

It was around this time that the winter break came up as an issue once again, only now it was suggested that taking a break had somehow stalled our momentum.

What I saw with my own eyes, in fact, was a lot of lads coming back fresher having enjoyed the benefit of some much needed time off. It was about recovery and getting our bodies ready for the rest of the season, not about guaranteeing results. Yes, the results weren't as good after the break as they had been beforehand but that could have happened anyway. It's far too simplistic to lay our downturn at the door of the winter break.

Having time off isn't just about that particular season either, it's about your entire career as a professional footballer because the fixture calendar is now so hectic that if you don't have some downtime, you just store up problems. We just had an off day at Watford and, to be honest, I'd rather have an off day with fresh legs than tired ones.

Chelsea ensured we would have a couple more blank weekends when they knocked us out of the FA Cup in the fifth round. This was the furthest we had gone in the competition since I had been at the club.

Usually the gaffer doesn't play me in early rounds of the FA Cup. He played me against Everton in my first season but since then, I had been an onlooker.

With the young lads having done so well against Shrewsbury, our attitude was definitely 'let's go and win it.' That was reflected in our team selection. We started well, generally showing our intent and creating chances that we were not able to take. Stamford Bridge is always a tough venue, though, and Chelsea ended up getting the better of us, running out 2-0 winners and ending any hopes we might have had of winning the treble.

There was actually more disappointment after losing to Chelsea than there was after Watford. We accepted the Watford defeat and were able to put it into context as our first league loss in a long time. But we also wanted to bounce back in our next game and we were unable to do that. It was the first time we had lost back to back fixtures in over a year and although our performance wasn't bad, Chelsea just clicked on the night and deserved to go through. If we had taken our chances it might have been a different game but we didn't.

For us, as players, we want to win every tournament we are

in and every game we play so, logically, this means we target every competition at the start of the season. It may or may not be realistic and it's clearly very ambitious but we want to win the lot. It's a mindset rather than a stated ambition and key to it is a commitment to take every game as it comes and never look too far ahead.

By the time we were coming out of winter, people were talking in terms of us doing the treble and this was a compliment in itself because it showed that we had managed to stay in contention on all fronts for so long. When you're still involved in all of these competitions after Christmas and you're quite far ahead in the league, it's inevitable that pundits will start asking whether we could win the treble and maybe also be invincible but for us, a club that had not won the league in thirty years, that had to be the priority.

We had won the Champions League but, when you sign for Liverpool, you understand how desperate everyone involved at the club has been to win the Premier League title. You understand the desire of the fans, those higher up in the club, Kenny Dalglish and all the other legends, people like that. It would be impossible not to understand how important the league title is. We wanted to win the Champions League and FA Cup as well but we're also well aware that we are in a profession in which losing is an occupational hazard, especially given every other team is also desperate to win.

Some people thought the wheels might had fallen off when we lost at Stamford Bridge but that was more to do with the standards we had set than anything else. We were still twenty-two points clear in the league and that was undoubtedly our number one priority.

Wearing my Scotland hat, I was able to take some consolation from this setback as Billy Gilmour gave a demonstration of the kind of ability that will hopefully serve our country well for years to come. I would've preferred it if he had saved it for another game but I loved how he went about his business on the night.

Billy is a lad I have kept an eye on because, as soon as he moved from Rangers to Chelsea, there was a lot of talk about him being too young – but I knew he was a top talent. At the SFA, they say he is a good lad and hopes are high that he could have a big future, so I wanted to see how he stood up to our midfield because it was strong that day. He ended up being named man of the match and, from a Scotland point of view, it was good to see him to put himself on the map with a very good performance.

I spoke to him afterwards and he gave me his shirt. I told him he had done well and that I looked forward to seeing him in a Scotland squad very soon. I had wanted our team to win and our team to get the better of him – of course I did – but he had stood up to the task against a Liverpool midfield and if he can do that, he can do anything.

While he looked forward to an exciting career, we had to come to terms with the FA Cup being put out of our reach. That was a disappointment but it was easier to take with the prize of a league title coming into view.

BIGGER THAN FOOTBALL

DRAINED, defeated and disappointed, the last thing I wanted was to be picked for a drugs test. Atlético Madrid had just won at Anfield and our reign as European champions was over. All I wanted to do was get home to start dealing with our loss. No such luck. Doc Andy Massey tapped me on the shoulder and told me I'd been randomly selected along with Adrian. Seeing as I'd missed an absolute sitter and Adrian had made a costly error, I didn't see much point in checking if either of us had taken anything that would enhance our performance. It is part of the job, though, and rightly so. We followed the Doc out of the dressing room, expecting to be put in another room with the two Atlético players who had also been chosen but a UEFA official told us this wouldn't be possible. We had to go into separate rooms as a precaution against infection. I lost my head.

Post-match adrenaline wasn't helping and neither was the result but even without those twin impostors I still would've been angry and confused. We had just been in close contact with the Atlético players and probably sixty others involved in the game in various roles. We had tackled one another, we had sweated, we had shaken hands and we had panted our way through one hundred and twenty gruelling minutes.

Yet here we were being told that we could not share a room with two of their players. I'm no scientist but I struggled with the logic of that. The doctor was from Switzerland and there were other medical staff from other parts of Europe. Had they been tested? How could I be sure that they didn't have something that they could pass on to me? The Swiss doctor probably had similar concerns himself but first he had to deal with mine. "How can you possibly split us up now?" I asked. "We've shaken hands. We've been in close contact all game. We've had 54,000 people watching us from the stands. And now you're saying we can't sit together. Really?" Everyone has their own moment when coronavirus invaded their consciousness. This was mine.

Even with the benefit of hindsight, I still can't get my head around everything that happened that night. When I was finally able to go home, someone told me about a story in *The Times* which said social distancing was set to be introduced. The story had obviously come from the government, the same government which had decided that mass gatherings such as football matches were safe to go ahead because the risks of the disease being transmitted were relatively low.

So you had medical professionals saying it wasn't safe for me to share a room with an opponent on the same night that tens of thousands had been allowed to congregate in close proximity. Forgive me for being confused. Excuse me for being concerned.

Like most people who had been at Anfield, I left the ground wondering what the immediate future held but not for a minute did I think it would be another three months before we were able to play there again. The reality of coronavirus was starting to dawn but its' tragic and long term impact was still to reveal itself. It was the final hour of my 26th birthday and things hadn't gone to plan but little did I know how much my life and everyone else's was about to change.

Again, I'm no expert, but looking back, it felt like Britain was looking at the damage that coronavirus was doing in other parts of the world without recognising that it would do the same here. I know we are an island but that doesn't make us immune to disease, especially in an age when international travel means people are coming and going every minute of every day.

I'm just an ordinary person like everyone else and I like to believe that those in power know what they're doing whether or not I agree with them politically, but I defy anyone to cast their mind back to the first days of March 2020 and not have concerns about some of the decisions that were made by those in authority. It's widely accepted now that the information we were getting at the time wasn't always ideal and that in certain instances it created a bit of naïvety and possibly a false sense of security too. Again, it is surreal when I think about it. We were all going about our normal everyday lives, in our case training, playing matches and looking forward to the possibility of winning the Premier League, but in the back of everyone's minds was a growing fear about an invisible killer.

We played Bournemouth at home on the Saturday before

Atlético and we won 2-1. For us, it was business as usual apart from falling behind early on, something that hadn't happened at Anfield since we'd faced Spurs in October. Mo and Sadio got the goals as usual to turn things in our favour but it was the left-back who was our hero that day. Not me, though, I was being rested for the second leg against Atlético.

This was Milly's day as he produced one of the greatest goal-line clearances I've ever seen to prevent Bournemouth from equalising. It was one of the moments of the season and it summed up everything that is good about our mentality. Here was one of our most experienced players operating out of position for a team which already had a twenty-two point lead at the top of the league and he couldn't bear the thought of us conceding an equalising goal. Every time I watched a replay I expected Ryan Fraser's lob to hit the back of the net, only for Milly to appear from nowhere to hook it away.

The clearance trended on social media afterwards which must have been the first time anything involving Milly had been trendy since about 1972. It was incredible, though, and it was a key factor in us opening up a twenty-five point advantage over City. I know by then there was a growing worry that football could be stopped before the league was won but we thought that, at the very least, the season wouldn't be interrupted until the international break which was due at the end of the month. Again, our thinking was influenced by what the authorities were saying at the time.

We did feel an urgency to get the job done but that was because it had been a thirty-year wait rather than any feeling that it could be taken away from us. We were only nine points away. Touching distance. I would be lying if I said any of us left the pitch after the Bournemouth game and feared it might turn out to be our last league game for months. We were only focused on reaching the finishing line and that moved clearly into view the next day when City lost the Manchester derby to United. Players don't usually like to admit to watching their rivals but we all watched that one, probably more out of hope than expectation because I think most people believed City would win. We knew, though, that United would play with pride at Old Trafford because we'd already experienced it and they were also going for the top four so it definitely wasn't out of the question that they could get a result.

I watched at home with a friend but I spent a lot of time on the players' WhatsApp group which became increasingly animated as the ninety minutes wore on. Most players are the same, you watch matches with a football head on but that game I watched as a fan. I was even a wee bit nervous before kick-off and I kicked pretty much every ball, which is out of character unless I'm watching Celtic in the Old Firm. Of all the games I have seen on television, this is the one that I watched as a Liverpool fan rather than as a Liverpool player. At least now I know what our supporters go through!

Anthony Martial gave United the lead. "City will come back," I said. Every time they attacked, I expected them to score but the goal didn't come. The seconds ticked by and became minutes. One half ended and another started. The seconds became minutes again. Stoppage time arrived and I was appealing for the final whistle to be blown as if I was out on the pitch. "Blow the thing," I shouted as if a referee 35 miles away was not only going to hear my demand, he was going to act on it. "It's ninety-seven minutes, blow the thing!"

The next thing, Scott McTominay, my Scotland team-mate, put me out of my misery with what will always be my favourite

Man United goal. Suddenly, I was literally jumping up and down on the couch, celebrating like I had when I saw Celtic win at Ibrox. I only stopped bouncing because my phone was buzzing constantly. The players' group chat had exploded into life. One caught my eye straight away. 'Campeones' it read. It was Virgil so I didn't need the smiley faces that followed to know it was partly tongue-in-cheek, but it was also the kind of message that could be sent if the league title was within our grasp. It was a big moment, I'm not going to deny that. When you're that close, just three wins away, and your closest rivals lose and you are able knock a game off without even playing, it is huge psychologically because you've effectively got a step closer without having to do anything.

I had been on a family break in Scotland when Wolves beat City earlier in the season but I hadn't even watched that game. I saw the result and obviously I was happy about it but it was far too early to make a big deal about it. The United game was different, though, because even though we all expected City to win there was also a feeling of fate about it. I suppose that's why we all watched it and experienced it as a group via our mobile phones.

The momentum was unquestionably in our favour and I noticed a bit of a shift from my family afterwards which wound me up a bit. I'm a bit superstitious in the sense that I don't want people around me thinking that something's done before it really is done. A light-hearted message from Virgil is one thing but I struggle when a result is called before it's been achieved, even if I am privately feeling the same way. I was the same when I was at Hull City and everyone thought we had reached the play-off final after a 3-0 win away to Derby County in the first leg of the semi-final. It was right that I was, too, because Derby beat us 2-0 in the second leg. I was also the same when we won 5-2 against Roma in the first leg of the Champions League semi-final. It's not done until it's done and Roma away was another example of that. That was why I wouldn't let anyone talk about Wembley or Kiev.

The first rule of 'final club' is that you don't talk about finals until you've got there and the same rules apply to title challenges. I didn't want us blowing up with just two wins needed or for the pressure to grow because the Holy Grail was so close. The only time I would talk about it would be when I had a winner's medal around my neck. Friends and family wanted to make plans for when they might be able to come down to celebrate it and that's only natural but I wasn't in the mood for making plans. I just wanted to make history.

Ideally, that would have happened in Europe as well as in England. We wanted to win the Champions League as well as the Premier League but for that to happen we had to overturn Atlético's first leg advantage.

We had a meeting at Melwood the day after United's win but the mood had definitely changed. In one respect, this was totally normal as you have to be able to switch your mindset depending on the situation otherwise you have zero chance of thriving at the highest level. But in another it was totally different because of the growing concerns about coronavirus. We were all asking questions about it and what it could mean. I've no doubt it was the same in workplaces across the country at that point because everyone had the same worries.

The gaffer was trying to be a calming influence because we needed to keep our focus on the game but there's no doubt that the build-up felt strange. Despite that, we knew the uncertainty wouldn't affect the outcome because we know that the minute we cross the line on a European night to be roared on by 50,000 of our fans there are no distractions, everything else gets forgotten.

Fixtures elsewhere were already being played behind closed doors, which was concerning because although the situation wasn't as serious in the UK at that stage it had started to feel like it wouldn't be long before it was. The virus was probably already establishing itself in this country by then but the majority of those who had it were either asymptomatic or hadn't been tested. Like most other people, my main concern was for my family. Taking football out of the equation, I have parents and grandparents and the information coming back from Europe, particularly Italy, was that they would be at greater risk than I was as a fit and healthy sportsman in my mid-twenties. I also have two children and even though their age meant they didn't fit in with that risk group it's still totally natural to worry for them at any time, never mind when a pandemic is breaking out.

At the team meeting, Ali had asked whether he should take his kids out of school and I totally understood where he was coming from. Against that kind of backdrop, it was probably inevitable that I would find it a bit strange that Atlético were allowed to travel to this country in the numbers that they did. Madrid was one of the hardest-hit cities in Europe at that stage and yet 3,000 of their supporters were permitted to come to Liverpool without any kind of testing. On top of that, the Atlético team brought around fity to sixty players and staff and 54,000 would be coming from all over to watch the game. Not that they were doing anything wrong. They were only obeying the rules as they stood and at that time the authorities were allowing stuff like this to happen. It's for others to decide whether or not this was the right decision but none of it was adding up to me.

The fact that people were so concerned created an additional tension around the game. I was on press conference duty the day before and there were more questions about the virus than there were about the game. Usually you go into the second leg of a last sixteen tie and the questions are about the aggregate, how you see the game going, what the atmosphere will be like and stuff like that.

This time around we were dealing with health issues and the journalists were right to ask those kind of questions but, equally, we weren't really the right people to answer them. It was all very strange. My parents were coming down for the game but if I'd had as much information as we had two or three weeks later I would have told them not to travel. The problem was that the guidance at the time was so clear. Mass gatherings were not being prohibited because it was not believed that doing so would have a major effect on the spread of the virus. I might have been struggling to get my head around it all, especially allowing foreign visitors to walk around our city untested, but the rules and the guidelines couldn't have been clearer. For us, it was game on but we knew it wasn't going to be the same – how could it?

In the dressing room before games, the gaffer is always pumped up and hugging everyone. It is as much a part of our routine as doing stretches and putting on our kit. But this time he was only fist bumping us which was a really visible change. When he went out for the warm-up, some of the supporters sat around the tunnel were putting their hands out for him to touch but he was having none of it. Normal behaviours were suddenly out of the window. Visitors had already been restricted at Melwood and other protocols were being put in place at workplaces up and down the country but seeing the gaffer, one of the most animated people any of us know, pulling his sleeves over his hands and reducing contact with others was a big eye opener for all of us. It definitely wasn't normal and only with time would we realise that it was the new normal.

The game itself must have been sensational for neutrals, especially given the circumstances. In the ninety minutes we were outstanding and had chances to put the outcome beyond doubt. From the moment that Gini put us in front there was only going to be one winner in normal time and although I thought we played really well, I have to credit Atlético for hanging on when most teams would have been blown away. They were not causing us many problems but they were still in the game and with every opportunity that we failed to take so the chances grew that we could be hit by a sucker punch.

The risk of that seemed greater when we went into extra-time because it is such a short period, the away goal still counts and if you do suffer a setback it can be difficult to respond given how much you have already put into the game. Even with the additional risks, though, we were still in pole position because we were very much on top and the sense that it would be another unforgettable Anfield night grew when Bobby put us 2-0 up. As the crowd erupted, it felt like the script was being written.

The most dramatic stories come with a twist, though, and on this occasion it arrived in the form of a mistake, one that none of us had seen coming. We were in total control when it happened. Trent played a standard back pass to Adrian who could have shelled it long but he didn't make a great connection and the ball fell to Joao Felix. We were exposed and before we had time to recover, Marcos Llorente scored in front of the Kop. Adrian was the first person to know he was at fault but football matches are very rarely won and lost on the back of one moment over one hundred and twenty minutes. Maybe we could have done more with the possession we had when the ball was in midfield. Maybe the defenders could have anticipated the problem quicker than we did. Who knows?

What I did know was Adrian had won us the European Super Cup and we had won every one of the twelve games he played at the start of the season when Ali wasn't available. He pulled off some unbelievable saves during that run but everybody makes mistakes and unfortunately when keepers make them they usually end in goals. We were annoyed because we'd worked so hard to get to 2-0 and then out of nowhere a mistake that ninety-nine times out of a hundred doesn't happen meant we were behind on the away goals rule. We needed another goal but psychologically it had all changed. The stuffing had been knocked out of us and Atlético hit us with another two sucker punches to knock us out altogether.

In any case, I was too busy focusing on what I could have done better to worry about anyone else. After a defeat the first question I ask myself is what could I have done differently? The way I see it is if I don't do that I won't be taking as much responsibility for myself as I should and I won't be giving myself the best possible opportunity to improve by learning from what's gone wrong.

After Atlético there was one moment that I kept going over in my mind, wishing I could go back and make it right. I knew the chance that fell my way in the second half was one of the best we had during normal time.

After Mo's shot was deflected, the ball spun into an area that I could attack in front of the Kop goal and it felt like everything had aligned in my favour. It was my birthday, I'd never scored at the Kop end before and I knew if I made a good connection there would be nothing that even Jan Oblak, who was brilliant on the night, could do about it. It had to hit the back of the net. It just had to. *Smash*. It hit the bar.

In fairness, Kieran Trippier leaned into me just as I made contact and that didn't help but that was the moment I replayed in my head constantly for the next twenty-four hours. I blamed myself, no-one else. I'd had another chance during the second half too, a shot that I couldn't have done much better with but Oblak dealt with it. The header was the one, though. Being self-critical, I was pointing fingers at one person and one person only and that was myself. The only consolation was that one of the greatest strengths about this Liverpool team is that everyone takes responsibility at all times so I knew we would all be putting ourselves through similar agonies in order to be better next time.

There was a real sense of despondency but it wasn't just because our reign as European champions had been brought to an end. As well as being wound up by the post-match drugs test and gutted about the result, the other thing that occupied my mind as I drove away from Anfield was the fear that it could be some time before we played there again. I didn't think that at all after Bournemouth but from what I had seen before and after we played Atlético and the stuff I had been seeing in the news, I just knew. I live in a country that hasn't experienced a pandemic or had war visited upon it in my lifetime but all of a sudden everyone was facing up to a future in which the only real certainty was that people would die.

All of our lives were about to change. I had seen that process start with my own eyes and in my own domain. Jürgen's behaviour changing. A drugs test without an opposition player in the same room. No mascots. No handshakes before the game. All small differences but each symbolic in their own way and together adding up to something much bigger. This was only the start too and as much as I try to keep myself informed nothing could have prepared me for what was to follow.

The game changer for football arrived when news broke that Mikel Arteta had been diagnosed with coronavirus. It was the day after we played Atlético and I had spent it with Rachel and other family because it had been my birthday the day before. I still found time to watch some football with Man United playing behind closed doors in Linz while Rangers played in front of a full house in Glasgow to add to the sense that Britain was not acting as decisively as European countries.

I got a message from a friend telling me about Arteta and, I think like everyone in football, it shook me. This was the moment that the virus arrived in our game. Arsenal said they would be closing their training ground and everyone who had been in contact with Arteta would have to self-isolate for fourteen days. It brought it all home to me. My first thoughts were for him. I knew he would be fit and healthy because he's clearly always looked after himself but, still, if there is a virus about, you don't want to be one of the ones who catches it.

Then came the realisation that it wouldn't just be Arsenal that would shut down, the entire Premier League would have to do it too in order to reduce the risk of it spreading. Even then, though, my instinct was that it would be a short break and we would come back after a few weeks or so, even if that meant playing behind closed doors.

Robbo roar: *(Top)* Showing the fans how good it feels after putting in one of our performances of the season to blow Leicester away on Boxing Day – less than five full days after winning the Club World Cup in Qatar. *(Above)* with Virgil and Joe after the game

Kids are alright: *(Left)* Curtis Jones after his wonder strike against Everton – a goal that was talked about a lot –by Curtis! *(Right)* I played against Spurs after receiving positive news about Rachel

Moment of truth: With Trent before the Manchester United game at Anfield in January. The fans started singing 'And now you're gonna believe us' and the hairs on the back of my neck stood up

My ball, pal: Along with the Liverpool lads, Robert Snodgrass is the person I'm closest to in football. We went one better than the previous season and got an important win at West Ham

Agony: Going out of the Champions League to Atlético on a surreal night at Anfield was hard to take. I came so close to scoring, only to see my header hit the bar –it was a chance that haunted me

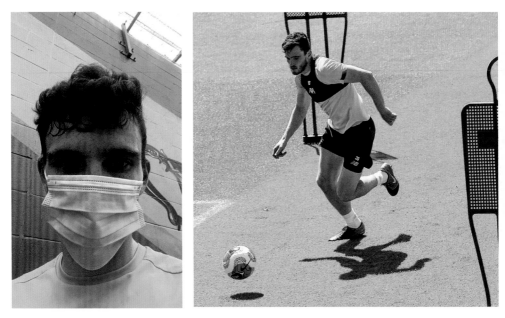

Me and my shadow: *(Left)* Face masks became essential wear in 2020. *(Right)* it was good to be allowed to train again after lockdown –even though we had to keep our distance from each other

Absent friends: Warming up before the Aston Villa game at Anfield on July 5th. This was the game more than most when I really missed the noise and colour of the Liverpool fans

Becoming a habit: Finding the net with my head again – this time against Burnley

Campeones! Enjoying the moment at Anfield with the boys after the Chelsea game. *(Above left)* at Formby Hall with Virgil and *(above right)* taking the knee in our final match of the season at Newcastle

Show us your medals: With the Ox and *(above)* party time in the dressing room. *(Left)* Rocco wearing the t-shirt – these are the best times

Four-midable: Personal picture at Anfield with the silverware – Super Cup, European Cup, Premier League trophy and the FIFA Club World Cup

Daring to dream: I'm so proud to wear the armband for my country. (*Above*) the personalised boots in honour of my Auntie Vera

The wait is over: Now it's time to *attack* our title ...

I went into training the following morning, in theory to prepare for the Merseyside derby that was due to take place three days later. When we arrived at Melwood, the gaffer let us know we would be having a big meeting after training and that's when we knew football was being placed on hold. We never have a meeting after training, it is always before, so we knew this was big and out of the ordinary. That created an atmosphere that I hadn't experienced before and I doubt very much I ever will do again.

While there was a tension about the announcement and the situation in general, there was also what I can only describe as an end of school feel to the place. The way we trained just felt more relaxed than is normal after a day off. It didn't feel like we were competing as we usually would. It was more like lads in the park or on the school field having a kick-around. It was like the competition was being taken away from us and so was our motivation. That was when it dawned on me that this could be our last session for the foreseeable future.

We all had to gather in the canteen at one o'clock but the penny had already dropped. The news about Arteta caused that to happen and so had the scene at Melwood which was already a very different place to the buzzing training ground environment I had been at just a couple of days previously. The number of staff members was clearly reduced – there was no-one on reception, nobody in from recruitment and catering staff was very limited – the entire training ground had a weekend feel to it but this was the Friday before one of our biggest games of the season.

The lads didn't really talk about what was happening and I think that was because we all knew what was coming. We were all clearing out our lockers and grabbing stuff that we might need while we were at home. This only usually happens in May when the season has ended but here we were in the middle of March preparing for time away from Melwood.

I headed to the canteen and sat with some of the staff. The gaffer came out of his office and perched himself on the end of the pool table. At that point we were all up to date on what coronavirus was, so he didn't need to go into that. He just told us that games were being postponed and that nobody would be allowed into Melwood for the time being so we should take anything that we need. He also said that the club would do whatever it could to help us and that the starting point would be the setting up of a WhatsApp group for us to share any concerns or issues.

Where the gaffer is really clever, though, is he deals with problems before they occur. He knew that at some point we would all start to worry about what this might mean for our hopes of winning the title so he dealt with that there and then. His message was simple: "You guys have earned this and you will get your chance. Don't worry about football for now. You are the best team in England and the most worthy champions there has ever been." He then explained to us why it was vital that football stopped for the time being and told us to have a breather. Effectively, he put us on holiday for a couple of weeks because he wasn't demanding anything from us and we weren't demanding anything from ourselves. I walked out of the canteen expecting to be away from the training ground for two, maybe three weeks.

There was never a spell when I stopped thinking about football altogether. There was too much at stake for us and it is such a focus in all of our lives that it is always in the back of my mind at the very least. It did become secondary, though.

The fact we were two games from winning the league seemed pretty irrelevant as we started to come to terms with the reality that a deadly virus that nobody could see was circulating without any medical solutions to deal with it. If this was a war you would be able to see bombs going off or planes flying over but this was an invisible killer and, in far too many cases, people didn't even know they had been infected by it until it was too late. I wasn't worrying about getting six more points during that period, I was worrying about my family. I have one grandparent in a care home and two who still live together so football slipped well down my priority list. This was more than football and we had to think about something else, something bigger.

Respite came in the form of the time that I was able to spend with the kids. Lockdown didn't happen until a week after we had been sent home from Melwood so at first it did just feel like I was off work.

We were able to take Rocco and Aria to the park for fresh air, to the beach for walks and just generally spend quality time with them. They were far too young to understand what was going on in the big world but in their small world that revolved around their home and family, they just knew that daddy was around a lot more than usual. I don't know whether that was a good thing for them but it was definitely a blessing for me.

The weather was good, another Godsend, as it made it easier to go out and about ahead of a period when everyone knew we would be spending a lot of time behind closed doors. Initially, at least, it was like I was on holiday with the sacrifices and focus that an everyday part of a professional football's life being put on the backburner. I was in full on dad-mode. There was no reason why I shouldn't be because I didn't have work but I actually loved it. Not that life at home didn't have its challenges.

There was one day when a message from Hendo popped up on the players WhatsApp group and it captured the kind of domestic bliss that I think most people in the country experienced at one time or another during lockdown: 'When will this end? I'm already pulling my hair out!'

I replied with a picture of Rocco potty training. He was facing the wrong way on the pot. Hendo might have been favourite to win footballer of the year but no-one was going to challenge my bid to become dad of the year. 'We need to get back to work ASAP,' I added. That kind of humour was vital and so was the camaraderie that we have as a squad. We are all just normal lads and normal dads and there was a spell when our WhatsApp group resembled a male version of Mumsnet but it definitely helped us to get through it all.

At first, we were just doing our own gym work because there was always a possibility that we could get called back into work and none of us wanted to be caught out if that happened. I only started running after our sports scientists got in touch and gave us all programmes to follow but there was definitely a feeling that we should also use the first couple of weeks to recharge our batteries ahead of a return.

I was doing my best to keep up with events but we couldn't watch the six o'clock news because that's dinnertime for the kids and afterwards we would be trying, but not always succeeding, to get them into bed. So we were trying to pick up bits of news when and where we could and like everyone else we could see that the picture nationally was worsening every single day. I phone my mum and dad most days anyway but it came even more important during that period. It kept them in touch with the kids, especially when it wasn't possible for them to see them in person, and it allowed me to find out how they and other family members were without looking like I was checking up on them too much. I was also speaking to my brother on WhatsApp every day, ringing my granny and grandad. You try not to give away that you're concerned but just by calling people more regularly you're showing that you are worried. Where I was lucky was that everyone in my family was fit and well. I will always be grateful for that because too many people were not fortunate in the same way.

This became increasingly clear when we went into lockdown. When football shut down I thought it was just a precaution as much as anything because we needed to avoid mass gatherings. That's fine in itself. As much as we like to think football is the most important thing in the world, in reality we know that it isn't and, as the gaffer put it, there was no way that games should be taking place if it puts people's health at risk. I came to terms with that side of things easily enough and this is why I was able to enjoy the first week or so in the knowledge that family and wellbeing were rightly being placed ahead of football. Realistically, the country can go on without it even if that does seem hard to believe sometimes.

When lockdown happened, though, with shops and businesses shutting down, workplaces grinding to a halt, hardly anyone able to go to work and everyone told to remain at home, that was when I became anxious. We had already known it was serious but just how serious it is really hits home when a government effectively closes down the economy. Then the death toll started to rise and it was just horrific. The numbers were difficult to comprehend because they were unprecedented and every day seemed to bring more bad news.

By then, our personal respite had become more basic as we became increasingly restricted to spending time in the garden rather than going out but at least it was something. Plenty of families don't even have gardens or outside areas that they can call their own and I have no idea how they coped.

The government's daily briefings became must-watch TV in the Robertson household. Rach and myself would make sure we made time for them because it was so important that we knew what was going on and were able to understand it. Like most people in the country, I was struggling with the way that the government was handling the situation but I also recognised that there were so many complexities at play that even the very best administration would have had a battle on its hands.

As it was, we had Matt Hancock, the secretary of state for health and social care no less, using up valuable time to tell Premier League footballers that they should be doing more to help. I was sat on the couch, on the same seat I had bounced on when McTominay sent me into raptures a few weeks earlier, when he said it. This time I didn't move. My jaw dropped and I just stared at the television in total disbelief. Premier League players "should take a pay cut and play their part," he said.

It was baffling how he could come out with something like that, particularly as reducing our pay would also have slashed the amount that we would contribute to the exchequer at a time of financial crisis. I would be the first to admit that footballers at the very highest level are privileged, having come from a background in which money is much harder to come by. I also accept that we have a responsibility to contribute and fully support the principle that our taxes are used to support the NHS, state schools, social care and the welfare state as a whole. Most footballers are the same in this respect. We tend to come from humble backgrounds, often working class, and we know how tough some people have it. It is this kind of knowledge and experience which means the collective social conscience in our sport is as strong as it has ever been. We don't need to be singled out, held up as a symbol of selfishness when the opposite is true more often than not.

Mr Hancock's comments were unfair and they were also uninformed. There was no mention of other wealthy individuals, in sport or other industries. The only people in the crosshairs were footballers. Whether it got publicised or not, a lot of players were very active at that time. I knew that from my own experience with team-mates making anonymous donations to local hospitals, children's charities, care homes, foodbanks, mental health organisations and other good causes besides.

Hendo had already set up a coronavirus fund for the NHS – Players Together – which the captains of all Premier League clubs got involved with on behalf of their team-mates. It only became a big story later in lockdown, but Marcus Rashford was supporting kids who were wondering where their next meals were coming from. The health secretary may not have been aware of this but when you're a government minister it's pretty easy to find out what individuals and groups are doing, but he didn't bother. He shot from the hip and we were the ones in the firing line.

I did have some guilt. Personal wealth was never something that I expected to have and I doubt I will ever be totally comfortable with it because I know a lot of people are struggling but I also saw the unfairness in the debate being taken in this particular direction.

If anyone from the government had wanted to have a conversation about how society can come together to ensure foodbanks are no longer a necessity, fine. I would have been all ears. Until then, footballers including myself will continue to support those causes because we know without that kind of support the type of poverty that is far too commonplace in cities like Glasgow and Liverpool will only worsen.

I hadn't wanted it to but a series of donations that I made to various foodbanks in the Glasgow area during lockdown got out into the public domain. I just wanted to help get food on the table for people who were desperate. The publicity that followed was of no interest but at least it helped highlight the kind of things that people in my profession were doing. I also made a donation to the Back Onside mental health charity at 3.30 one morning. That happened because I was trying to get the kids into a good sleep routine. Before lockdown, they were God-awful at sleeping. The eldest would climb over his gate, run into our room and not go back to sleep so drastic action was needed. I said to Rachel: "Let me have lie-ins in the morning and I will get up with him in the night and get him into a routine. I'm going to get him sleeping during this lockdown and nobody is stopping me." So that is why I was awake at 3.30am, waiting to tell him what was what if he got back up.

I was lying on the landing, looking at my phone when I came across a charity back home that needed support. Obviously, mental health was a hidden problem during lockdown with the number of people suffering on the increase because everyone was stuck inside so I went online and made an anonymous donation on the JustGiving page. You can't forget where you come from and you also need to have empathy with other people, not least because you never know when you might need support yourself.

I don't think it would be possible to have the kind of up-bringing that I had and not have a social conscience. We were from a big working class family but my mum and dad tried to give my brother Stephen and myself the best possible life that we could get. We were able to go on holiday every single year; when the new Celtic strip came out they would always try to get it for us; we had season tickets; we had a privileged life compared to a lot of others but we were not wealthy and what made the biggest difference to us was having a support network. We have a big family, we have always been really tight as a unit and still are. Some people do lack that support network, some feel on their own but we were nalways protected by a big wider family and that helped massively. I am very conscious of that. So at a time of national crisis, it did hit me that a lot of people did not have that level of support.

Could I have done more? Yes, I could have and that's why have I started making steps to set up my own charity AR26. Since I have been at Liverpool I have started to understand that my voice can carry a message so that gives me greater responsibility. It will definitely be strange for my mates who know me best but if I say something, maybe more people will listen simply because I am a Liverpool player. That's why, when I was donating to those good causes, I was already starting my own charity behind the scenes because I believe that will allow us to help make a difference as a family.

Football didn't quite become irrelevant while all of this was going on. I'm not sure it ever could, simply because it serves as an escape for so many. People were still talking about it and wondering what the game might look like if it was able to return. I was definitely thinking about it. We were so close to an incredible achievement that I had to try to prepare myself for various possible outcomes that started to emerge when the Premier League's owners and chief executives began to hold discussions about what the future might hold.

Various information found its way into the media and it quickly became clear that three main options were emerging: the season could be completed behind closed doors, the season could be decided by points per game or the season would be null and void. That was when I started to worry. None of the alternatives were ideal and all of them needed to be viewed through the lens of how much the country was suffering, but when you have put so much effort into something it's inevitable that you will want to finish the job in the best way possible. That's just human nature.

The problem was, none of the options would allow this to happen with even the best of them – behind closed doors – having the obvious drawback of football being played without fans. The other alternatives were much worse, though. We knew we were already champions in all but name but we wanted to win the league on the pitch, not be handed it as a result of an administrative decision. Having said that, we would have taken that all day long over the season being declared null and void, an alternative that would have meant all of our hard work would have gone to waste.

It was obvious that different clubs had different agendas depending on where they were in the table. If I put myself in the shoes I was wearing four years ago, bottom of the league with Hull and relegation a near certainty, do I want it null and void so we get another year in the Premier League with the money? Of course. You need to look after yourself at the end of the day but then there is also a responsibility to do what is right for the sport.

The relegation battle actually gave me reason for optimism because it was so tight at the bottom and it would have been totally unfair for the outcome to be decided anywhere other than the pitch. If the league had ended it there and then, nobody would have questioned us being league champions. It wouldn't have been an ideal way to win it, but we would have won it and nobody could have doubted that we were deserving champions. Everything else would have been brought into question, though – how relegation had been decided, how promotion had been determined, whatever happened to the teams in and around the play-off places, how European qualification was settled.

We were twenty-nine games into the campaign and although some outcomes were nailed on, others were up in the air. There was far too much at stake. Relegation can cost people jobs and clubs a lot of money and what about the teams hoping to come up? Leeds United, for instance, had been waiting for a long time to get back into the Premier League. There's no way that those situations could be resolved by a formula or, worse, not decided at all. Anyone with any interest whatsoever in fairness and sporting integrity had to at least try to find a way for the season to be completed. Anything else would have been of no benefit to football and the spirit of the game.

Did we fear null and void? Yes. There was a couple of weeks when it was very much a live issue and I can vividly recall being told about a column that Karren Brady had written calling for the season to be made null and void. I didn't think that was right. As I've said, clubs and individuals at clubs were entitled to hold those views and to do what they believed was in their best interests but these views should have been restricted to Premier League meetings. This was obviously an attempt to shape public opinion and all we could do was hope that it didn't pick up any speed.

Our situation was so difficult because if we had come out and said we wanted the season to finish, there would have been those who accused us of being selfish for wanting football to continue while people were dying. There was no way we could win in a situation like that and, in any case, we had to put the values of our own club first and that meant going about things the right way, no matter what others might have been doing.

Thankfully, the gaffer had set the tone for that early on so the rest of us were not in any doubt about what the club's position was. In an open letter to supporters, he spelled out exactly how we viewed football in the context of a pandemic.

'I've said before that football always seems the most important of the least important things,' he wrote. 'Today, football and football matches really aren't important at all. Of course, we don't want to play in front of an empty stadium and we don't want games or competitions suspended, but if doing so helps one individual stay healthy – just one – we do it, no questions asked. If it's a choice between football and the good of the wider society, it's no contest. Really, it isn't.'

Spot on.

We had no interest in deviating from that view. Not because the optics wouldn't have been great if we had but because it was the only context that made any sense of football at a time of global tragedy. Of course we wanted football to return but only at a time when it was deemed safe for that to happen. As much as all of us wanted the league title, none of us wanted it so much that we would have put people at risk for it. But the longer we were in limbo, the more we realised that winning the league on the pitch wouldn't come down to whether or not we were good enough, it would be determined by the impact of the virus and the ability of society in general and football in particular to cope with it.

Supporters probably believe that players get inside information but most of the time we're just waiting for formal announcements like everyone else and that was certainly true in this case. Every day the death rate and infection rate were rising so as long as that was happening we knew, and respected, that it would be difficult for football to return.

The only time when we felt that we were better informed than most was when the Bundesliga was given the green light to resume and having a German manager meant he was able to keep us up to date with everything that was going on. We were behind Germany in this country and it was clear that we would be taking our lead from them. The way that Germany as a nation had dealt with the virus gave us cause for hope but, equally, we knew that if twenty or thirty players and staff got infected after returning to training in early April it would have been difficult for their league – and therefore our own – to restart.

Thankfully that didn't happen and it became a case of learning from their protocols and how German clubs had gone about making football safe. By this stage, Project Restart had gone from being an ambition to an actual work in progress so it was definitely beneficial that there was a workable template to follow. That's why most people in English football watched the return of Bundesliga and I was among them, spending a sunny afternoon in mid-May at home to see how Borussia

Dortmund fared against Schalke. The result wasn't of any great interest but the circumstances surrounding the game were. Seeing the substitutes and staff wearing masks, the players avoiding handshakes, no celebrations after goals and the stadium without supporters was definitely a lot to take in because it went against everything that we are accustomed to, but it worked and it was safe. That was all that mattered.

Not that all leagues were giving us similar cause for hope with the season being curtailed in France, Belgium and Holland. For obvious reasons, Scotland was the one that had the biggest impact on me. Celtic were awarded the league and rightly so because they were so far ahead of the rest. I was just happy that they were one step closer to ten in a row. I wouldn't have liked us to win the league like they did but as a supporter I was delighted and relieved that it was done. The Celtic players would not have wanted it to finish in that manner either, they would have wanted to do it on the pitch and enjoy the moment with their fans but these things were being taken out of everyone's hands so it was just a case of making the best of a very difficult situation. There is more money in the Premier League than there is in the Scottish Premier League and maybe some clubs couldn't afford the testing so curtailment was the only option for them.

Fortunately, Celtic had built up a big enough lead that null and void couldn't be a realistic option. If it had been a one or two point gap between Celtic and Rangers, there would've been uproar in Glasgow if they had gifted Celtic the trophy. Of course, Rangers argued against the decision. If roles had been reversed Celtic would have done the same because that's the nature of the rivalry. But I firmly believe Celtic had won the league already – like I thought we had won the league.

THE ANFIELD ROAR

I T was literally a primal scream, a release of frustration, passion and relief that seemed to come from the pits of our stomachs and reverberated around the dressing room like no noise I had ever heard before. Just when I thought it would stop, it carried on, becoming louder and more intense.

Not satisfied by the sound of thirty-odd men shouting in unison and a noise that must have sounded to anyone outside like a rumbling storm getting closer, I added to the racket, banging on the door of my locker until my hand was red raw. *Bang. Bang. Bang.* Thirty seconds became a minute. The commotion still did not diminish. There wasn't even a pause. Nor were there any words. Pure release. No words, no tune and definitely no premeditation. It was totally surreal but, at the same time, it could not have felt more right.

I have been in football dressing rooms since I was a kid but never had I experienced anything like this and I very much doubt it will happen again.

What caused it? We had just beaten Crystal Palace 4-0 but it wasn't just that. This was the sound of a team which had moved within two points of becoming Premier League champions. It was a collective cry by a group of people who feared that everything they had worked for could be taken away from them. It was a holler which told the world that Liverpool's thirty-year wait to be crowned champions was all but over.

Fifteen weeks had passed since my last game at Anfield and everything that had built during that intervening period was pouring out. It had been a period dominated by concerns over a virus which had brought life, as we had known it, to a halt and inflicted tragedy on so many. So much pent up emotion being released and shared that only those who were there could possibly understand what it felt like. I've no doubt a psychiatrist would find other deep and meaningful reasons for it that even we haven't considered, but one thing is absolutely for certain – it was one of the most special moments of my entire life and I've no doubt that everyone involved feels exactly the same. Who would have thought acting like cavemen could be so powerful?

The fact we were in a dressing room at all was a big thing. There was a period when the return of football had been in serious doubt. A debate had taken place about whether or not sport should even be on the agenda. My own emotions were conflicted. I would find myself worrying about the season being ended, just when we had the league title within our grasp – then I'd immediately question my right to harbour such concerns when so much suffering was going on around me. Maybe there was a bit of Catholic guilt going on but whatever it was, it wasn't pleasant and it didn't make me feel good about myself.

I know it is often claimed that top footballers live in a bubble. I fully accept that we have certain privileges that support this view, but we are not disconnected from the world, certainly not to the extent that any of us would place more importance on our jobs than is appropriate during a time of global crisis. I would turn on the news and it was dominated by deaths, illness, hospitals being under massive strain, suicides going through the roof and people losing their jobs.

Most of the arguments put forward against a resumption made sense. No further strain could be placed on the NHS. Football is not a special case. Health has to come first. Undue risks could not be incurred. There was consensus on all of these issues and many more. Did some try to take advantage of these concerns for their own ends? Possibly. Only those involved could answer that question but, in the main, I have no doubt that most of the voices expressing doubts about football coming back did so for legitimate reasons. It wasn't as if legitimate reasons are hard to find during a pandemic, put it that way.

The phrase that seemed to be being continuously overlooked whenever the possible return of football was discussed was 'when the time is right'. Anything else would have been an affront to humanity and, besides, no-one was interested in playing when the virus was at its peak.

I recognised that a time would come when some sort of normality would return and when it did, the return of football would be legitimate. I felt strongly that twenty-two men kicking a disinfected ball around a pitch would help in terms of being a step in the right direction and, hopefully, a sign of better times ahead. Yes, it is only a game at one level but it is an escape which invigorates and entertains many and also an industry which employs countless thousands of people.

Like a lot of players, I had my own red lines. Had the return of football only been possible by taking testing capacity away from the NHS, I wouldn't have been able to go along with that. From the conversations I was having with players at Liverpool and other clubs, I firmly believe that this view was widely held. I also would not have even considered going back had doing so put myself and others at risk.

But if assurances could be provided on those fronts and others, I also felt that football could play a small part in helping the country to get back on its feet. We knew games would be behind closed doors but the fact that football would be on television would provide an incentive for people to stay at home, which was what we were all being told to do. I also believed that by playing we could provide a welcome distraction at a time when one was needed more than ever before.

Thoughts like these eventually became more widely held, providing the thrust for Project Restart and giving the football industry the opportunity to prove that it could operate safely and in a way that would be morally justified.

Central to that was testing. As players, we needed to be sure that the risk of infection was being controlled, but at the same time there was not a chance that any of us would take priority over NHS staff or key workers. Their needs had to come first – anything else would have been indefensible – but, thankfully, a solution was found which allowed us to be tested without impinging on vital public sector supplies. For me, this was a big breakthrough.

Hendo played a blinder for us throughout this process, taking part in God knows how many Zoom calls with other club captains, the Premier League, medical experts, the PFA and anyone else who had information that might be beneficial to us. If we had any questions or concerns, we just had to post them on the players' WhatsApp group and he would raise them on our behalf. Hendo was on it from day one, so it was good to see him getting wider recognition for the leadership he showed – not just for us but for English football as a whole.

We were also being looked after well by Liverpool. We had fitness staff laying on yoga classes via Zoom three times a week; we had coaches preparing tailor-made routines for if and when we could return; we had a sports psychologist on call and we had the player liaison department taking care of some of our most basic needs. We also had nutritionists and kitchen staff preparing food for us. Mona Nemmer is the club's head of nutrition and she does an amazing job, making sure we're in prime condition. She is outstanding at what she does.

So, this was definitely a club pulling together. Our Foundation and our fans were also doing an incredible job, providing support to those who needed it most in our local communities. Plenty is said and written about what makes a club successful at any given time but if anyone wants to find Liverpool's 'secret', they could do a lot worse than look at this period. On top of it all, we had owners and leaders who were doing everything in their power to make sure that football could return, to repeat that phrase, 'when the time was right'. In terms of leadership, innovation, comradeship and unity in the face of adversity, this was a pivotal time and it set the tone for everything that followed.

When the green light was given for us to return to individual training in early May, it felt like a massive breakthrough. Only three of us were allowed to be at Melwood at any one time and we could only be outside. Pretty much all we could do was run and contact was totally out of the question, but just being out on a training pitch gave us all a big psychological boost. We were desperate to get back into it.

It still felt strange, of course. The coaching staff were only allowed to stand a safe distance away which meant they had to shout louder. If it was windy, we would struggle to hear. We had videos put on the WhatsApp group which explained all of the protocols to us. We had to bring our own clothes, water and balls and we had to follow one route in and one route out, so it was all very different.

We are obviously used to everything being done for us at Melwood and I hadn't had to take my kit home to be washed since I was a teenager at Queen's Park. It was like being an amateur footballer again because we had to be responsible for everything ourselves. There wasn't even a changing room that we could use and no showers either, so we would have been in a bit of a smelly mess had it rained heavily. Thankfully, the weather was really good at the time.

Not surprisingly, the first person I saw was Milly. He was on the pitch already and had no doubt already done about 35 laps when I arrived for my first session. It was me, Milly and Virgil and we did our runs on three separate pitches while having a conversation from about 50 yards away, shouting at each other and giving one another some socially distanced stick! It wasn't ideal but it was better than FaceTime or Zoom. Just knowing they were on the same pitch gave me a feeling that we were nearly back.

Beforehand, we all had to be tested to make sure we did

not have coronavirus and while this was a pretty straight-forward process for everyone else, it ended up being pretty complicated for me. We had to go to the Academy in Kirkby where a drive-thru testing centre had been set up so that we could remain in our cars while being checked.

It had already been established that the test involved a swab to the back of the throat and then up the nose. Inevitably, we ended up joking with each other which somehow managed to make us simultaneously feel better and worse about the whole experience. Adam was through before I was so he watched my test getting done, shouting at me from his car. It was all that I could do to stop myself laughing as I gagged on the swab. When it was over, I then made sure that everyone behind me was left in no doubt at about how horrific it was by telling them it had been one of the worst experiences of my entire life. It wasn't, of course, but if this was the new normal and if part of it was not particularly pleasant, we needed to make it as light-hearted as possible. It really was funny too, at least until the joke rebounded on me.

Forty of us had been tested at Kirkby. Thirty-nine of the results were negative. One was inconclusive. Guess whose?

I knew there was something wrong when I checked my phone while I was in the garden with the kids and realised I had missed four calls in quick succession from the doc, Jim Moxon. I rang Jim back straight away and he said: "I've got some bad news. Your test is one of three in the whole of the Premier League that was inconclusive. They got nothing, so a guy needs to come to your house now and do another test." I immediately told Rachel to stand back, as if that was going to make any kind of difference, seeing as I'd constantly been with her throughout!

Doing another test didn't particularly appeal to me. I thought about a phone video Adam had made of his own test – he was so reluctant he was almost fighting with the poor bloke trying to swab the back of his throat. He nearly ended up in the back of his car trying to get away from it. Up until that point, it was one of the funniest videos I had ever seen but all of a sudden it didn't seem quite so amusing.

The next thing, there's a fella in full PPE and white overalls knocking at my door. I got the kids out of the way and took him in the second living room so that he could do his job. He was clearly the hitman who doesn't miss because he was straight up my nose like he was drilling for oil. As the tears streamed down, I consoled myself in the knowledge that this was one test that couldn't be anything but conclusive. He definitely got everything he needed – and probably a bit more besides.

We were due to start group training the following day so I called the doc and asked him to do everything he could to make sure that my test results were back in time. The last thing I wanted was to miss training. Luckily, it came back early and the result was negative. The man in the white overalls might have made me cry but he had got the job done.

The mood was brilliant from the moment that group training started. All of the lads were happy to be back out on the pitch and to be in one another's company again after thirteen weeks of communicating via WhatsApp and Zoom. It felt like the first day of school after the summer holidays when the weather is still decent and you get to see all your mates together again for the first time in ages.

Aside from the camaraderie, there was also a sense of urgency and a collective desire to get the job done. We would not be playing games for another few weeks so while we were enjoying our work, there was also a heightened desire to make it count. There was no point us being out there if we didn't get ourselves in the best possible condition because our first three fixtures were Everton away, Palace at home and City away. We might only have needed six points but it doesn't matter who you are, if you're not in good shape for a run of games like that you could find yourselves struggling for form and confidence and then even a small target can become more difficult than it should.

It's at times like this that the coaches really come into their own. Don't get me wrong, we don't need any reminders of their quality because we see it on a daily basis but this was a new and unprecedented challenge. We could only work in groups of five initially and this was on the back of the longest spell that any of us had ever had away from football, barring injuries, so the coaching staff really had their work cut out.

The only saving grace for them was that they had plenty of time to think and plan. But even with this advantage, the positives were definitely outweighed by the negatives in terms of preparing players for matches, particularly in comparison to what we were used to. I wouldn't say I was worried because I've got complete faith in the manager and his staff but I was intrigued to see how they would go about things.

In the event, it couldn't have been better. From the word go, the sessions were brilliant. You might ask what can you do with just five people but it wasn't too dissimilar to having eleven on the park and we managed to make it work. Whether it was just having a left centre-back, winger and midfield working together, they put on fantastic sessions. When you come back from pre-season you expect poor crosses and passes but, to be fair, the lads were totally on it. Part of that was down to the excitement about finishing the job. That's what got us going and ensured the quality was so high from such an early stage.

Our fitness levels kept improving but it was only when we were able to train together with everyone involved that the rhythm fully returned. We played an eleven versus eleven game at Anfield and the standard was very high. That was when I knew we would be okay. Playing behind closed doors was going to be anything but ideal, especially for a team like ours which thrives on the passion of our supporters. Not having the power of Anfield behind us was definitely a concern but our fitness and quality were not in question and this gave us the belief we would be able to play the way the manager expects.

Given the circumstances, things couldn't have gone much better until a couple of weeks before the derby when I felt my quad go while we were doing a crossing and finishing session. I leant back as I went to strike the ball and felt it straight away. I went straight in to get it looked at.

I knew something wasn't quite right and a scan confirmed that I had a grade two tear. I never feared missing the rest of the season but I was worried that I might not be fit enough to be involved when the league was there to be won. We were two games away from winning the title and I was a big, big doubt so I gave everything to get back as quickly as possible and I believed I'd done enough to give myself a chance of being on the bench for Everton.

I told the gaffer I was ready for that. I had done everything that had been asked of me up to that point and all that was left for me to do was long balls and crosses. I felt fit and I was ready to push myself. Just as I was convinced that I could be involved, our head physio Lee Nobes – 'Nobby' to us – was equally convinced that I shouldn't. This is where a player's logic and sports science pull in different directions. In my mind, I was ready to play. In Nobby's, there was a risk that if I did play, I could potentially re-injure myself which would benefit no-one. We both had the best interests of the team and myself at heart but we were coming at it from different angles.

Nobby stuck to his position and even though it was frustrating for me because I was back in full training, I respected that. The gaffer spoke to me twenty-four hours before the game and told me I would not be involved. He said: "We pay experts to be experts at this club and, as manager, I have to respect them."

There was also a resolve to get me fit to play ninety minutes against Palace and the best way of achieving that was by me working on my fitness rather than being on the bench at Goodison and maybe getting on towards the end of the game. I had missed two weeks of training and a couple of practice games so I was behind the rest of the lads. The gaffer told me that if I was substitute he could end up being too tempted to bring me on and this made total sense after Milly got injured during the first half. That might have meant me playing more than an hour. The way Nobby and the gaffer dealt with it was spot on, even if it was hard for me to deal with.

So I ended up watching the derby at home. While the rest of the lads headed to Goodison in their face masks I was sat on the couch with the only saving grace being that City had beaten Arsenal a few days earlier which meant we couldn't win the league against Everton. If City had lost, leaving us one win away from being champions, I would have had to have found a way to get into the ground even if it meant going in dressed as a steward!

It was definitely weird watching a Merseyside derby without

fans. I had seen most of the televised fixtures up until then but this was the game when I really felt the absence of supporters. Goodison is never an easy place to go. Everton fans always get up for the derby, the same as our supporters at Anfield, so it felt very different without them being there. Even when you're on the receiving end – as I often am at Goodison – it's still preferable to the sound of silence. You could tell that from the way both teams responded to the situation too.

The lads took a point which was a decent result given the circumstances but their performance still prompted a fair bit of criticism. I couldn't get my head around that. We hadn't played a competitive match for three months, we had drawn at the home of our local rivals and moved within five points of winning the league and yet the post-match analysis was more negative than positive. For me, every one of the players – both from Liverpool and Everton – deserved credit for getting themselves back out there and putting a decent game on. It certainly wasn't a classic but we had blown off a few cobwebs at the same time as extending our unbeaten run against Everton. I was struggling to find any negatives in that, with the obvious exception of the knocks picked up by Milly and Joel.

I was definitely a bit nervous going into the Palace game. It was nothing to do with the match, I was just worried I wouldn't be able to last the full ninety minutes. Palace are a good team with good wingers. I hadn't played a game in a long time and that was nagging away at me. I was also still about five days ahead of my injury schedule. It wasn't that I thought the injury could flare up. I had looked after myself throughout lockdown and my recovery had gone well but whenever training is disrupted, it's inevitable you will have a few concerns about your fitness.

Within five minutes of the game kicking off, I knew I would be fine. I felt good, fresh and sharp. The incentive of getting the win that would move us even closer towards achieving our dream also helped. We knew we couldn't win the league against Palace but we knew if we did secure victory, we would only be a couple of points away from doing so. Then it would be up to City to win their fixture against Chelsea the following night or else the title would be ours. Anfield behind closed doors was never going to be anything like it is when there is a full house but we didn't have to go looking for motivation, we just had to look at the league table.

Sometimes when the finishing line is in sight you can tense up a little bit but we didn't feel any pressure even if we were aware that it existed. As with Leicester away, I knew we were on it from the very first whistle. In the opening five minutes we won the ball back so many times and started to create plenty of chances so I thought if any of the lads did feel any pressure they were definitely using it the right way.

There is pressure in every game. Even Barcelona at home when there was talk of us having a free hit, I felt there was a pressure to perform, to prove that we could compete with one of the best teams in Europe and to do our fans proud. It is the same when we play City because we know beforehand that there is so much at stake. What we have learned to do as a team is to use that pressure to our advantage so that it turns into positive energy. I think that was one of the reasons why we performed as well as we did against Palace.

There was a lot of focus on the fans not being allowed into the stadium but, as disappointing as that was, Anfield is still our home; it is still the place where we have gone unbeaten in the league since Palace won there in April 2017. We have so many fantastic memories there and each one of them serves as an inspiration and a reminder of what we can achieve on home soil.

Even in their absence our supporters still made the Kop look incredible. I was told that Spion Kop 1906 and other fans had worked with the club to make sure as many flags and banners as possible were in place and when I saw it for the first time, it took my breath away. When fans go to that kind of effort, you do feel an added responsibility to repay them on the pitch. Even though they were not in the ground, they were still motivating us.

The performance was top class. The counter-pressing, the ability and skill we showed and the goals we scored were all fantastic. Trent's free-kick, Mo's goal from Fab's pass, Fab's strike from 25 yards and then Sadio's finish to top it all off were brilliant and we kept a clean sheet which was also important. It was a proper all-round display that every one of us contributed to and we took a lot of heart from that. Our fans get praised at Anfield – and rightly so – but we showed that when we had to, we could put in a high quality performance in front of an empty ground.

Every time I think about that scene in the dressing room afterwards and what it meant, it sends a shiver down my back and makes the hairs stand up on the back of my neck. It's right up there with singing 'You'll Never Walk Alone' in front of the Kop after the Barcelona game because in that moment, all of the lads were together and we all knew exactly what it meant. As I've said, the noise that came out of that changing room is something that will live with me for ever.

I'll also never forget a couple of things that were said to me on that night because they meant so much to me. The first came from Bobby Firmino at half-time when he told me that the difference when I do and don't play is incredible.

The two of us have a great relationship, even though I don't think he can understand a word I say! We are always smiling and hugging, we both get on really well – so for him to say something like that meant an awful lot. Lads don't often compliment each other. In interviews, yes, you talk each other up but to each other's faces you are much more likely to talk one another down. Virgil is possibly the best centre-back to have played the game, he doesn't have a weakness, but I still criticise him from time to time and I can say with absolute certainty that he does the same to me! That's part of football and I love it. But for Bobby to say something like that blew me away. I was playing with confidence anyway and just loving being out there but I went out for the second half with even more belief, simply because of what he had said.

Next, the gaffer got in on the act. Nobby had been talking to him about when I would be coming off because it was my first game in such a long time but the gaffer left me out there for as long as he could before biting the bullet with around ten minutes remaining.

We had just scored our fourth goal but I was knackered so I sort of stumbled into him as he gave me a hug and he said: "I love watching when you're playing football."

For someone who has a sense of insecurity which will always be there, this was massive. Usually I will go over the things that I feel I haven't done well in a game before going to sleep but this was one of the first times I've gone to bed and not doubted myself.

I thought: 'If he thinks that, I must be doing something right.' That felt really good.

Another thing that helped me sleep easily was the knowledge that we had played like champions. That mattered to all of us. We didn't need an outstanding performance to prove our worth, the league table was more than sufficient to do that, but it was definitely a shared ambition to embellish what we were doing with something a bit special and we showed all of our qualities that night. Not one person played beneath their level and there were no mistakes really, which was remarkable given this was only our second competitive game since mid-March.

Having played like champions, we then celebrated like champions back in the dressing room. We knew that if City dropped points against Chelsea twenty-four hours later it would be done and dusted.

The following morning, the gaffer spoke to us at Melwood and said that we would be meeting at Formby Hall later that day so we could watch the match together.

He said: "I've been in this game long enough to know that tonight is going to be compulsory because if it does happen, it's not the same if we all FaceTime each other. We have to be together."

We were ahead of him on that, to be honest. We'd discussed what we could do but the moment we shared in the dressing room crystallised everyone's thoughts – we had to be together as a squad. If City had won and nothing happened, fine, but we had nothing to lose. We had seven days before our next game anyway. It had to be compulsory attendance on the basis that there was a chance that something could happen.

"You all have to be there," the gaffer stressed. "We meet at six o'clock and let's hope it goes well into the night. If it doesn't then we go home and we've had a nice barbecue."

ROBBO

CHAMPIONS AT LAST

WHAT should you wear if you are a Liverpool player preparing for what could turn out to be the greatest day of your football career so far? Easy – a Chelsea shirt. As the rest of the lads were getting ready for a barbecue that we all hoped would turn into a title winners party, I went into my wardrobe and pulled out the shirt that Billy Gilmour had given me a few months earlier. Putting it on, it felt a bit snug but I was going for the colour, not the fit.

A quick selfie followed and I posted the picture on our group chat straight away. 'Lads, what's the dress code for tonight?' I asked and a series of uncomplimentary responses and emojis sent my phone into overdrive. 'Shorts and t-shirt it is then,' I thought. Not that I'd been serious anyway. I just wanted to give the lads the chance to have a pop but there was no doubt that for one night and one night only, everyone of a Liverpool persuasion would be supporting Chelsea. All they needed was a draw and we would be champions.

By this point it was only a matter of time anyway. Even if City won at Stamford Bridge, it was still a question of *when* rather than *if* we would finish the job. But having waited for thirty years to win the league, no-one associated with Liverpool wanted the delay to go on any longer. Yes, we were in a luxury position and if all we had taken from the night was some decent food and drink, none of us would have complained but when a trophy is so close that you can almost reach out and touch it, you just want someone to thrust it into your arms.

I didn't say this to anyone else, but I was in no doubt that this would be the night. It felt fated and it felt that way from the moment we came off the pitch after beating Palace. The hope had been that we would win the league at Anfield or, if that didn't work out, then the fans were letting us know that it would be nice to be crowned champions at the home of one of our rivals. But from the moment we gathered at Formby Hall, the expectation grew that it would happen there.

We are used to watching games as a group but usually it's in a professional setting and there's definitely no booze on offer, so for once it felt like we were just a group of lads enjoying a match in the pub. We were all sat in rows, watching intently, and there was a bit of conservative celebrating when Chelsea took the lead towards the end of the first half. We were all Chelsea supporters for the night but it was still far too early for getting carried away.

Things got a bit more interesting when De Bruyne equalised because that just added to the tension and we were all shouting at the television whenever a decision didn't go our way or a Chelsea player made a mistake or missed a chance. We got really involved in it all – you would never hear forty blokes go as silent as we did whenever City went forward, especially when Sterling hit the post.

For the first time, I realised what I put my family through whenever I'm playing a big game. God help them. Being a player can be stressful, particularly when there is so much at stake, but at least you are master of your own destiny to a large extent. As a fan, all you can do is hope that others will deliver on your behalf which is why we spent the second half urging Chelsea on as if our shouts from Formby could be heard two hundred miles away at Stamford Bridge.

I actually owe Tammy Abraham an apology because I was cursing him when he missed a couple of chances to give Chelsea the lead. The ball was bouncing around in City's six yard box and big Tammy had to score but the ball somehow didn't go in. It was only when a replay was showed that I realised Fernandinho had used a hand to deny him. It hadn't even entered my head that anything untoward had happened. "Penalty," I shouted. "You've got to give that." As VAR got involved we saw another couple of angles that showed how blatant it was. "He's got to go!" At that moment, we were like everyone in the red half of Liverpool, screaming at the television and trying to shape events by sheer willpower.

There shouldn't have been that much tension, it was totally illogical. No matter what happened, we would still have seven fixtures from which to glean the single point that we would need in the event of City winning. Football isn't rational, though. We feel it and when it really matters emotions take over. That's why we were all hollering at a broadcast of a game that we could not affect on a night when history could only be delayed, not denied. It's also why we celebrated like we were on the Kop itself when Willian scored the penalty after it had finally been given. Not only were Chelsea 2-1 up, City were down to ten men due to Fernandinho's sending off. All that remained was for the minutes to tick down and we would be champions.

I headed straight for the toilet. This wasn't nerves, it was a tactical decision. I knew if Chelsea hung on, the celebrations would be massive and I didn't want to miss a second. I had been sat at the front next to Hendo and up until Willian scored I'd been having a bit of fun at his expense, telling him to start getting his shuffling feet ready – until he put me back in my box. "Will you shut up Robbo," he said. "Aye, no problem. That's me told." If City had gone ahead I reckon he might have killed me there and then, so I didn't do it again. There was no way I was taking any chances.

I wasn't feeling any tension but, understandably, others were. Ali went inside for the last ten minutes because he couldn't bear to watch. Probably the only person in the world who would have been more nervous than him at that stage was my dad. I was texting him, my mum, Rachel and a few of my pals throughout the game but as the seconds ticked away I was too focused on what was happening on the screen to bother with my phone.

Ten, nine, eight, seven, six, five, four, three, two, one . . . . "Campeones. Campeones. Olé, olé, olé! Campeones. Campeones. Olé, olé, olé ..."

After three decades, a group of Liverpool players could finally sing that song. We got into a huddle and danced. Every bounce felt like it could take me higher. Every word seemed louder. Euphoria was wasting no time, it was already kicking in. I've got to be honest, though, as we were all hugging one another and saying "we've done it" – I found it hard to take in. It was too big to sink in so soon. I knew that we were the champions but I didn't feel like a champion, not yet anyway. I was celebrating but I was celebrating for Liverpool, not for myself. "Campeones. Campeones. Olé, olé, olé!"

I couldn't describe what it meant to me at that stage. I'm not the type to become teary in those situations. I didn't cry when we won the Champions League either. I'm more giddy than anything else, jumping around like I'm on an invisible pogo stick and generally getting myself lost in the moment.

The gaffer got emotional. We all saw him crying and then he went around every single one of us, giving us a hug before leaving the room. He just put his head in his hands and said: "I've got to go, I've got to go." He was literally overwhelmed and that hit home more than anything else after we were confirmed as champions.

When you see a manager of his stature react like that and you know that we have all contributed to it, it can't help but move you. Winning the league was massive for all of us but at that moment I think we all realised that, if anything, it was possibly even bigger for him. Becoming the first Liverpool manager to lead the club to the Premier League title is off the scale as far as achievements go. As a Celtic fan, I know all about Bill Shankly telling Jock Stein that he was "immortal now" after the Lisbon Lions won the European Cup in 1967, and similar sentiments applied here.

We had the big screens on and another Celtic legend, arguably the greatest of them all, appeared. There was a bit of a hush because we all wanted to hear what Sir Kenny had to say but the look on his face, illuminated by emotion and pride, told us all we needed to know. Thirty years ago, when he guided Liverpool to their last league title, they probably didn't even celebrate that much because it was the norm by then. They just lifted the trophy and walked off. The fans probably took it for granted and who could blame them. Then a whole generation followed without the bread and butter arriving. Supporters of twenty-nine-years-old had not seen Liverpool win the league. Even those who had won the lot had pined for the title to return. That's why everyone was so emotional.

Sir Kenny has won everything in the game but he showed his emotions thirty years on because he knew better than anyone else how big this was. We saw how much it meant to the gaffer and various Liverpool legends and that's when it really hit home. When you see Sir Kenny – a man who has a stand at Anfield named after him – crying because of something that we had achieved, you can't help but feel proud.

As soon as I got a chance, I found myself a quiet space so that I could FaceTime my family. We had all been given 'Champions' hoodies so I put mine on and it was a good job I did because we couldn't hear each other properly. The pictures told the story anyway. I could see they had a bottle of champagne and they could see I had my hoodie on.

I didn't cry but I was emotional. I think I had too much excitement and joy for tears and there was also an element of coming to terms with what had just happened, but seeing what it meant to my family was massive for me. They are the ones who have kept me going when I have needed support and they are also the ones who have driven me on. I can't ever repay them for that but being able to bring them so much pleasure is definitely one of the best things about winning the league.

I don't need to drink to have a good time but at parties I do like a drink – my dancing is terrible, so at least I can blame it on the beer. We danced that night. 'Show Me Love' was the highlight. That was the one that brought everyone onto the dancefloor and the good thing was that it was so crowded that it would have been hard for anyone to pick out my moves.

The last time I had been able to enjoy a drink like that was Madrid more than a year earlier, so I was determined to make the most of this opportunity. These aren't just good times, they are the very best times, and you have to enjoy them as much as you possibly can. Even before the fun really began we were already letting our hair down as anyone who saw a live TV interview with Trent and Virgil being gatecrashed could testify. I eventually got to bed shortly after 5am, having decided to stay at the hotel rather than going home because I didn't want to wake the kids up.

For whatever reason, I didn't have a hangover when I woke up but I was knackered as I'd only had a couple of hours' sleep on the back of a day of high adrenaline and excitement. I went home, spent some time with the kids until I was forced to give in to my tiredness and go up to my room for a couple of hours. I could have slept for a lot longer but I wanted to enjoy the moment with Rocco and Aria. I got up and we took them out for a walk so that they could let off a bit of steam with so much excitement going on.

When we got back, there was a massive box waiting for me which had been sent out by the club. The kids ripped their way through the wrapping paper like it was Christmas Day and they found all kinds in the box but their favourites were definitely the 'Champions' flags and hoodies.

So much effort had gone into it and that made it even more special for us as a family. Usually you would expect to have your kids on the pitch with you at some stage after winning the league and you would all be able to milk in the atmosphere but that wasn't possible, so the club helped us to create a special moment at home and it was great for them to share it. My kids are young but they still knew their dad had won something and getting a massive present to open no doubt made them wish it would happen more often.

We had a couple of days off which was great and I'm definitely taking the credit for that because I'd done an interview with LFCTV where I said we needed to get the gaffer drunk so he might give us a bit more time off to enjoy the moment! We were given the Friday and the Saturday off – so he must have listened to me.

When we returned to training on the Sunday, it was business as usual. Yes, there was a sense of achievement and everyone was buzzing, but we had a big game to prepare for against Man City and we didn't want to go to the Etihad as champions and let ourselves down.

The fact that we went on to lose 4-0 meant a lot of people accused us of taking our eye off the ball and enjoying ourselves too much but nothing could have been further from the truth. We prepared for that game like every other game and that's why the perception of what happened is totally wrong. It also fails to take into account that we probably created more chances in that game than in any of our previous matches against City, certainly in my time at Liverpool.

We'd won the previous fixture 3-1 at Anfield but we had created four good chances and taken three, it wasn't as if we had run amok. This time we weren't clinical but if Mo's chance had gone in instead of striking the post I would have fancied us to go on and win.

City taking the lead from the penalty spot meant the game suited them, though, and after they got their second it was a long way back for us – particularly as we didn't have to win, no matter how much we may have wanted to. For whatever reason, our timing was a split second off and that's a big problem against a team like City who had shown since lockdown that they can play like it's a training match. They are so relaxed and obviously they are phenomenal technically so I just think we got caught by a team which was sharper on the night.

This was underlined by their third goal when I got attracted to the ball and left a space behind which Phil Foden exploited to score. As soon as I did it I thought: 'What are you doing? Hold your position.' But I had spent most of the season looking to nip in front of attackers in situations like that so we could get on the front foot. This was the first time I had really been caught out, so I just needed to take it on the chin and move on. One of the main reasons why we became champions was that willingness to be aggressive and play on the front foot. We don't want to change that and we accept the risks involved because the potential rewards are so great.

City would probably look back at the game at Anfield and say that, in certain moments, we were a split second ahead of them and it made a big difference to the outcome. It's often stuff that people watching won't even notice. If Bernardo Silva hadn't been momentarily attracted to Virgil when Trent played the switch, I probably would have come under more pressure and it would have been more difficult for me to put a cross in like I did. Silva didn't do anything wrong. He just made a decision that would have been fine ninety-nine times out of a hundred but the brilliance of Trent's pass with his wrong foot exposed the space that had been left. We are all under a lot more pressure in these games because the small margins are more crucial than ever. This was a night when they all seemed to go in City's favour and we had a couple of sloppy moments, too, which they took advantage of. It definitely wasn't nice to find ourselves 4-0 down but City can do that to any team in the world.

The only consolation was that it didn't end up 5-0. This may not seem totally logical, but most footballers will tell you that the psychological impact of losing 4-0 is on one level and losing 5-0 is on another level entirely. We managed to stabilise after going four down and we created a couple more chances, but that was pretty irrelevant because we were never getting back to 4-4. At least we had stopped the bleeding, though. Then, out of nowhere, Riyad Mahrez goes through and scores a fifth. I was gutted. The game was long since gone but this was one last kick in the bollocks so I was massively relieved when the goal was disallowed.

We all hated losing in that fashion and Hendo and the gaffer let everyone know in the dressing room afterwards that it shouldn't have happened. Had it been mid-season with everything still to play for I've no doubt the inquest would have been harsher still, but the fact that we had already achieved our objective of becoming champions meant some perspective had to come into play. We were all raging at ourselves but there was also a sense that we should not go overboard here because this is a blip and it's much better to have a blip after you've won the Premier League than before.

I also wondered whether it would have been different if City had beaten Chelsea as then we would have faced them knowing that if we avoided defeat we would win the league. That's totally hypothetical, of course, so the overriding feeling was that we were annoyed. When you play for a club like Liverpool you don't want to lose any game and you definitely don't want to lose heavily.

It was difficult in a way that we were no longer playing for something. Since I first moved to Liverpool, we've been playing for something until the very last game of the season. In my first season we needed to win our last game to qualify for the Champions League and then we had a Champions League final against Real Madrid. In the next, we were fighting for the title and then had another Champions League final. This time around, we've won the league with seven games to go, we were out of the cup competitions and technically we had nothing to play for. Obviously we didn't want it to happen, but even if we had lost all of our remaining fixtures, it wouldn't have changed a thing that happened to us or detract from what we had achieved.

In ourselves, we definitely wanted to keep performing but there is no question that the incentive to keep winning is much stronger when you are trying to win a league than it is when you have just won it.

A few took the opportunity to take a few cheap shots at us after City and the narrative that we had taken our eye off the ball couldn't have been more wrong, which was why it was so important to all of us that we responded in the right way and we did with a 2-0 victory over Aston Villa.

This was our first game back at Anfield since becoming champions and I couldn't help thinking about what the atmosphere could have been like. Of all the games behind closed doors, this was probably the one that impacted on me the most because Anfield would have been sensational that day if the fans had been there. I was disappointed for us in this respect but I was even more gutted for the supporters. As it was, all we could do was be professional and we did that. It was also nice to see Curtis get another goal after Sadio had given us the lead and nicer still to make it seventeen wins out of seventeen home games.

Despite the criticism that followed our defeat at City, we knew our focus was still right and we demonstrated that again with a 3-1 win away to Brighton.

We scored three really good goals, Mo chipping in with a couple with Hendo getting one from the edge of the box in between, but by the time the final whistle went I was already worried because the captain had gone off with a knee injury. I had no idea how bad it was at that stage but I knew full well that Hendo isn't the type to go off with a knock unless he absolutely has to, so I was concerned.

The moment I knew it was serious was when I went in to get some treatment on my hip because I'd taken a bang and I saw Hendo sat in the corner with a towel over his head. That's when I realised it could be really bad. There was just silence in the changing room. We had been buzzing when we won but then we settled back in and realised that Hendo might have a bad one.

When a situation like that happens, there's literally nothing anyone can say that is going to help, so I knew I would be better off just leaving him be. It was a tough one because automatically I started worrying that he might need an operation and then it hit me – will he even be able to lift the trophy? By the look of things, it was already a given that he would miss the rest of the season, so the concern switched to whether he would be able to get onto the podium. I can't think of another player who's ever deserved to lift the Premier League title more than Hendo and, for me, he was player of the year, so it was difficult seeing him like that. All we could do was hold our breath, say our prayers and hope that when the scan took place the following day the outcome wouldn't be as bad as we all feared.

At the outset, we realised that the best case scenario was probably six weeks out and the worst was nine months. The two big worries were that we could be without our captain for a long time and also that, if surgery was required, lifting the trophy might not be possible. Knowing Hendo and the guy he is, I couldn't see him going up on crutches or with a big brace on his knee.

All of the lads were asking about it during recovery at Melwood. It was all any of us could think about. Then Jim the doc got a call with the scan results and you could literally hear a pin drop. Nobby was stood next to him like a puppy waiting for a biscuit, knowing he probably wasn't going to get one. I saw Jim sigh with relief and the next thing he was off the phone celebrating with Nobby and Dave Rydings, who looks after player rehabilitation. They had planned for the worst, a nine-month rehab, so to find out it was only six weeks and that Hendo was back for next season was a massive relief.

I texted Hendo and said: 'If you ever doubt your importance at this club, you should've been at Melwood when the news came through.' I've never seen a six-week injury get celebrated so much on a training ground.

It gave me a massive boost because I know how much being Liverpool captain means to Hendo and how much responsibility he takes for all of us, so I went into the Burnley game on a bit of a high. That feeling became even stronger when I scored the second headed goal of my career from Fab's brilliant cross – more proof that if you close your eyes and hope for the best good things can happen.

It wasn't anywhere near as important as my goal against Villa but it definitely looked better and it was also nice to get a bit of praise from Peter Crouch who knows better than most what it takes to score a header. Hopefully one day he'll be able to tell me what I did!

We deserved that goal too. We were well on top, creating plenty of chances and if it hadn't have been for Nick Pope, we could have been out of sight by half-time. For seventy minutes we were in control but Burnley stayed in the game and when their chance came, they took it. Credit to them for that. Yes, we had dominated possession and we had carved out plenty of opportunities but they showed plenty of resilience and you have to admire that and the job that Sean Dyche has done for them. It was disappointing for us as we had wanted to maintain our one hundred per cent home record, but that wasn't why I was so frustrated at the end of the game.

The main reason was I felt we should have had a stonewall penalty when Jóhann Gudmundsson brought me down late on. I knew he had got a slight touch on the ball but it was his follow-through that toppled me as I went into the box and, for me, it couldn't have been clearer. David Coote, the referee, thought differently and there was no intervention from VAR.

My head went. It doesn't matter if we are champions, we still have that will to win and that is why it was so annoying. It would have been no different if it had happened at the start of the season. I wanted to win and, in my opinion, a bad decision stopped that from happening so I spoke to the referee after the game had ended to register my disapproval.

With there being no fans in the ground, my complaints were picked up and became a big deal on social media – like pretty much everything does these days. I don't regret anything I said, but if I could go back and have the conversation again it would be in a different manner. The ref told me that Gudmundsson had touched the ball and that just set me off. Football is about emotion and, on that occasion, I allowed mine to show.

Dropping two points as champions shouldn't really be a problem, regardless of our obvious desire to win, but this was a period when we were being judged by targets that were set by others rather than ourselves.

At the start of the season, not one of us had said: "Let's get one hundred points." No-one was saying it, even when we had ninety-three points with three games to go. If anyone wants to take it to extremes, we missed our 'target' in October when we drew at Old Trafford because we set out to win every single game we played in. Maybe we became victims of our own standards in this respect as, in some quarters, it stopped being good enough for us to win the league, we needed to bring up our century or else there would be a tinge of disappointment.

So, when we lost at Arsenal and the one hundred-points mark went out of reach, it gave some the opportunity to place a question mark next to our achievement. They had tried the asterisk and that hadn't worked so there had to be some other form of punctuation. I've checked my Premier League medal and it doesn't have a points tally on it, it just says 'champions'.

All we set out to be was the very best that we could be. Nothing was mentioned about points or records. Our priority was to win the league, anything else would be a bonus. Our incentive when we faced Arsenal was to win. It was that simple. It should have happened too. I got an assist for Sadio's goal and, as against Burnley, we were well on top but the second never came. We made a couple of mistakes that Arsenal took advantage of and they hung on.

It was one of those games that happens every now and again when your dominance isn't rewarded and your opponent gets a victory against the run of play. I'm just glad it came after the league had been won.

City lost nine league games but there was only the odd one when they weren't the better side. At least when it happened to us against Burnley and Arsenal it didn't cost us a great deal. The league title was in the bag and now all we needed to do was celebrate it in style.

ROBBO

PARTY TIME

F OR the second season in a row, I ended up sharing an unforgettable night with Sir Kenny Dalglish. This time, rather than a hotel function room in Madrid, we were stood on the Kop at Anfield – him wearing a face mask and me a smile as wide as any in my entire life.

In keeping with tradition, he had a flight to catch and we had a trophy to celebrate. Our prize gleamed just as the European Cup had a year earlier and the red ribbons that adorned it told the world that finally, after all these years, the Premier League belonged to Liverpool Football Club. All that remained was for the ritual to be observed – a pair of shuffling feet to dance on the stage followed by a quick spin and the silverware to be thrust into the sky.

Even with a strapping around his injured knee, Hendo pulled it off to perfection. His signature move had been delivered and it happened in the presence of the last manager to make Liverpool champions way back in 1990. For us, as a team and a club, this was as close to perfection as it gets.

The only ingredient that would have made it even better still was the fans. Between them, the club and the Premier League could not have made the presentation better in the circumstances. Hendo's idea to collect the trophy on the Kop was perfect. It summed up our relationship with the supporters even in their absence and it showed how much they mean to us and how much this moment was for them as much as anyone.

But there was no getting away from the fact that we all would have given anything for them to be there. Collecting the Premier League trophy in front of empty seats definitely wasn't part of the dream that everyone associated with Liverpool FC had shared for so long. It doesn't take a great deal of imagination to visualise what Anfield could have looked and sounded like had things been different and I've no doubt that there wouldn't have been a dry eye in the house, either in the stands or on the pitch had normality not been so brutally ripped away. This was the new normal, though, and like everyone else, all we could do was make the best of it and we did that. There was also a realisation that we could not feel too hard done by, not when so many families had been torn apart and so many people were suffering. As much as we might have wanted things to be different, we all understood why they couldn't be. Perspective definitely comes easily at a time of tragedy.

I had been concerned about how the trophy lift would look without fans in the ground and I wasn't the only one. At one stage, Hendo actually said to me that he wasn't sure whether he would have the same emotion and I definitely understood where he was coming from. My response was typically blunt but there was also a bit of bravado on my behalf. "Of course you will," I said. "One million per cent. Once you see Sir Kenny handing out the medals and all of us gathered together on the stage, the emotion will come." It did too. Having our families there helped, especially after it had looked like they would not be able to attend.

What also helped was the powerful sense that this was the end of two incredible journeys – for Liverpool as a club and for us as a group of players. One had taken thirty years and the other only twelve months but each required closure and this was the moment it had arrived. No wonder we went nuts as fireworks ripped into the Merseyside sky along with the silverware that all of us had longed for. Hopefully we can win the Premier League again and lift the trophy in front of our fans because they deserve that so much, but we knew we were never getting this moment back so we had to make the best of it and we did that. It was the first time for most of us and we will remember it for ever.

We still haven't given up hope of a parade either. All of us want to share this success with the supporters. We would like nothing better than to see our people take to the streets again to celebrate what we have achieved together, but we also know that health has to come first. The most important thing was that we delivered the trophy. We brought a long wait to an end and we did that for every single Liverpool fan who has been desperate for their club to be champions again, including those who are no longer with us.

The fact that we lifted the trophy having accumulated ninety-six points was also poignant. I am not normally one for coincidences but this felt like fate. It also meant that on one of the club's greatest nights, its darkest hour was in everyone's thoughts. For me, this is how it should be. No matter how much time passes, we have a duty to remember those who died at Hillsborough and to preserve their memory. Trent actually mentioned the symbolism of the points total the following day but it was something that a lot of people, ourselves included, had all been thinking.

Liverpool's past always informs its present and rightly so. One of my first thoughts when I woke up on the morning of the lift was about the great players who had gone before us. Being a proud Scot, my mind wandered to old images showing the likes of Sir Kenny, Graeme Souness and Alan Hansen parading the trophy around the pitch but I also reflected on local lads like Steven Gerrard and Jamie Carragher who had deserved a league title as much as anyone, only to be denied.

Both thoughts gave me a feeling of enormous privilege and I hope that all of our former players and managers were able to enjoy our success because, one way or another, they had all played a part in making this club what it is. They laid the foundations and set the standards. The current generation definitely recognises this, albeit in the knowledge that the time had come for us to make our own history. It is also why we could not have a more fitting leader than Hendo. He was signed by Sir Kenny and played alongside Stevie and Carra. The baton had been passed along, connecting past and present, cultivating institutional memory and upholding everything that Liverpool FC stands for.

As well as thinking about the past, I was also incredibly excited about what lay in store. I had the feeling you get in your stomach that you only get when you know it's a really big day. It is totally natural and can't be created at will, it just happens and when it does it can't be switched off, even if you try. I tried to calculate how many days it had been since Liverpool were last crowned champions but I gave up when I realised I would have to work out the leap years too. All I knew was that it was a big number.

I knew my mind was racing but I also had a game to focus on and given the way I was feeling it was probably inevitable that I felt hugely confident about that. Chelsea are a very good side and they are improving all the time, but I firmly believed that we were going to put on a great performance. Nothing was going to get in the way of us winning the trophy in style. Not that I believe the occasion would have been ruined in any way had we lost because the league had been won over a season and a bad result would not have changed that. But there's no question that defeat would have put a wee bit of a dampener on things for a few minutes. That's why we had kind of split the night into two separate events anyway – the game and the trophy lift. In our minds, this meant that whatever happened during the ninety minutes we would put behind us as soon as the match finished so that we could focus solely on our crowning glory.

I went into training at Melwood on the morning of the game and I could see straight away that people were excited. Some of the lads were doing the Hendo shuffle and there was just a buzz about the place that can only happen when everyone knows it's going to be a special day. I sat with Hendo for lunch after he had joined us following his rehab and he was still in planning mode. He was so determined that everything would be just right. As soon as he sat down he asked: "What do you think I should do in the dressing room depending on whether we win, lose or draw; should I have the music pumping out?"

I said: "If we lose or draw, give the lads five minutes or so to get over it because that is what we would all want but I'm telling you now, we are one hundred per cent not losing tonight." Maybe that was a bit daft on my behalf but I had this incredible feeling that nothing was going to stop us, so I went with it. This was going to be the perfect day and that meant winning the game as well as lifting the trophy. If you can't believe on a day like that, when can you believe?

For once, my prediction was pretty much spot on. We were excellent on the night and we showed why we are champions. We probably also showed a wee touch of post-lockdown slackness too because although we scored five really good goals, we conceded three that were pretty poor by the standards that we set for ourselves. Maybe the first one couldn't have been avoided; Ali made an unbelievable save and Olivier Giroud was just the first one to react. The second and third definitely could have been avoided at various stages and should have been dealt with but the five goals we scored were frightening. Naby's piledriver was a joke, Trent's free-kick was a joke, Gini's was a brilliant instinctive finish, Trent delivered the perfect ball for Bobby's header and Ox put the top hat on with a great strike from my cross.

If I had to pick a favourite I would choose Bobby's. It wasn't the most eye-catching of the five but seeing him scoring his first league goal of the season at Anfield meant a lot to all of us. As soon as Trent's cross went over it looked like it would be a goal, Bobby couldn't miss and he didn't. As soon as the ball hit the net I knew we had the perfect day that I had been hoping for.

I'm still to score at the Kop end and hopefully that will happen sooner rather than later but on this occasion I genuinely wanted him to get a goal more than I wanted one for myself. What he does for the team goes unnoticed by some people but everyone at Melwood appreciates it because we know that he sacrifices his own goals for others and for the good of the team. The thing that is unique about Bobby is that number 9s are naturally selfish but Bobby isn't at all and sometimes that's his downfall, in the eyes of some at least. What can't be calculated is the number of goals that we score because of his movement, because of his willingness to drag defenders away to make space for others and because he always puts the team first. I doubt he will ever be the Premier League's top scorer but his value to us goes way beyond that and we all recognise his contribution, even if there are those who overlook it.

As soon as Ox got our fifth, I wanted the final whistle to go so that I could get my hands on that trophy. I'd been excited about it throughout the game and, at one point, I actually asked Andre Marriner, the referee, whether he was staying to watch us lift it! I don't know whether he did stick around but he enjoyed the joke.

Emotions were running high for many reasons, it wasn't just about euphoria. I walked into the dressing room and the first person I saw was Adam. His contract was almost at an end and we all knew that this would be the last time he would be at Anfield as a Liverpool player.

I gave him a big hug and he said: "Don't Robbo, please don't," and that set him off. He was gone. That was how much it meant to him to play for this club.

The gaffer put him in the matchday squad and had probably wanted to give him some minutes but the opportunity didn't really emerge because there were some big challenges going in. It would only have taken one heavy tackle and it could have potentially ruined the move he had agreed to Brighton. He was about to be out of contract and was still young enough to continue a fantastic career, so the gaffer made the right call.

Otherwise, it was going off. 'Show Me Love' had become our unofficial title-winning anthem so Hendo had that blasting out. I was spraying champagne over all of the lads and then Virgil, Adrian and Bobby got involved too. We were all soaked to the skin.

Then the gaffer came in and made a short speech. "What you have done is absolutely outstanding," he said. "Each of you has made history. Champions of Europe. Champions of the world. Champions of England." As soon as he said that, it went off again. 'Campeones. Campeones. Olé, olé, olé!'

The gaffer wasn't finished, though. He turned to Andy Lonergan and I love what came next. "Andy Lonergan – champion of England, champion of Europe, champion of the world. What a guy!"

Next thing, everyone was singing 'Andy Lonergan' to the tune of 'Baby, Give It Up' and it wasn't just because we like the song. For me, if there is one person who sums Melwood up it is Andy. He was our fourth choice keeper and some probably don't even know who he is. He had spent his whole career in the Football League and had a great career at that level but now here he was, as the gaffer put it, a champion of everywhere.

A couple of weeks earlier, somebody asked the gaffer if squad players like Andy deserved a winner's medal and I understand why the question was asked but for us there was no doubt about it. They totally deserved a medal because of the way that they trained and what they bring to the squad. Whether or not they got onto the pitch was absolutely irrelevant. Andy and the rest had played their part and they deserved their medals.

Then the gaffer came for me. "Eight million pounds! What a buy." He had a pull on his vape and went again. "Nobody wanted him apart from us and we took him!"

Everyone was in stitches. Gini was next.

"Gini Wijnaldum, you were quite expensive weren't you?! Who else was in for you Gini?"

"Tottenham wanted me boss."

"And now you're a Premier League champion – you made the right decision!"

The gaffer then turned around and spotted Smally. "And Smally." We were all waiting for what followed but the gaffer just gave him a massive hug, which was lovely. It showed the respect that we all have for him.

We had another bounce around the dressing room before getting changed into our 'Champions 19/20' shirts and heading back out for the presentation. It wasn't long before I had another bottle of champagne in my hands. This time I was chasing our head of fitness Andreas Kornmayer around the pitch with it which was only right seeing how much running he's made us do over the years. Everyone was just buzzing and the celebrations continued inside the stadium as we headed up three flights of stairs, past the boardroom, singing 'Allez Allez Allez' on the way to meet up with our families.

Formby Hall beckoned again but this time it was a bit different for me as in my eyes the party was as much of a farewell to Adam as it was a celebration of what we had achieved. The two of us have had a really strong relationship since I first came in. He was injured a lot and it was tough at times because I could see how much it affected him but from the moment I arrived, I realised straight away that he was a great guy and our bond got stronger and stronger.

Then it started dawning on me that he won't be with us next season and it hit me that it won't be the same without him and not just because he's my drinking partner. Milly and Hendo are both teetotal while, on the very rare occasions when we are able to indulge, Adam and myself are always the ones who drink similar amounts.

He's got a fantastic move to a really good club, he's looked after his family, he will move closer to where he's from, and he will play. It was brilliant for us to have Adam as a squad player but there comes a point where these guys are too good to sit about and it's great that the gaffer and the club respect that. Ingsy was too good to sit on the bench for us and he's proved it with twenty goals in a season for Southampton. Adam will go and be Brighton's best player next season, I firmly believe that.

It is hard for us on a personal level because we want lads like Adam to stay forever but football doesn't always work like that. It was similar with Dejan, another player who has always done a job for the team. He also leaves Liverpool as a Champions League winner and a Premier League winner, not to mention the scorer of one of the most famous goals in the club's history. The two of them were emotional as we celebrated our success and we were emotional with them. You can't win big honours unless you have a good dressing room and it's hard to imagine there have been many better than ours. The flip side of that is it does hurt when good lads leave, but all we can do is wish them the very best and look to fill the void in whatever way we can.

Amid the singing, the dancing, the photographs with the four trophies we had won in just over a year, the drinking and the reminiscing, I also took a bit of time to reflect on everything that we had achieved and the big thing that hit me was how proud I am to be part of this team and this club.

It means everything to me and winning the league with Liverpool is the absolute ultimate. This doesn't mean I will be resting on my laurels because I want to win again and again and again but this club, the biggest in the world for me, had not won a league title for thirty years and that hurt. I'm not bothered about rival fans who have used it against us, that goes with the territory, but people were entitled to question us because, by the standards that have been set since 1892, this was a failure.

I looked at the lads bouncing about on the dancefloor without a decent move between them and I realised that, as a squad, we had taken Liverpool back to where this club belongs. Competing for trophies is what Liverpool is all about. The great teams of the past might not have won every time but they did compete for trophies year in and year out and this is something that we hadn't done for far too long. Yes, they won the Champions League in 2005 and we won it in 2019 but in between that, there was only one FA Cup and one League Cup. We had not been competing for the Premier League on an annual basis. It's now two years that we've been in the running for it and hopefully this run will continue because that is what should always be expected of this club. There are no guarantees but if we're still competing and challenging we will still have brought Liverpool back to being one of the best clubs in the world, even if we do fall short. We have to be there or thereabouts, it is as simple as that.

The good thing is, we are well placed to kick on. The journey didn't end with Hendo's shuffle on the Kop and, if anything, the feeling that gave all of us has only inspired us to do everything we can to experience it again. What the fans probably aren't able to see as much as we do is that the club has been sorted from top to bottom. The gaffer coming in has obviously been key but it was also crucial that the owners gave Michael Edwards and himself the backing they needed to put their stamp on the team. You only have to look at the group of players we have now to realise how much this approach has paid off.

As the gaffer pointed out in the dressing room, they also brought me in for eight million pounds which I'm sure a lot of people thought was a big fee to shell out for a player who had just been relegated to the Championship. The day before we lifted the Premier League trophy was the third anniversary of me signing for Liverpool so when I saw Michael with two of our most senior scouts Barry Hunter and Dave Fallows after the Chelsea game, I made sure I reminded them about how much value for money I was providing. I said: "Three years ago, I got yous all a job for life!" and they just burst out laughing. As usual, big Barry was loving it: "You're right there to be fair Robbo, but I also got you a job for life too so don't you forget it!" Point taken.

Michael and Barry were both big factors in me coming here. All the initial contact between Liverpool and Hull was done by Barry and my agents dealt with him as well. Michael got the deal done and while they may have a few regrets in terms of having to put up with my banter, I think they have proven that they are very, very good at what they do.

As players we are in the public eye and we get a lot of praise but in terms of team planning, recruitment, scouting and building a squad that is capable of winning the biggest trophies, I think these fellas deserve a lot more credit than they actually get. Along with the gaffer and the owners, they have transformed this club. They could do with listening to me a bit more than they do, though. If it was up to me and I was under Michael Edwards, the whole team would be Scottish. I've put pretty much everyone in the frame who was born on the right side of the border but nothing has come off up to now, but I'll keep trying! Everyone knows that one of Liverpool's greatest ever sides was 'The Team Of All The Macs' so the more Scots the better as far as I'm concerned.

Another who gets overlooked is Mike Gordon, probably because he is based in America and likes to keep a low profile. The supporters would probably be surprised at just how hands-on he is. There was a period when I was ill – it was just a bit of flu but it really laid me low – and Mike was on the phone to me every day, checking how I was and telling me to let him know if I needed anything at all. He is the co-owner of Liverpool Football Club but he is very down to earth and very approachable.

I was travelling to London for the PFA awards with my family in April 2019 and Mike was on the same train as us. He came over and spoke to my mum and dad and the conversation lasted pretty much all the way to Euston. My mum and dad were like: "Who's that?" because he is such a normal bloke that you wouldn't know he is the co-owner of one of the biggest institutions in sport. That's why he connects so well with the club. He has the kind of humility and commitment to the cause that Liverpool FC and Liverpool people are renowned for and when that kind of tone is set at the very top it will seep right the way through the club.

We know that the season after winning the league will be tougher still. As City discovered during the 2019/20 campaign, opponents try to find more ways to counteract your strengths and identify your weaknesses when you are champions. Teams always want to beat Liverpool but now there's an added incentive, especially when they come to Anfield.

That's a challenge that we need to be up to. We have to deal with the expectation and the demands and I also believe we will need to be a lot more patient. The perception outside of the club may be that we are a team which is at its best when it is responding to adversity. I can certainly understand that. By winning the European Cup after losing a final and winning the Premier League on the back of missing out by a point, we have definitely shown that we can get up off the canvas. Now we have to show that we can handle success. The dynamic is very different now. A different energy, a different motivation and a different mental approach are all required.

We are a team and a club who have proven people wrong and now we're champions. That's a big change. What I would say, though, is that the process of going from having an underdog mentality to the outlook needed when you're one of the top dogs is already underway. It started on the podium in Madrid and along with the burning desire to end a thirty-year wait to become champions, we were also inspired by a determination to have that winning feeling again. We didn't want to have that feeling just once.

As much as any other during the entire campaign, our final game of the season underlined what we are all about. The job had long since been done, we had just celebrated being champions and, on top of that, it was a sunny afternoon on Tyneside when neither Newcastle nor ourselves really had anything to play for.

We even went a goal down inside a minute, so all the ingredients were in place for us to rest on our laurels if we wanted to, but we're not built like that. We knew we would have a long wait until our next game and we wanted to finish the season on a high. That didn't change even though we had already won the league. We didn't want to end on a defeat – and we didn't.

To a man, we left it all out there with Virgil getting us back into the game and leading by example along with Milly in Hendo's absence. It would have been easy to go through the motions but as a team we all drive each other on. In my case, I always feel like I'm fighting for something, whether that's proving myself or representing our supporters. I also look to create my own personal incentives, like the assist challenge that I have with Trent every season. Nothing is at stake – there are no prizes and no forfeits – but because it is me versus him and we are so close it definitely gives both of us an added edge. I had gone into the Newcastle game 13-11 down and it looked like Trent had it in the bag, but I was playing while he was on the bench so I had a chance to make up some ground on him. I wasn't really expecting an assist when I knocked Virgil's long pass back to Divock but the big fella pulled one of his golden shots out of the bag and I had one.

As soon as he scored I knew exactly where Trent was because I'd taken a throw-in there a few moments before. I turned around, put my index finger up and said: "One more." He was saying: "No chance," so I held my hands together like I was praying. He was desperate to get on. These are small things but when you're so competitive it matters in your own mind. Also, he was four points behind my all-time fantasy football record for defenders from the '18/19 season but he needed an assist to break it, so when he came on he held up four fingers to me. We were playing properly but there was an additional motivation.

It is a healthy competition that drives the two of us on. I didn't manage to get another assist at Newcastle, it was Bobby who provided the final pass before Sadio scored our third, which meant I finished one behind Trent for the second season in a row. Over those two campaigns, he got 25 assists and I got 23. Every season won't be like the last couple but we will keep pushing each other and that can only help. Put it this way, when I see Trent bombing up and down the pitch creating chances it spurs me on and in its own way this captures the essence of this team – no matter what, we will always look for something to give us an added edge. If necessary, we will create one.

We do allow ourselves to enjoy the odd moment when we reflect on what we have done but only when the time is right. It happened when we got off the plane back to Liverpool from Newcastle and we were all sharing hugs and congratulating one another on a fantastic season at the same time as looking forward to a good break. The gaffer went around everyone thanking them for their efforts and it was just nice that we were all able to do that before we went our separate ways.

At the same time, though, the gaffer has created a new mantra for us that we won't *defend* our title, we will *attack* it. It's brilliant psychology because it creates a positive energy by establishing a new target to go at, rather than making us fear that we have something to lose.

We know it will be tough. City will come back stronger than ever. United and Chelsea will carry on improving. That's just the top four. The promoted teams will fight for their lives again, just as we discovered in our away games at Sheffield United, Aston Villa and Norwich City, all of which went in our favour but only by the smallest of margins.

Everyone in between will be looking to push on too, none more so than Tottenham, Arsenal, Leicester, Wolves and Everton, who will have the top four in their sights. Everywhere you look there is a challenge, which is exactly how it should be. We won't fear that but we have to be aware that it exists and if there is one thing that I can guarantee it is that this Liverpool team will give its all once again. Time will tell whether or not this will be good enough and we have total respect for all of our rivals but we are all determined to do everything in our power to make the '20/21 season as special as the one that went before it.

This doesn't just apply to club football either.

At international level, Scotland are two play-off wins away from qualification for Euro 2020 which will actually take place in 2021 due to the coronavirus. This is a real opportunity for us. It has been at the back of people's minds because of everything else that's been happening in the world but by the time it comes around, everyone will realise how big it is. At the end of the day it's a two-game shootout for the Euros and it is a long time since we qualified for a major tournament so we have to give it our all. The last time we did it was 1998 and I was only four years old, so all I can remember about it was watching on television as John Collins scored a penalty against Brazil while we were at a family party to celebrate the occasion.

The Scotland team has always been very important to my family as a whole, none more so than my auntie, Vera Murchie, who passed away at Christmas in 2013. The only times I have worn personalised boots – the play-off final with Hull, the Champions League final in Madrid and an international against Cyprus that I scored in – it has been in her memory. I have her date of birth, 27.05.56, on one boot and 'Cheeky

V' on the other. A Cheeky Vimto was her favourite drink at family parties, she used to mix her own, and it's something that I remember her by.

When my mum, dad and Auntie Vera were growing up, Scotland qualified for every tournament, it was like Liverpool winning the league, and now it's been far too long.

This team has the potential to right that wrong. Our individual quality is there for all to see but now we have to show it as a team and deliver as a team. I have confidence that we will only get stronger and the sooner the better.

Having just ended a thirty-year wait with Liverpool, I now want to end a twenty-two-year wait with Scotland. If that happens, I'll be having a Cheeky Vimto in memory of my Auntie Vera.